Wealth of an Empire

Wealth

═ of an ═

Empire

The Treasure Shipments That
Saved Britain and the World

═══

ROBERT SWITKY

═══

Potomac Books   Washington, D.C.

Potomac Books is an imprint of the
University of Nebraska Press.

Library of Congress
Cataloging-in-Publication Data
Switky, Robert, 1961–
Wealth of an empire: the treasure shipments that saved
Britain and the world / Robert Switky. — First Edition.
pages cm
Includes bibliographical references and index.
ISBN 978-1-61234-496-6 (hardcover: alk. paper)
ISBN (invalid) 978-1-61234-497-3 (electronic) 1. World War,
1939–1945—Economic aspects—Great Britain.
2. World War, 1939–1945—Naval operations, British.
3. Naval convoys—Great Britain—History—20th century.
4. Bank reserves—Great Britain—History—20th century.
5. Great Britain—Foreign economic relations—United
States. 6. United States—Foreign economic relations—
Great Britain. I. Title.
HC256.4.s85 2013
940.53'1—dc23   2013013185

Printed in the United States of America on acid-free
paper that meets the American National Standards
Institute z39-48 Standard.

Potomac Books
22841 Quicksilver Drive
Dulles, Virginia 20166

First Edition

10 9 8 7 6 5 4 3 2 1

Contents

Illustrations

Preface

In the summer of 1940, a convoy of five Allied ships sailed from Britain to Halifax, Canada, carrying more wealth than the gold extracted from the California gold rush, that formed the Klondike gold rush, the gold hauled out of Mexico by Cortés, and Pizarro's gold take in Peru combined. The special consignments on board HMS *Revenge*, HMS *Bonaventure*, and the ocean liners *Monarch of Bermuda*, *Batory*, and *Sobieski* were part of an operation that consisted of more than three hundred top-secret shipments sent to North America between 1938 and 1941. The gold and financial securities on board these ships helped Britain buy the materials it needed for World War II and prevent the wealth of the British Empire from falling into Nazi hands. Had this special convoy and the other treasure ships been lost at sea or—worse—captured by the Germans, Britain could have been forced to sue for peace with Nazi Germany long before an American declaration of war would shift the war's momentum. In this long-running operation, a select group of government, military, and banking leaders were gambling with their country's financial and political future as no great power ever had.

The story of the evacuation of so much of Britain's wealth is crucial to our understanding of why Britain survived the war—and ultimately why the Allies won the war. Britain's transfer of wealth took place within a broader financial context in which Britain sustained the Allied war effort until the U.S. Lend-Lease program took effect in 1941. Isolationist sentiment in the United States and legislation passed by Congress in the 1930s put a great strain on Britain's finances and indirectly led the country to take great risks with the relocation of its liquid assets.

This story also raises many important questions about what might have been. If some or most of the shipments had been lost or captured, would Britain have been so weak as to pave the way for Hitler's command of all of Europe? Would such an outcome have encouraged Germany and Japan to consider an earlier attack on the United States? Would the United States have chosen to declare war long before Pearl Harbor? Would the Nazis have attacked the Soviet Union sooner?

Despite the enormous military, political, and financial stakes involved, the transfer of Britain's wealth to North America is a generally unknown chapter of the war. One might even be tempted to ask if the gold shipments actually took place. Numerous official, declassified documents and eyewitness accounts confirm that the shipments were, in fact, genuine. Historical records on ships, the amount of gold or securities they carried, and the ports of origin and destination are not always precise, but considerable evidence on both sides of the Atlantic attests to the reality of this immensely risky undertaking.

Why, then, the surprising inattention to this operation? First, the documentary evidence covering the shipments is not exhaustive. For good reason, the British and Canadians kept mum about the many phases of the operation, as did—albeit with less diligence—the Americans. When Bank of England and British Treasury officials met to plan the shipments, no secretaries were present and no minutes were taken.[1] In addition, Royal Navy regulations forbid an officer from keeping a private diary while on active service ashore or afloat.[2]

Key political figures left few documentary traces about the operation. Trawling through their writings yields less than a researcher would hope to find. Winston Churchill, a prodigious writer, made only a passing reference to the so-called special shipments in his multivolume work on World War II.[3] One might have expected Neville Chamberlain, the British prime minister from the prewar years until May 1940, to make at least some mention of the issue, but his papers at the University of Birmingham in England yielded few clues. Robert Self's compilation and review of Chamberlain's letters and diary contain no references to the special shipments.[4] Outside of a few declassified British government documents—from the Foreign Office, the Treasury, and War Cabinet meetings—Chamberlain said nothing specific about the shipments in Self's analyses.

Similarly, one might have expected to learn important information from the lengthy diary of John "Jock" Colville, who served as assistant private secretary to both Chamberlain and Churchill.[5] In violation of the rules, Colville kept a diary starting in 1939, but he failed to mention British wealth heading to North America. There are also no references in the lengthy diary of Alexander Cadogan, the permanent undersecretary at the Foreign Office.[6] Either Colville or Cadogan (and other mid-level officials) knew of, but kept secret about, the shipments, or they were deliberately kept out of the loop.

Another explanation for the lack of information on this topic is the code of silence among war-era banking representatives. For example, some high-level employees working at the Bank of Canada kept quiet even after the war for fear of losing their jobs or pensions.[7] It was also true that some key government and banking representatives felt as if they were simply doing their jobs. They were, thus, uninterested in boasting about the historical importance of their wartime actions.[8]

Others found the transfer of British wealth unworthy of special attention. At the start of his memoir, for example, Cdr. Oliver Lascelles wrote, "I have been consistently nagged at by the family to put down something about what I did in the war. I can't think why but still I'm doing my best now as it doesn't seem to be all that interesting or outstanding." This British naval officer, who served on HMS *Malaya*, did not believe his family would find it interesting that his ship carried "tons of gold" across the Atlantic to North America. When Lascelles passed away in 1999, his friend Roderick Corrie's address for the "service of thanksgiving for the life of Lascelles" only mentioned the gold in passing: "Oliver was then posted to the HMS *Malaya* and the arduous duty of taking our gold reserves across the Atlantic. Then after service in Force H taking convoys to Malta."[9]

Another explanation for the dearth of coverage is negligence amid other facets of the war. World War II is replete with momentous events that have rightly attracted the attention of scholars from around the world. Extensive theoretical debates have taken place over the proximate and underlying causes of the war. Libraries have gorged on works related to Hitler's strategies, motives, and psychology. Innumerable studies have addressed the ideological confrontations between liberal capitalism, fascism, and Marxist-Leninist-Stalinist socialism. The march of events in World War II would eventually submerge the story of the greatest transfer of wealth to this point in history. In the dreadful summer of 1940, as most of the treasure crossed to North America, the great air confrontation between Britain and Germany—the Battle of

Britain—took place. By the end of that year, the bulk of the treasure shipments had been completed, but still to come were the Japanese attack on Pearl Harbor; Germany's declaration of war on its former ally the Soviet Union; the worst of Nazi atrocities against Jews, Slavs, and others; the battles for Iwo Jima and Okinawa in the Pacific; the Battle of Stalingrad; the Battle of the Bulge; and, of course, the dropping of the atomic bombs on Hiroshima and Nagasaki.[10]

The public did not learn about this operation until November 1955, when Pulitzer Prize–winning author Leland Stowe published his research in an article in *Reader's Digest*. Stowe first heard about Britain's World War II financial flight in the spring of 1955 from A. J. Stump, a journalist based in Santa Barbara, California. Stump shared an office with Sidney Perkins, who—fifteen years earlier—had been at the center of the operation. In 1940 Perkins was in charge of processing gold and securities worth millions of dollars arriving on board Allied ships in Halifax, Nova Scotia. Through the spring and summer of 1955, Stowe—with extensive help from Perkins—pieced together the broad contours of the story.[11]

The only full-length book devoted to the subject is Alfred Draper's *Operation Fish*—although the operation did not go by that name or any other.[12] Writing in the 1970s, Draper built on Stowe's research, much of which was vital but did not fit into the narrow confines of a magazine article. Draper covered the evacuation of gold from Britain as well as from several other European countries, particularly Norway, the Netherlands, and France. Without the efforts of Draper and especially Stowe, very little would be known about Britain's massive transfer of wealth during the war.

Much of the research for *Wealth of an Empire* supports Stowe's and Draper's broad conclusions for why Britain undertook the operation. However, this book extends our knowledge of the treasure shipments by highlighting how security breaches were more extensive than previously believed. It also demonstrates that the German submarine threat to the ships heading to North America in 1939 and 1940 was more complex than portrayed by either Stowe or Draper.

It is perplexing that most books on World War II, even the large-scale histories, fail to mention the operation altogether.[13] The basic facts about the treasure shipments do not appear in the seven-hundred-plus-page *Simon and Schuster Encyclopedia of World War II* or the comparably long

Oxford Companion to World War II.[14] In addition, the story is absent from published books on the Battle of the Atlantic, such as those by Bernard Ireland, Marc Milner, and David White.[15] In Thomas Parrish's book, *To Keep the British Isles Afloat*, a good deal of space is devoted to the crucial year 1940 and even to Britain's financial problems, but the author includes no specific discussion about the shipments of gold and securities.[16]

In the few books that do address aspects of Britain's wartime financial flight, only passing references are provided. For example, Peter Fleming's book on Operation Sea Lion—the code name for Germany's planned invasion of Britain—carries only a single paragraph on the subject, and that is based on the Stowe article.[17] The subject is given only slightly more space in *The Last Ditch* by David Lampe, *Nineteen Weeks: America and Britain and the Fateful Summer of 1940* by Norman Moss, and *The Duel: The Eighty-Day Struggle between Churchill and Hitler* by John Lukacs.[18]

In his extensive review of World War II, David M. Kennedy simply writes, "Anticipating a German invasion, the British government [sent] a shipment of gold bullion and securities, code-named *Fish*, to Canada for safekeeping."[19] In his five-hundred-page *North American Supply*—a detailed organizational study of the methods by which Britain gained its war supplies from North America—H. Duncan Hall used only brief and bland language to describe the treasure shipments.[20] Two valuable historical studies published in the 1990s—about the Bank of England and the Bank of Canada, respectively—provide important banking-related information but leave out much of this multifaceted story.[21] Finally, the many websites devoted to World War II either ignore the subject or provide only snippets of information.

It is rare for such an important and exciting topic to evade the eyes of history watchers. It is hoped that *Wealth of an Empire* will help make this a more widely known subject of World War II history. Studies of the Battle of Britain have helped demonstrate how close Britain came to losing the war in 1940; the story of the shipments of British wealth helps explain how close Britain came to losing the war for lack of money.

The research for *Wealth of an Empire* stands on the shoulders of Stowe, Draper, and others by fleshing out the nature of the risks involved in shipping so much of Britain's wealth and by amplifying the British, Canadian, and American political and military facets of the operation. The materials gathered by Stowe are housed in the Wisconsin Historical Society on the campus of the University of Wisconsin in Madison. This book is also based on primary sources gleaned from the Chamberlain Papers at the University of Birmingham, the Churchill Archives at Churchill College, and Britain's National Archives, the Imperial War Museum, and the Bank of England, all based in London.[22] Additional archival material was acquired from the Bank of Canada in Ottawa and the Library and Archives Canada in Ottawa. Duncan McDowall's study of earmarked gold in Canada from 1935 to 1956 was particularly instrumental in organizing the Bank of Canada's many archival records about wartime gold, facilitating the job of subsequent historians.

Many people provided assistance in the creation of this book. At the Churchill Archives at Churchill College in Cambridge, the staff was extremely helpful, and a special thanks goes to Elizabeth Wells. The archivists at the Chamberlain Archives at the University of Birmingham offered excellent assistance as well. The archivists at the Bank of England, Ben White in particular, proved invaluable in navigating some of the more complicated files covering the Bank's role. I spoke with many of the staff members of the National Archives in London, and without exception, they were very helpful. The staff members at the Imperial War Museum in London were considerate of my many questions, and I appreciated their patience in escorting me frequently through the circuitous route to and from the museum lobby and the reading room. On the western side of the Atlantic, Jodi-Ann Ouellette, Andy Weston, and in particular Jane Boyko at the Bank of Canada Archives in Ottawa guided me to vital information about Canada's banking role in the operation.

Nigel West offered crucial insights into German intelligence capabilities. On the same subject, David Kohnen of the Naval War College provided both invaluable assessments and suggestions for further research. Michael Santos of Sonoma State University in California answered numerous questions about banking and finance. Portions of the book benefitted from reviews by Richard Ned Lebow of King's College London, Jonathan Schwartz of the State University of New York at New Paltz, Sherri Anderson, Judy Abbott, and Director Kathy Charmaz and other members of the Writing Program at Sonoma State University. At

Potomac Books, I'd like to thank Elizabeth Demers; Kathryn Owens; Melissa Jones, who helped polish the work for publication; and especially Don McKeon, who raised many important questions. Thanks, as well, to the many presenters of the 2010 San Francisco Writers Conference who taught me how to navigate the choppy waters of the publishing business.

I also wish to thank my wife, Karen Thompson, who was instrumental in the completion of this project. She offered both encouragement and superb editorial recommendations on every draft of the manuscript, delivering indispensable advice regarding style and substance. In addition, she patiently endured the time I spent on the project over the years and graciously accepted the cancellation of more than one vacation. I am also grateful to Kathy Switky, who edited the initial draft of the manuscript with care and diplomacy. Her tireless and patient work to secure many of the images used in this book was greatly appreciated as well. My agent, Robert Shepard, showed not only an interest in the art and minutia of writing but in the details of World War II history as well. Any author he works with should feel fortunate to have such a dedicated advocate. The book is much stronger because of the work of all of these individuals. Any errors remain my responsibility.

1

Shoring Up Support

On May 17, 1939, an enthusiastic crowd in Québec City cheered as the *Empress of Australia* sailed into port. The Canadians had gathered to greet King George VI and Queen Elizabeth, the first reigning British monarchs ever to visit North America. During the monthlong visit, journalists feasted on the pomp and personal details of the royal couple. Journalist Dixie Tighe reported that "at Quebec's Citadel the King and Queen slept in narrow beds in separate rooms . . . [and although] the King and Queen had running water in their private bathrooms, members of their entourage had to use old-fashioned wash basins."[1]

On their first day in the New World, the King and Queen dined at the magnificent Château Frontenac. *Time* magazine reported that lobster tails were served as well as "grilled breast of chicken and a Grand Marnier soufflé which neither the King nor the Queen accepted."[2] On the second day of the trip, the monarchs visited Montréal, the biggest city in Canada. In a baseball stadium, they sat in a Buick convertible near home plate and listened to fifty thousand children sing while nine hundred of them formed a great Union Jack. The King and Queen witnessed more grand spectacles as they worked their way westward by train. In the central provinces, *Time* described the Canadians as having a "hearty blend of U.S. hail-fellowship and a reassuring, yeoman love of King and Country that was truly British."[3] In Winnipeg, the crowd's warm greeting brought tears to the Queen's eyes. "Isn't it wonderful?" she told the King.[4] In Vancouver, on Canada's western coast, a headline from the newspaper *The Province* proclaimed, "The Greatest Day in the City's Whole History."[5]

After touring much of Canada for the better part of three weeks, the King and Queen then spent several days in the United States, drawing especially large crowds in New York City. According to one estimate, nearly 3.5 million people lined the streets to see the monarchs.[6] After a visit to the nation's capital, several papers ran the headline "The British Take Washington Again."[7] During the monarchs' stay with President Franklin Roosevelt and his family at Hyde Park, New York, the press continued to focus on the lighter side of the tour: the unusually informal settings, a visit to the local Episcopal church, and an American-style picnic during which the King "shed his necktie, ate hot dogs, and drank beer."[8]

The public and the press were so caught up in the hoopla of the royal visit that the real agenda had been masked. Despite the pleasantries detailed in the news media, grave political developments in Europe had motivated the monarchs' trip to North America. Anxiety had been growing across most of Europe as a result of Adolf Hitler's aggressive actions in Austria, Czechoslovakia, and elsewhere. Just weeks before the royal visit, George Bolton of the Bank of England reported that the "tension and strain in England [are] increasing daily and . . . the latest move of the Germans in sending their navy to Spain is regarded as very serious."[9]

In light of Germany's mounting threat to European stability, the trip by the King and Queen was designed in part to "stimulate Canadian affection" for Britain.[10] Officials in London had doubts about Canada's commitment to the British cause. Canadian prime minister Mackenzie King had made several public statements in support of Britain, and he was personally committed to helping the British. But, on occasion, the prime minister had played up the need for independence in Canadian foreign policy.[11] As recently as March 30, 1938, he had told the House of Commons in Ottawa that Canadian involvement in an eventual war would not be guaranteed:

> The idea of every twenty years this country should automatically and as a matter of course take part in a war overseas for democracy or self-determination of other small nations, that a country which has all it can do to run itself should feel called upon to save, periodically, a continent that cannot run itself, and to these ends to risk the lives of its people, risk bankruptcy and political disunion, seems to many a nightmare and sheer madness.[12]

Animosity on a personal level between the Canadian and British prime ministers contributed to the tension as well. The current British prime

FIG. 1.1. The British monarchs in Toronto, Canada. The King and Queen received enthusiastic welcomes nearly everywhere they went in Canada and the United States. Public interest in the monarchs likely distracted the press from investigating the secret cargo in the ships that accompanied them to Canada. *Courtesy of Wikimedia Commons*

minister, Neville Chamberlain, in particular, had doubts not only about Canadian loyalty but also about Mackenzie King's competence. After an Imperial Conference in June 1937, Chamberlain described the Canadian prime minister as "the weakest vessel in the team." Elsewhere he described King as "inclined to be pernickety and critical."[13]

Another prominent critic of strong Canadian ties to Britain was the mayor of Montréal, Camillien Houde. A folk hero and a prominent political figure during the monarchs' visit to Canada, Houde, nevertheless, publicly stated his intention not to register for conscription and urged others to join him in disobeying the law. Houde was just one of many Canadians who saw the brewing conflict in Europe as a British and imperial war in which Canada should play no role.[14]

In addition to securing Canadian solidarity, the royal visit to North America was designed to improve British-American relations and, more specifically, to gain military commitments from President Roosevelt in the event of war.[15] Among other things, King George VI sought American help in enhancing the safety of ship convoys that would be traversing the Atlantic. Britain was short of warships so the King proposed that Britain acquire dozens of World War I–era American destroyers in exchange for American access to British naval bases in the Caribbean. He also addressed the need for U.S. naval patrols to support Britain's own convoy escorts in the Atlantic. For his part, FDR saw the royal visit as an effective way to dramatize U.S.-British cooperation, as historian David Reynolds explained, "for the benefit of the dictators and the American public."[16]

After their sojourn in the United States, the King and Queen returned to Canada for a tour of the Maritime Provinces. When they left Canada on June 16 on board the *Empress of Britain*, the monarchs could look back on having accomplished much during their visit. The trip helped reinvigorate imperial sentiment in Canada, and the connection between Canada and Britain seemed much closer after the visit than before. In a letter to the King, the premier of Ontario, M. F. Hepburn, described the monarchs' visit as "unparalleled in Canadian History.... [I]t should be a source of great encouragement to the British Empire to receive the joyous word that you and the Queen won completely the hearts of all of us who live in the Heart of Canada."[17]

For his part, Prime Minister King wrote to a representative of King George that the visit could not have been improved upon: "It has left the best of feeling in all parts of Canada, and as between Canada and the United States, I do not think the peoples of the two countries were ever happier than they were at the time of the visit, or that any event has left so much of common interest to be continuously recalled."[18] And as one enthusiastic provincial premier in Canada told a senior aide to the King, "You can go home and tell the old country that any talk they may hear about Canada being isolationist after today is just nonsense."[19]

Britain would reap the rewards of its successful public relations tour of Canada two years later when, during the most harrowing months of the war, all thoughts of letting Britain go it alone had vanished. On June 12, 1940, Mackenzie King told Britain's Earl of Athlone that Canada was "young in nationhood, but ancient in steadfast loyalty to the British Crown."[20]

The monarchs' visit to the United States had also remarkably improved American perceptions of the British. According to the FDR Library, "due in no small part to the King and Queen's visit, [Americans now] sympathized with England's plight; Britons were no longer strangers or the evil colonial rulers from the past but familiar friends and relatives with whom Americans could identify."[21] The *Chicago Tribune*, a newspaper opposed to strong U.S.-British ties, took the conciliatory position that attacking the royal visitors would seem "tactless and inhospitable."[22] Ronald Lindsay, the British ambassador to the United States, deemed the royal visit a great success. In the event of a grave crisis, he wrote, "this [visit] might have decisive results."[23]

On specifics, however, the meeting between King George and President Roosevelt left much to be resolved. The King's proposal to exchange destroyers for access to British bases, for example, would require excruciating and drawn-out negotiations. In the end, the Roosevelt administration failed to offer significant aid because the specter of repeating the horrors of World War I loomed too large for Congress and the American public. The lack of a dependable commitment from the United States established a theme that would endure during the bleakest months of the war.

Completely overlooked by the crowds and nearly every journalist covering the royal tour was the secret cargo aboard HMS *Glasgow* and HMS *Southampton*, the two warships that escorted the King and Queen across the North Atlantic. Each ship transported a consignment of £15 million in gold from the Bank of England.[24] In 1939 the value of the cargo was worth more than $120 million—the equivalent of nearly $4.5 billion today.[25]

In Québec City on May 17, 1939, beyond the gaze of the well-wishers and the curious, the two ships were met by teams of dockworkers who spent the next seven hours unloading the gold. How the gold from the *Glasgow* and the *Southampton* was bundled is unknown, but we know from later shipments that workers usually packed four gold bars with sawdust into wooden crates bound with metal straps. Gold is a particularly heavy metal with bars typically weighing approximately 27.5 pounds (400 troy ounces). Thus, each crate weighed 125 to 130 pounds. The gold was eventually transferred to armored trains for the trip to the Bank of Canada in Ottawa, the country's capital. Security was overseen by the Royal Canadian Mounted Police (RCMP).[26]

To hide evidence of this secret and very large gold delivery, the Bank of Canada took several precautions. The entry record on customs documents did not show the vessels involved, and the routine publication of gold transfers was delayed a month to avoid linking the gold transfer to the royal visit. Donald Gordon of the Bank of Canada worried, however, that the operation's security may have been compromised. In a letter to George Bolton of the Bank of England, Gordon wrote, "[O]n the morning of the unloading, the Admiral-in-Charge had invited on board a fairly large party of Québec city officials and other dignitaries. . . . [T]his party was on board during a period of unloading. It may be that after the reporters get back to normal activity someone will remember the story, but at the moment it looks to be a reasonable supposition that in the general excitement of the visit no one paid any attention to the labors of the stevedores."[27] In Ottawa, a "stray journalist" had seen the gold train arrive, but the security breach proved to be limited.[28] As it turned out, by May 22, Gordon confidently reported to London that "everything passed off without a hitch."[29]

The crew members on board the warships seemed far more concerned about their role in escorting the royal passengers than about the special consignments of gold. George Purkiss Haskell, a crewman on board HMS *Glasgow*, wrote,

> In those days a seven-week prestige trip to the East coast of Canada was the kind of foreign travel only the well-heeled could consider. For the Royal Navy it would be all in the day's work—one of the perks of naval service. . . . *Glasgow* and her sister ship HMS *Southampton* were therefore ready at Spithead [an anchorage off Portsmouth] on May 6th 1939 to take up their Royal escort duties. The fresh coats of paint on our super-structure had been laid on with enthusiasm, our brass work polished, decks honed and bunting displayed—we had never looked smarter than on that bright morning. *Glasgow* was <u>our</u> ship, we were <u>her</u> crew, and we had <u>pride</u> in her.[30]

Haskell made no mention of the stash of gold.

The need for secrecy was twofold. First, and most obviously, the British and Canadian authorities did not want any of the gold to be stolen. Second, if made public, shipments of large amounts of gold from Britain were likely to unsettle financial markets in North America and Europe given the tense political climate. An early sign of this concern was evident the year before when Otto Niemeyer, a leading figure at the Bank of England, made an apparently innocuous visit to New York. According to a report in the *Sydney Morning Star* on January 22, 1937, Niemeyer had to dispel rumors that the "war scare in Europe" was real and that Britain was sending "an alarming amount" of gold to the

United States.[31] The *Morning Star*'s use of the phrase "alarming" overstated the situation at the time, but the newspaper unknowingly anticipated what would become a truly alarming situation three years later.

The idea of shipping gold under cover of the royal visit was formally proposed late in the trip's planning stages by senior British Treasury official Frederick Phillips. Like others at the Bank of England, Phillips had grown increasingly nervous about political developments in Europe and anticipated the need to get large quantities of gold safely to Canada. The gold would pay for the many goods Britain would need in case of war. On April 27, 1939, Phillips sent a secret memorandum to the British Admiralty explaining, "In the event of the heavy expenditure which would be incurred in North America in the event of war, the Lords Commissioners of HM [His Majesty's] Treasury are anxious to arrange the dispatch of gold to Canada in substantial amounts under conditions of secrecy."[32] Phillips did not elaborate on what he meant by "substantial amounts," but his definition of the term would expand greatly after the start of the war. Basil Catterns, deputy governor of the Bank of England, concurred with Phillips and suggested that in case "the royal visit were postponed for any reason, our need is so great that we should want them to make fresh efforts to send the gold in any other way."[33]

As it turned out, the £30 million in gold sent to Canada in mid-May 1939 would be dwarfed by future shipments. As the first year of the war progressed Britain's demand for military and civilian goods from Canada and the United States increased dramatically. As a result, more gold and financial securities were shipped across the treacherous waters of the North Atlantic. Britain eventually needed to authorize "special shipments" from the rest of the Empire as well, especially Australia, India, and South Africa.

Britain's urgent desire to get its liquid assets to North America was driven in part by the experience of World War I. As in 1914, Britain was going to depend heavily on Canada for manufactured goods, wheat, and other commodities during the war.[34] Further, Britain would have to depend even more on weapons and manufactured goods from the United States. As French prime minister Édouard Daladier told the American ambassador to France William Bullitt, if the Allies were "to win this war, we shall have to win it on supplies of everything from the United States."[35] Thus, British military planners and banking leaders knew that in order to pay for the vast stores of civilian and military goods, they would need to get gold—and lots of it—tucked safely into vaults on the other side of the Atlantic.

Some of Britain's gold would have to go directly to the United States, a neutral country and a supplier of much of what Britain needed. Canada offered its own advantages as a home for Britain's wealth. Canada was a member of the British Commonwealth; it was geographically removed from the European theater of war; and it was in close proximity to the United States, in particular the Federal Reserve Bank in New York. In a pinch, British ships could also reach Canadian ports more quickly than U.S. ports. Those contemplating the worst possible outcomes also believed that Ottawa could serve as the new location for the British government if Germany succeeded in capturing the British Isles.

Britain's Defence Advisory Committee agreed with the need for substantial imports from North America and was fully aware of the risks involved. As in World War I, the most dangerous areas for Allied shipping would be the western approaches to the British Isles into which the shipping lanes converged.[36] During World War I, German submarines had destroyed 11.1 million tons of Allied and neutral merchant shipping. British planners could not know it at the time, but the losses would be even greater in World War II.[37]

Representatives of the Bank of England and the British Treasury began making rudimentary preparations for war as early as 1936. As tensions flared in Europe over the next two years, the pace of their activities quickened. In March 1938 Harry Siepmann, a special adviser to Bank of England governor Montagu Norman, sent a cable stamped "Very Secret" to Graham Towers, the governor of the Bank of Canada, inquiring about the possibility of storing very large quantities of gold in its facilities in Ottawa. To accommodate the British request, the vaults in the Bank of Canada's new headquarters in Ottawa had to be expanded, because they lacked the storage capacity for so much gold.[38] And even though the war was some time off, Siepmann let Towers know that, in order to facilitate war purchases, the Canadian mint could melt down British gold coins held in Ottawa to add to Britain's deposit of gold bullion.[39]

Thus the gold that accompanied the King and Queen in 1939 was not the first shipment sent to North America. At the end of April 1938, the navies of Britain and Canada, in coordination with the Bank of England and the Bank of Canada, had dispatched HMS *Montclare* and its sister ship, HMS *Montcalm*, to Canada. Each carried 965 gold bars worth £2.5 million.[40] And more shipments followed. Montagu Norman told his Canadian colleagues that some British gold would "reach you by devious and unexpected ways" so as not to excite alarm in England.[41]

Banking and naval leaders arranged several shipments in the fall of 1938, including the September delivery by the *Queen Mary* of the relatively modest quantity of 159 gold bars. In October more substantive deliveries were made by the *Empress of Britain* (1,100 gold bars) and the *Aurania* (1,070 gold bars).[42] The gold shipments continued into 1939. Shortly before the royal visit, approximately £9 million in gold was delivered to Canada by the *Duchess of Richmond* (983 bars), the *Andani* (1,000 bars), and the *Ascania* (1,000 bars). Shortly after that, the *Montclare* delivered another 1,006 gold bars. By the time the King and Queen had arrived in Canada, from these and other shipments the Canadian National Railway had transported more than 10,000 gold bars to the Bank of Canada alone.[43]

The prewar precautions taken by British political and military leaders—and in the case of the secret gold shipments, by the banking communities in London and Ottawa—were based on the assumption that Hitler would drag Europe into war. But no one knew for sure whether Hitler truly wanted war; many believed that diplomatic maneuvers could mollify the dictator's desire for more territory. Perhaps war was not inevitable. Pessimists, however, had much to worry about.

Leading up to the May 1939 royal visit, the King was concerned about leaving Britain at a time of serious political unrest in Europe. The trip's potential long-term public relations benefits, however, held sway. Chamberlain worried about the monarchs' safety during the trip, noting that one could "never exclude any possibility with dictators."[44] In fact, the Germans had begun detailed planning for the war in Europe a month before the King and Queen set sail for North America. And, a week before the royal visit, Hitler had given instructions to concentrate warfare against Britain and, as a second priority, against France.[45]

Britain's secret plan, which would finance the war and safeguard its wealth, would require treasure shipments of previously unimagined magnitude compared to the modest shipments that had already crossed the Atlantic.

While the Americans watched safely from a distance, British leaders worried that help from the United States was not guaranteed. And in the first half of 1939, no one knew what Hitler's strategic objectives were. How ambitious were his goals? What were the limits, if any, of his territorial demands? Was the German submarine fleet growing so fast that nothing traveling to North America and back would be safe?[46] Would the combined forces of Europe's democracies—especially the French army and the British Royal Navy—be sufficient to restrain Hitler's ambitions? Those anticipating war had little doubt that devastation would occur on a large scale, but most failed to foresee how awful the coming year would be.

2

For the Sake of the Realm

During the King and Queen's triumphant tour of North America, few in Britain realized that their nation's wealth would soon be in danger. While an atmosphere of false hope seemed to grip many of Britain's political leaders, first among them Prime Minister Chamberlain, many of the nation's financial leaders were deeply worried by the political events developing across the European continent.

Near the end of the 1930s, Germany's economy was booming and its foreign policy ambitions were growing bolder by the month. When Adolf Hitler came to power in 1933, he almost immediately began defying the provisions of the 1919 Treaty of Versailles, which had been designed to punish Germany for its role in World War I. In March 1936, in violation of both the Versailles Treaty and the 1925 Locarno Treaty, Hitler sent thousands of troops to occupy the previously demilitarized Rhineland, an industrial region in western Germany rich in mineral resources. And in March 1938, Hitler forced Austria into a union with Germany (the Anschluss). Hitler's moves exposed the lack of political will in Britain and France to restrain the dictator's increasingly aggressive policies.

Although Britain's Royal Navy and merchant marine constituted the most formidable maritime presence in the world, Britain's leaders knew that the country was unprepared for all-out war. The British economy, which was still feeling the strains of the Great Depression, relied heavily on imports for many basic goods, including food, oil, and armaments. Somehow, these necessities would have to be financed.

Britain's financial situation was the focus of numerous and sobering prewar Cabinet discussions. Minutes from the July 3, 1939, Cabinet meeting expressed concern that Britain's economic troubles combined with the need to ramp up military spending had contributed to the reduction of nearly 40 percent of Britain's gold stock in the previous eighteen months:

> Up to the present the disadvantage of our gold loss has been largely political. It must discourage our friends and encourage the Axis Powers. If it continues swiftly it will soon become also a serious economic anxiety even in peace. . . . But the greatest anxiety is that it may gravely affect our staying power in war. Our gold stock, together with such assets as we may be able to sell or mortgage in wartime to countries overseas, constitutes our sole war chest.[1]

Two days later, the Cabinet held another broad discussion about the implications of a potential war. A consensus had formed that Germany's navy (Kriegsmarine) was not large enough to supply the Nazi-run country with the war and civilian goods it needed. Sir Richard Hopkins, second secretary at the British Treasury, explained that Germany did not have "command of the seas and could not expect to import goods except from adjacent countries. Her plans had therefore been drawn, on the basis of self-sufficiency." Hopkins added, "If at any time Germany was short of a particular commodity and had to buy from countries overseas, her lack of gold would be the determining factor."[2] The Cabinet meeting's minutes do not address this point, but Germany's ability to finance its war purchases could have been improved significantly with the capture of Britain's treasure shipments.

During the Cabinet meeting, discussions also centered on enhancing Britain's war chest with privately held securities. The government did not own stocks and bonds, but it considered selling requisitioned shares to acquire much-needed U.S. dollars. In return, the private holders whose shares had been requisitioned and sold would be remunerated with British pounds. In July 1939, the government concluded that it could requisition at least £200 million worth of foreign securities that could then be sold in the United States.[3] Over time, the British would send to Canada some 200,000 American securities, as well as others from Argentina, Belgium, Canada, France, Holland, the Dutch East Indies, Norway, Sweden, and Switzerland. The securities included Canadian municipal bonds (both federal and provincial), industrial shares, and mining and oil stocks.[4] Indicative of both the severity of wartime conditions and the imperative of maintaining secrecy, British citizens were not consulted about the scheme.[5]

Troubles for Britain were looming on the political front as well. No one knew for certain how European states would array themselves in the great clash of fascism, communism, and democratic capitalism. Leading politicians in Britain and other major European countries believed that the appeasement of German demands was required to avoid such a clash. Up to 1938, the strategy appeared to be working even as war clouds continued to gather.

Remembering the nation's huge losses in World War I, Britain was hesitant to engage in another military confrontation. In the face of Hitler's provocations, the initial political strategy shared by British prime ministers Ramsay McDonald (1931–1935), Stanley Baldwin (1935–1937), and Neville Chamberlain (beginning in May 1937) was to seek diplomatic solutions. A 1937 report from the British military service chiefs warned that hostile policies toward Germany could ultimately overextend the British armed forces. The committee reported that Britain should not underestimate the need to acquire allies and reduce the number of potential enemies.[6]

For those who supported it, appeasement meant conflict resolution through compromise and other peaceful means. The appeal of appeasement, wrote Chamberlain biographer Keith Feiling, was that "a war postponed may be a war averted."[7] In case war eventually came, appeasement was expected to give Britain a breathing space within which to mobilize the necessary military and economic resources. This interpretation of appeasement was partially established by a young John F. Kennedy in his 1940 book, *Why England Slept*.[8]

The last, and most infamous, major application of the appeasement policy occurred in late September 1938 during a series of meetings in Munich. There the leaders of Britain, France, Germany, and Italy agreed to allow Hitler to take control of the Sudetenland, a western region of Czechoslovakia. According to historian John Keegan, in a series of "craven meetings" Chamberlain and French prime minister Édouard Daladier conceded to Hitler "even more than he had initially demanded."[9] Nevertheless, at the conclusion of the conference, many in Europe were happy with what the British prime minister had achieved: Hitler's territorial demands had been satisfied and the alternative—another pan-European war—had been avoided.

For bringing "peace in our time," Chamberlain's cautious approach received enthusiastic support from Britain's political elite and the public at large. In February 1939, Wilson Carlile wrote to him expressing a view common among those in Britain: "Forgive an old man of 92 writing to such a busy man as yourself. In the Church Army [an evangelical form of the Salvation Army] we are full of thankfulness and even thrilled at the results brought about from your visits to Germany and Rome, and believe that goodwill and peace will be the outcome. God grant it may be so."[10]

Carlile, along with much of the British public, knew all too well about the consequences of war. Nearly a million service personnel from throughout the British Empire had died in World War I.[11] And despite the sacrifices and the lofty proclamations of the victors, the world had *not* "been made safe for democracy" as had been promised. In addition, since the 1920s, many Britons had come to believe that Germany had been wronged by the Treaty of Versailles. Chamberlain's decision to allow Hitler to have a little land seemed an appropriate concession. A public that believed he had crafted a deal to prevent another world war sent Chamberlain such gifts as fishing rods, salmon flies, a thousand tulips from Holland, and cases of Alsatian wine. He even received a request from a man in Greece who wanted to make a religious icon from a piece of Chamberlain's umbrella.[12] As W. W. Hadley put it, "Whatever happens, no one can say that [Chamberlain] did not do all in his power to preserve peace."[13]

Positive views of Chamberlain's dealings with Hitler extended to North America as well. Canadian prime minister Mackenzie King was "temperamentally as well as politically attracted" to appeasement and was initially persuaded by Hitler's "great sincerity."[14] King later sent Chamberlain a telegram of appreciation and in his diary wrote, "It really looks as if the dam were breaking from behind the darkest of all clouds. What a happy man Chamberlain must be, and what an example he has set to the world in perseverance of a just cause."[15]

From Los Angeles, California, British actor Basil Rathbone wrote to Chamberlain explaining how he had received "many hundreds" of letters expressing support for the prime minister. Rathbone, widely known from stage and screen, said that the letters he had received "were heartily in support of everything you have done from Munich onwards."[16] For its part, the *Chicago Tribune* claimed that the Munich agreement had removed all cause for war in western Europe.

Those who *opposed* the policy of appeasement believed the Munich agreement did nothing but pave the way for war, since it exposed how fainthearted the British and French were in the face of Hitler's demands. After Hitler was essentially given free access to the Sudetenland, the Führer's appetite for territory increased, as he was encouraged by the belief that France and Britain would be unwilling to stop Germany's future land grabs.

Winston Churchill was contemptuous of appeasement from the start and of the Munich agreement in particular. In the House of Commons on October 8, 1938, he delivered this blunt assessment: "I will . . . begin by saying the most unpopular and most unwelcome thing. I will begin by saying what everybody would like to ignore or forget but which must nevertheless be stated, namely, that we have sustained a total and unmitigated defeat, and that France has suffered even more than we have."[17] In a letter to a friend, Churchill wrote, "We seem to be very near the black choice between War and Shame. My feeling is that we shall choose Shame, and then have War thrown in a little later, on even more adverse terms than at present."[18]

Many of those who supported Prime Minister Chamberlain's decisions at Munich held negative views of Winston Churchill. In July 1939, for example, conservative member of Parliament Joan Davidson wrote a "Personal and Confidential" letter to the prime minister warning him of Churchill's meddling:

> I feel I must write . . . to say how much I hope you will not put [Churchill] into the Cabinet. . . . I regard him as the greatest danger, not only because he has no balance or judgement, but because he cannot refrain from intriguing, and from taking actions that will enhance his position and give him excitement. His restlessness is such that no sooner is he in one department than he wants to interfere in the works of others. . . . I go so far as to say that if Winston were in Government, and we managed to maintain peace in the world, he would in short time be agitating for war in order to create that excitement without which he is never happy.[19]

In fact, before the start of the war, Churchill's reputation was far from what it would become. As historian John Lukacs put it, "people in Britain thought Churchill [was] impulsive, erratic, wordy, unduly combative, a maverick, perhaps a publicity hound; in one word, unsteady."[20] Permanent Undersecretary Alexander Cadogan, a Chamberlain loyalist, used two words: "Churchill useless."[21]

Regardless of the merits of appeasement, it would appear that Britain had violated the admonishments of respected military strategists. In the fifth century BC, Sun Tzu counseled that in peace, prepare for war. In the fourth century AD, the Roman Publius Flavius Vegetius Renatus, issued similar advice: he who desires peace should prepare for war. Britain wanted peace but began preparing for war very late. The delay in putting the country on a solid war footing forced Britain to risk transporting its vast wealth to North America with weaker naval- and air-support capabilities than would normally have been prudent. Officials at the Admiralty, the Ministry of Supply, and the Bank of England worried constantly that if more "special shipments" had to be authorized, there might not be enough escort ships to protect them on their westward journeys. The limited supply of convoy escorts was also the result of misguided findings from a 1937 Naval Staff report, which concluded, "the submarine would never again be able to present us with the problem we were faced with in 1917."[22] As a result, according to historian David McIntyre, "no provision was made for convoy escorts beyond the existing . . . force of some 150 destroyers, half of which were veterans of the First World War."[23]

The policy of appeasement also indirectly resulted in a severe shortage of military aircraft. In 1938 the British had only three thousand aircraft fit for war duty. Only a few of these were deployed on reconnaissance missions, notably for spotting submarines. This meant that imminent gold shipments would be launched at greater risk. It would not be until 1941 that Britain, having mobilized its resources fully, would have more than twenty thousand aircraft.[24]

Building up the military usually went hand in hand with the funneling of resources into counterespionage. Here again, the appeasement strategy was indirectly linked to the relatively small budget devoted to MI5, Britain's counterintelligence agency. With thousands of people ultimately involved in the gold's shipping and handling, spies would have many opportunities to learn about the operation. Would MI5's limited resources inadvertently lead to devastating breaches of security?

Churchill's understanding of German motives differed from Chamberlain's (and that of Canada's Mackenzie King) in part because of their different assessments of Adolf Hitler. Churchill saw Hitler as a menace who could be stopped only by force; Chamberlain, however, seemed too apt to suffer from wishful thinking. After meeting Hitler, for example, Chamberlain commented, "In spite of the hardness and ruthlessness I thought I saw in his face, I got the impression that here was a man who could be relied upon when he had given his word."[25]

Chamberlain's appraisal of Hitler eventually coincided more closely with Churchill's, but Chamberlain remained convinced that appeasement had been the correct policy all along. According to Robert Self, the editor of Chamberlain's diaries, "Chamberlain went to his grave with the unwavering conviction that when the history of those final tumultuous years was written, 'the broad outlines of the story [would] be plain enough' and his policy and reputation would be fully vindicated."[26] Shortly before his death on November 9, 1940, Chamberlain wrote to Joseph Ball about the vast quantity of letters he had received that dwelt on the same point: without the appeasement of Germany at Munich, the British Empire would have been destroyed in 1938. Chamberlain added, "I should not fear the historian's verdict."[27]

Nevertheless, as opponents of appeasement contended, failure to stand up to Hitler encouraged more aggressive behavior by the Nazi leader. Such aggression might have been discouraged if the appeasement policy had not also delayed the buildup of Britain's military forces. In March 1939, Churchill tried again to warn Chamberlain of Britain's lack of preparations for war. With a man like Hitler, Churchill wrote on March 21, "anything is possible. The temptation to make a surprise attack on London or on the aircraft factories about which I am even more anxious would be removed if it was known that all was ready."[28]

Even as British political leaders hoped for the best in high-level negotiations with Germany, they nevertheless authorized what the *Los Angeles Times* referred to as "the greatest amount of treasure ever carried by a man-of-war" on board two American warships. In October 1938, the cruisers USS *Nashville* and USS *Honolulu* were visiting northern Europe on a goodwill tour when they were each asked to secretly ferry $25 million in gold from Britain to New York. For their efforts, more than a year later, on December 23, 1939, the ships' captains were each given a bronze plaque from Treasury Secretary Henry Morgenthau Jr. and a personal letter of appreciation from FDR.[29]

Like Britain, France was sending its gold to Canada and the Federal Reserve Bank in New York for safekeeping. Reflecting the widespread concern about a war in Europe, gold stored at the Fed, for example, amounted to $652 million in March 1939 but had jumped to $1.35 billion by August.[30]

Britain's gold transfers made good strategic sense in light of Hitler's provocative moves on the Continent. In March 1939, as the British were finalizing arrangements for the royal visit to North America, Hitler broke the terms of the Munich agreement and invaded the rest of Czechoslovakia. A month later, on April 28, Hitler abrogated the German-Polish Non-Aggression Pact. The very same day, Germany renounced the Anglo-German Naval Agreement of 1935, which restricted the German navy's surface fleet tonnage to 35 percent of the Royal Navy. These signs ominously pointed to further German aggression and a buildup of its naval forces.

As the leaders of Britain, France, Italy, Germany, and the other European powers wrangled over political questions, the British banking community increasingly focused on the consequences of their leaders' decisions. Bankers have a tendency to be cautious and conservative. These instincts meant that a certain degree of skepticism about appeasement was warranted. The British Treasury and the Bank of England studied the preparations that had been made before World War I and applied the lessons in anticipation of a second world war. According to Bank historian Elizabeth Hennessy, arrangements were made for staff members of the Bank to move underground in the event of German bombing raids—raids that were almost certain to come.[31]

The Bank's medical officer, Dr. Donald Norris, provided courses in first aid, lectures were offered on air raid precautions, first aid stations were established, and, in late 1938, everyone at the Bank was required to wear a gas mask for five minutes each week. This precaution was taken at other banks as well. According to Bank secretary Alma Arnall-Culliford, "I joined the secretarial staff of Barclays Bank, 54 Lombard Street, London, in 1938 aged almost 17 and even then we had been issued with gas masks which we had to wear for half an hour each week whilst typing."[32]

Bankers also made provisions to produce banknotes outside London in what became known as Shadow Factory. In order to avoid a catastrophic loss in an attack on the Bank's central location in London's financial district, its officers established facilities in Roehampton, Stoke-on-Trent, Hurstbourne, Overton, Whitchurch, and elsewhere. "Gradually," Hennessy recounts, much of "this almost wholly urban staff settled to an unfamiliar rural life, lived communally and in many cases far away from family and friends, although some of the married men did manage to find suitable housing locally and were reunited with wives and children."[33]

The war scare, and eventually the war itself, presented the Bank with unusual staffing challenges. For example, male military service reduced the pool of available employees, so a special court decision suspended the rule requiring women to leave the Bank upon marriage. Given the growing demands on the institution, the governor of the Bank of England, Montagu Norman, set up his own living quarters at the Bank's main office on Threadneedle Street. He slept there two or three nights a week for almost three years. The Bank also took measures to ensure that an adequate number of its employees obtained training in firefighting.

═══════════

Although Chamberlain and his domestic and international supporters thought that the world would have peace in their time, Hitler's machinations with Czechoslovakia would be followed by an order for all-out war. Between August 19 and 21, 1939, twenty-one German submarines (U-boats) sailed from their home bases and took up positions in the North Atlantic, North Sea, and Mediterranean in anticipation of hostilities. Germany's large warships set sail on the 21st and 24th to take up stations in the North and South Atlantic. Of the eighteen U-boats waiting to the north-northwest of the British Isles, none apparently saw the Canadian Pacific steamship *Montrose* sail to Canada. It arrived in Canada without incident on August 24 with a shipment of 251 wooden boxes containing 1,001 bars of gold.[34]

On August 31, Germany launched an offensive against its eastern neighbor Poland—a ruse designed to convince the world that the German military was merely responding to "Polish aggression." Few accepted the farfetched propaganda ploy, but German military forces nevertheless marched into Poland on September 1. Two days later, Britain and France declared war on Germany. In a radio broadcast on September 3, Chamberlain told his people that they were now at war despite his every effort to prevent it. "We have a clear conscience," he said in a grave tone. "We have done all that any country could do to establish peace. But the situation in which no word given by Germany's ruler could be trusted, and no people or country could feel itself safe, had become intolerable."[35] At 12:56 p.m. the same day, U-boat radio operators received this message from the commander in chief of the navy, Erich Raeder: "Commence hostilities against Britain forthwith."[36]

Also on September 3, Prime Minister Chamberlain appointed Winston Churchill First Lord of the Admiralty, despite important policy differences between the two men. A sense of relief and enthusiasm permeated the Royal Navy. Petty Officer Raymond Dutton of HMS *Ramillies*, one of the gold transport ships, recalled that the Admiralty marked the occasion with "a cryptic signal to the whole Fleet. 'Winnie is back!' It certainly raised our morale, as we knew that the Navy would be well led, by a man who had the necessary fighting spirit."[37] On HMS *Emerald*, a cruiser that would eventually make several gold runs during the war, Capt. Augustus Agar read to the crew the contents of the telegram announcing the war. He then called for "Three cheers for the King." He had never heard cheers "given so sincerely or more enthusiastically."[38]

Britain's churches that day "were packed with worshippers, many of whom had not been seen in church for a long time."[39] The British government issued new regulations affecting nearly every corner of civilian life. One of the more peculiar orders was directed at zookeepers. Within a few hours of the declaration of war, all poisonous snakes, spiders, and scorpions were to be destroyed in case they broke free during bombing raids. The zoo's air raid precautions staff included a small reserve of "trained riflemen" who were to be at the ready to deal with the larger animals if necessary. The riflemen were later ordered to add German paratroopers to their list of potential targets.[40] *Time* magazine also reported that "beauty parlors were crammed with women seeking one last hairdo before fleeing to safety or reporting for emergency jobs."[41]

In a futile attempt to persuade Germans not to follow Hitler, British planes began dropping thirteen tons of leaflets in Germany with this message: "Your rulers have condemned you to the massacres, miseries and privations of a war they cannot ever hope to win."[42] The warning was prophetic, but its promise would not be realized for years to come.

Just as precautionary measures were being taken on land, several shipments of gold from the Bank of England were on the high seas en route to the United States. The *Samaria, Arandora Star, Van Dyck, Antonia, Empress of Britain,* and *Empress of Australia* each carried roughly £3 million in gold. The famed *Queen Mary* was also heading to the United States when the war broke out. Its twenty-five hundred passengers, including actor/comedian Bob Hope and his wife, learned mid-voyage that Britain and France had declared war against Germany. The cargo hidden from the bewildered passengers was £10 million in gold.[43]

British and Canadian leaders knew that there would undoubtedly be more gold shipments to finance the war, but they could not anticipate how many would be required. Much depended on Hitler's ambitions, of course, but much also depended on America's reaction to the war.

3

Seeking Refuge from the Storm

London seemed "half-deserted and silent" after more than a week of war. On September 11, 1939, *Time* reported, "London had changed . . . with the eerie air of a city of no children, when their absence from the parks and the playgrounds, the lack of their racket in the streets, reminded people how much their unnoticed daily presence had contributed to the life of the city." *Time* also offered this generally positive image of the British prime minister:

> In the trenches amid mud, vermin, bad food and the repeated shock of shells exploding all around, the 70-year-old body of Neville Chamberlain would probably become a physical wreck in a few hours. But at the end of last week the British Prime Minister had been through 13 days of such labor, strain and anxiety as would have wrecked the constitution of many a man under 30. And Mr. Chamberlain emerged from it rather fatigued but quite unshaken. Fortunately the old do not need much sleep.[1]

In his diary, Chamberlain simply wrote, "Here again after a week of war which seems like a year."[2]

Over the next few months, German forces dealt serious blows to the British cause. On September 17, 1939, the German submarine U-29 sank the British aircraft carrier *Courageous* with the loss of over five hundred men. By the end of October, U-boats had sunk nearly seventy ships.[3] In November Karl Dönitz, head of Germany's U-boat fleet, issued Standing Order No. 154: "Rescue no one and take no one aboard. Do not concern yourself with the ship's boats. Weather conditions and the proximity of land are of no account. Care only for your own boat and strive to achieve the next success as soon as possible! We must be hard in this war."[4] In the middle of November, German bombers struck British soil for the first time. Even though the raid did only minor damage to an unoccupied house on the Shetland Islands, it was an omen of things to come. The attack symbolized the vulnerability of the British Isles to German air attack.[5]

The threat of Nazi domination was so serious that many in the Allied countries began to contemplate radically new ideas about the relations of nations. The governor general of Canada, Lord Tweedsmuir (John Buchan), offered an optimistic vision in which the Allies would prevail. In a letter to Prime Minister Chamberlain, Lord Tweedsmuir wrote that "the only way to safeguard the future of civilization is by some kind of federal system, which would begin by including all the Powers who accept the Reign of Law. Its members should have a common denominator in the shape of a political creed, and there should be a surrender, where necessary, of certain elements of national sovereignty."[6] Tweedsmuir's 1939 vision is similar in many ways to the realities of today's European Union.

What disturbed most citizens of Allied countries was a different scenario—a nightmarish scene of Europe dominated by Nazi Germany. If Europe were to succumb to fascism, the fate of the rest of the world's democracies would be in jeopardy. In the early months of the war, many in Britain—including members of the armed forces—were convinced that Germany would soon attack Britain with horrific consequences. In a letter to his sister in mid-October, Chamberlain wrote, "I still retain my skepticism about any major attack either on land or from the air. But I am bound to say that the soldiers are all against me. They think an attack is imminent—it might even come today and they say you can't pile up so many divisions and then do nothing with them."[7]

Given the gravity of the situation in Europe, one of the biggest questions was, what was the United States going to do? American entry into the war would fundamentally alter the balance of power, giving Britain, France, and the rest of Europe's democracies a much greater chance of survival. Concealed behind this strategic question about U.S. participation, however, was a far more urgent question for the short term: If the United States stayed out of the war or delayed its entry, how would Britain arm itself sufficiently? And if the United States demanded payment for arms and other supplies up front, how would Britain pay for them? If the United States obstinately remained aloof, Britain would be forced to arrange more risky shipments of gold and securities.

Before the war, and even during its first few months, it would have been foolhardy to count on American intervention. In fact, any hopes that the United States would declare war against Germany in late 1939 faded quickly owing to overwhelming American opposition to the war. Relying on the geographic security afforded to it by the Atlantic Ocean, the United States sought to isolate itself from the deadly troubles of the Old World.

The isolationist, anti-interventionist mood in America led Congress to pass two vitally important pieces of legislation that compelled Britain to take tremendous risks with its wealth. The Johnson Act, passed by Congress in 1934, prohibited loans to any government that was already in debt to the American government.[8] The act severely constrained Britain, which still owed the United States about $4 billion, much of which was from World War I.[9]

As early as 1921, Winston Churchill had complained about American stubbornness over the debt. His comments were as relevant in 1939 as they had been nearly twenty years before: "It was uphill work to make an enthusiastic speech about the United States at a time when so many hard things are said about us over there and when they are wringing the last penny out of their unfortunate allies. All the same there is only one road for us to tread, and that is to keep as friendly with them as possible, to be overwhelmingly patient and to wait for the growth of better feelings."[10]

In August 1939, the British government sent Lord Riverdale of Sheffield to Washington, New York, and Ottawa to sound out attitudes about the potential war. He reported back to London that "in every direction, in private discussions, and in cartoons in the newspapers, the non-payment of the War Debt by Great Britain is quoted in rather an antagonistic spirit, and while this is very detrimental, I do not think that in the last resource it would stand in the way of the abolition of the Johnson Act if war actually occurred."[11] Lord Riverdale's optimism was not shared by Second Secretary to the Treasury Sir Richard Hopkins. In a letter to the Bank of England, Hopkins wrote, "It seems to me possible that, when it came to the pinch, American help would be found to be accompanied by awkward and embarrassing limitations or conditions."[12] In fact, when the war came weeks later, the Johnson Act remained in effect, impeding Britain's ability to buy its much needed war matériel or vast stocks of civilian goods on credit.

The isolationist mood in Washington influenced a second important piece of congressional legislation—the 1935 Neutrality Act prohibiting the sale of arms and war matériel to belligerent states. The act was revised in 1936 to include a ban on loans to countries waging war and in 1937 to include what became known as the cash-and-carry provision. Cash was required to purchase goods, and the goods would have to be carried away on non-American ships. Congress included this provision, in part, to prevent American ships from coming under attack in a future war. FDR, who encouraged the provision, knew that the cash-and-carry plan would benefit Britain and France—the only countries with sufficient gold and dollar resources to pay for massive quantities of wartime goods *and* the shipping capacity to carry the purchased goods away.[13] Leaders in Europe's national capitals, including Berlin, most certainly came to the same realization.

Back in March 1939, after Germany occupied Czechoslovakia, Roosevelt sought to include arms sales in renewed cash-and-carry legislation. Congress would have none of it. Lawmakers were in no mood to give the perception that the United States was arming Germany's enemies. With or without the ban on weapons, it remained uncertain how much British gold would have to be shipped. Almost two weeks into the war, the *Wall Street Journal* reported that the pressure to ship gold to the New World was so great "that it was understood all available cargo space—except on German boats—has been engaged for the next two or three weeks."[14] The flow of the precious metal would eventually turn into a deluge with each major German military victory.

Concerned about the effects of Congress's neutrality legislation, Chamberlain wrote in his diary on February 19, 1939, that the United States "has drawn closer to us, but the isolationists there are so strong and so vocal that she cannot be depended on for help if we should get into trouble."[15] Three months later, during the royal visit to the United States, King George VI thought that FDR might find a way to work around the Johnson Act's prohibition of further loans to Britain, but the King came away from the discussion empty-handed. Resigned to the realities of the American political climate, the King wrote, "Better not reopen the question. Congress wants repayment in full, which is impossible, and a small bit [of loan repayment] is of no use, as they will want more later."[16]

If today's debates about the wars in Iraq and Afghanistan use, correctly or not, the Vietnam War as the launching point for comparative analysis, Americans of the 1930s and early 1940s used World War I as their main reference point. In addition to the number of individuals wounded and the disruptions to the lives of millions, 127,000 Americans died in World War I.[17] Americans understandably wanted to avoid repeating the horrors of the Great War, and to most that required staying uninvolved in Europe's conflicts.

In the 1930s the American public's isolationist stance meant that the Roosevelt administration would withhold the financial and military help the Chamberlain government so desperately hoped to receive. Despite his sympathies for Britain's plight, the president sometimes sounded the isolationist call himself. In his annual message to Congress in January 1936, Roosevelt said that as part of a consistent policy the United States declined "to encourage the prosecution of war by permitting belligerents to obtain arms, ammunition or implements of war from the United States."[18] FDR was more forceful in a speech to a joint session of Congress on September 21, 1937: "Our acts must be guided by one single hard-headed thought—keeping America out of this war!"[19] For FDR and Congress, there was no doubt that "this war" meant another great war.

Isolationism ran deep in American society. Isolationists included among their ranks politicians, celebrities, students, and most of the general public. As war in Europe became increasingly likely, and to some extent even more so once the war began, isolationists in Congress frequently lobbied the Roosevelt administration to keep the United States out. Prominent isolationists in Congress included Senators William Borah (R-ID), Bennett Clark (D-MO), Hiram Johnson (R-CA), William Langer (R-ND), Gerald Nye (R-ND), Robert Taft (R-OH), and Arthur Vandenberg (R-MI).

After Germany's swift victory over Poland in September 1939, the Neutrality Act, with its cash-and-carry component, was renewed in early November. This time, however, the arms embargo was lifted.[20] In response, an unhappy Senator Vandenberg wrote in his diary, "In the name of 'democracy' we have taken the first step, once more, into Europe's 'power policies.' . . . What 'suckers' our emotions make of us."[21] Speaking at an April 1940 meeting in Pennsylvania, Senator Nye told the audience that the European war was not "worthy of the sacrifice of one American mule, much less one American son."[22] Senator David Walsh (D-MA) said, "I do not want our forces deprived of one gun, or one bomb or one ship which can aid that American boy whom you and I may some day have to draft."[23] In July, the chairman of the Senate Foreign Relations Committee, Key Pittman (D-NV) argued that Britain's position was so hopeless that it should accept Nazi domination and send its fleet to North America. In his view, it was fruitless for Britain to fight on and fruitless for the United States to send it weapons.[24]

High-ranking members of the U.S. military were also opposed to joining the war in Europe and even resisted sending arms to Britain. Many military leaders believed that American weapons sent to Britain would eventually be used against the United States if Germany defeated Britain. Britain, hoping to place significant orders for airplanes and engines, faced stiff resistance, for example, from the Army Air Corps. Opposition to aiding Britain came not only from military leaders like Gen. Henry "Hap" Arnold, the head of the Air Corps, but also from Secretary of War Harry Woodring and his assistant secretary Louis Johnson. They refused to support British arms purchases in part because they wanted to conserve weaponry the United States might eventually need if it got dragged into the war.[25]

Isolationist feelings also hampered military cooperation between Britain and the United States. Shortly after the start of the war, for example, the Chamberlain government offered the United States access to Britain's ASDIC technology for locating submarines. (ASDIC was similar to sonar.) The British Air Ministry insisted that, as part of the bargain, the United States should provide the secrets to its Norden bombsight technology. The Americans, likely influenced by the desire to avoid too close a relationship with Britain, were unwilling to complete the deal.[26]

Many college students were also fervent opponents of giving aid to Britain. Nearly fifteen hundred Yale students signed a petition stating that the United States should "grant no credits, give no supplies and send no men . . . even if England is on the verge of defeat." Among those who signed the petition was future U.S. president Gerald Ford. Similar antiwar gestures were made by students at Princeton University, City College of New York, the University of Virginia, the University of Kansas, and elsewhere.[27]

One of the most prominent antiwar groups, the America First Committee (AFC), had many well-known industrialists and politicians on its membership roll. It advanced four basic principles. First, the United States must build an impregnable defense. Second, no power can attack a prepared America. Third, American democracy can be preserved only by keeping out of a European war. And fourth, aid short of war weakens national defense and threatens to involve America in war. The AFC's most prominent member was its spokesperson, Charles Lindbergh. Other members included Gerald Ford, future Supreme Court Justice Potter Stewart, and former general Robert E. Wood, chairman of the Sears, Roebuck & Co board.[28]

Joseph P. Kennedy, the U.S. ambassador to Britain since 1938, believed the United States was ill-prepared for war, a view shared by the popular press. Even as late as May 1940, U.S. Army maneuvers in Louisiana had gone so poorly that *Time* magazine reported, "Against Europe's total war, the U.S. Army looked like a few nice boys with BB Guns."[29] In June 1940, as FDR tried to rally the nation to Britain's defense, most military observers were aware of how inadequate U.S. defenses truly were. The U.S. Army was ranked eighteenth in the world—behind even Portugal, Spain, and Switzerland. Germany had 6.8 million men under arms while America had slightly more than half a million.[30]

Another prominent isolationist was Henry Ford. Demonstrating that isolationists were motivated by many things, Ford was also anti-British and anti-Semitic. Among his gestures to oppose the war, Ford refused to build airplane engines in his factories after learning that some of them would be used by the British.[31]

Isolationism was strong on the political left as well. Socialist Party leader Norman Thomas argued that war was inevitable in Europe, but that the only way for the United States to build a new socialist society was to stay away from the fighting.[32] Socialist organizations in general tended to characterize the coming war not in terms of a great power struggle but in the context of Marxist-Leninist concepts. (The journal *Christian Century* took a similar position, arguing that war would involve rival imperial powers.[33]) For example, the platform of the Keep America Out of War Congress (KAOWC), a pacifist-socialist group organized in March 1938, stated that the United States should withdraw from imperialist involvements, end conscription, and terminate foreign alliances. The group was primarily concerned that FDR would gain dictatorial powers and that the government would initiate a program of censorship.[34]

The fear of a Roosevelt dictatorship ran so deep that it worked its way into a campaign speech by Republican presidential candidate Wendell L. Willkie in September 1940. At a campaign stop in Coffeyville, Kansas, Willkie told his fellow countrymen,

> I deny that Franklin Roosevelt—whatever his intentions—is the defender of democracy. First, I charge that his influence has weakened, rather than strengthened democracy throughout the world. And secondly, I charge that here in America he has strained our democratic institutions to the breaking point. I warn you—and I say this in dead earnest—if, because of some fine speeches about humanity, you return this administration to office, you will be serving under an American totalitarian government before the long third term is finished.[35]

Thus both KAOWC and the Republican candidate for the presidency saw U.S. involvement in the war as a prelude to American fascism.

Given the intensity of isolationist sentiment permeating American society, pro-British members of the Roosevelt administration knew that they had to tread carefully. Treasury Secretary Morgenthau counseled the British on the public relations risk of coordinating their stocks and bonds sales in the United States through J. P. Morgan & Company. In World War I, the company, as broker to the British, collected a commission that Morgenthau considered properly earned. Nevertheless, Morgenthau warned that there was a "certain phobia" against the company because it more or less symbolized "the one institution that got us into the last war. . . . The children in the schools are taught that."[36]

British pleas for help could sway neither Congress nor an intractable American public. On September 11, 1939, a week after Britain and France declared war on Germany, newly appointed Minister of Information Hugh Macmillan wrote to Chamberlain advising him on the most effective approach to take with the Americans. Macmillan—who described himself as having "probably as large an American acquaintance as any Englishman living"—wrote,

> American psychology has changed considerably since 1914. Her people, on the whole, are exceedingly well-informed about international questions. . . . But at the prevailing moment the mood is fear—quite honorable fear. She

descended into the pit in 1929 and has now managed to crawl a certain distance out of it. But she is in terror—all classes—of slipping back again . . . [r]ightly or wrongly, she puts down all her economic troubles to the last war.[37]

Lord Lothian, the British ambassador to the United States, offered similar advice for dealing with U.S. officials. He warned his colleagues at the Foreign Office in London not to antagonize the Americans for legislation blocking aid to Britain "for that will simply inflame the present isolationist argument that America is being driven to supply first arms, then money, and then armies."[38] Lord Riverdale, the head of the British Air Training Mission, wrote in mid-August 1939 to the minister of supply, Leslie Burgin, that under no circumstances should the British be seen as trying to evade the Johnson Act or the Neutrality Act. He added, "Nothing would give the pacifists and the isolationists better ammunition than our having employed roundabout methods to evade these Acts."[39] The counsel offered by Lothian and Riverdale mattered significantly because, as Roosevelt administration official Edward R. Stettinius put it, many in Congress "believed that the U.S. shouldn't be dragged into another war because of 'cunning allied propaganda.'"[40]

As head of the Admiralty and later as prime minister, Churchill adopted this delicate approach to the United States in general, and to FDR in particular. According to historian Keith Sainsbury,

Churchill was aware, from the beginning of the relationship, how important it was for Britain that he should cultivate and conciliate Roosevelt. . . . [H]e disciplined himself to show uncharacteristic patience and restraint in his dealings with the President, but he lacked the personal sensitivity that would have enabled him in any real sense, to "manage" Roosevelt. . . . Insofar as Churchill and his British associate[s] were able to "persuade" the President, it was essentially by providing facts and figures, the weight of evidence, which convinced Roosevelt and his associates of certain necessities, rather than Churchill's inherent persuasiveness.[41]

By the summer of 1939, with the war still two months away, officials in Britain debated the likelihood of U.S. help. During a Cabinet meeting in early July, Viscount Halifax, secretary of state for foreign affairs, said that if "the war should last longer than we anticipated, it would be reasonably safe to assume that . . . the attitude of the United States would be sufficiently favorable to us to enable us to win the war." Sir

Richard Hopkins at the Treasury, however, argued that Britain had to proceed on the assumption that the United States would not be willing to give Britain "unlimited financial resources" in a long war.[42]

Aware of the doubts and hesitations in the United States, Prime Minister Winston Churchill wrote to President Roosevelt in mid-June 1940 to express in dire terms the fragility of his country's independence: "Although the present government and I personally would never fail to send the fleet across the Atlantic if resistance was beaten down here, a point may be reached in the struggle where the present [Cabinet] ministers no longer have control of affairs and when very easy terms could be obtained for the British Islands by their becoming a vassal state of the Hitler empire."[43]

Through the first year of war, the British came to feel that the United States was committing two strategic mistakes. First, the United States failed to realize the threat to the world posed by Hitler's ambitions, and second, it believed that it could permanently avoid becoming entangled in another European war. Many in Britain also complained that as the war progressed, the U.S. Congress failed to understand how greater assistance to Britain was in the national interest of the United States. Few knew or had any appreciation of the risks Britain was taking with its clandestine shipments of gold and securities.

Isolationist sentiment in the United States highlighted significant differences between the two countries despite their historical, political, and cultural similarities. At times, it seemed as if the two great powers were still strangers to each other.[44] Even among high-ranking officials in Britain, the basic framework of the American political system needed to be clarified from time to time. For example, British officials working with U.S. government and corporate representatives were reminded that the U.S. Congress was more powerful than the British Parliament.[45]

The disconnect between the British and American positions extended into cultural arenas as well. For example, Sir Alexander Cadogan, the permanent undersecretary at the Foreign Office, wrote in his diaries perhaps the oddest put-down of America's pastime ever: "Spent about 5 minutes watching a baseball match. It's the silliest—and the dullest—game I've ever seen. I'd no sooner play dominoes with mangeldwurzels [beets]."[46] The lack of understanding between the two countries, as well as their different strategic perspectives, meant that Britain's financial situation would remain precarious through the most danger-ous months of the war.[47]

Smoothing over differences between the two countries was not facil-itated by FDR's assessments of several high-ranking British politi-cians. According to Sir Arthur Willet, who spoke with FDR in April 1939, "The President was bitter about appeasement. He had no use for Chamberlain. He thought [Chancellor of the Exchequer John] Simon and [Lord Privy Seal] Samuel Hoare about the worst foreign ministers [Britain] ever had."[48]

The person ideally situated to help bring the two countries together—the American ambassador in London—actually muddied the diplomatic waters further. Joseph Kennedy, among American officials with cru-cial links to the British government, was perhaps the most pessimistic about Britain's ability to withstand Nazi Germany. In 1940 Kennedy declared, "Democracy is finished in England. It may be [in the United States as well]. Because it comes to a question of feeding people. It's all an economic question. . . . It's the loss of our foreign trade that's going to threaten to change our form of government." He had been making similarly defeatist remarks since early 1939. The man that *Time* maga-zine described as the "official eyes, ears, head and heart of the U.S. in Great Britain" was of little use to the British.[49]

Chamberlain, Halifax, and Cadogan initially liked Kennedy, but many in the British government had doubts about Kennedy's diplo-matic value from the start. As one official in the Foreign Office put it, "according to a 'very reliable journalist' with 'excellent' sources," Ken-nedy was chosen to be ambassador to the United Kingdom "in order to get him out of the way. He is in a position to control 25 million Catho-lic votes."[50] In this interpretation, the Democrats' electoral needs dic-tated the choice and retention of Kennedy, not his policy disposition or diplomatic skills. In fact, according to Kennedy biographer, David Nasaw, the new American ambassador to Britain "had never demon-strated any interest or knowledge of foreign affairs, and he was among the least diplomatic men in Washington."[51]

One of the harshest accusations about Kennedy came from J. V. Perowne of the Foreign Office. Perowne wrote that one of his "trusted sources" had described Kennedy as the biggest "fifth columnist" (internal enemy) in Britain. "His attempts to influence neutral journalists were described as persistent. Kennedy is alleged to have told journalists that

Hitler would be in London by August 15 [1940]." Sir Balfour replied to Perowne saying that "whilst we do not consider Mr. Kennedy as anti-British, we consider that he is undoubtedly a coward."[52]

Roosevelt's own opinion of Kennedy was not always flattering. As he told Treasury Secretary Morgenthau, "Joe Kennedy . . . has been an appeaser and always will be an appeaser. . . . If Germany or Italy made a good peace offer tomorrow, Joe would start working on the [British] King . . . and from there on down to get everybody to accept it. . . . He's just a pain in the neck to me."[53] Nevertheless, FDR kept Kennedy at the post of top U.S. representative in London during the first year of the war, much to the chagrin of the British, who so desperately needed a more sympathetic White House liaison. Kennedy eventually announced his retirement and returned to the United States on October 23, 1940, citing his intentions to devote his efforts to the "greatest cause in the world—helping the President keep the United States out of war."[54] Kennedy's faith in American isolationism persisted into 1941, when he stated that it was "nonsense to say an Axis victory spells ruin for us."[55]

While British leaders hoped for greater U.S. involvement in the war, many had grown restless. The United States had, after all, "gone very far in seeking refuge from the storm," as Allen W. Dulles put it.[56] Frustrated by the political realities of the time, Colville wrote in his diary, "The U.S. is aloof, and critical of what everybody in Europe is doing and thinking, without showing the least inclination to step in to redress the balance of the Old World."[57]

———————————

The United States was not completely indifferent to the British cause, however. Despite the choppy relationship between the United States and Britain, some of the onerous roadblocks in U.S. neutrality legislation were removed after Poland's defeat in September 1939. More specifically, after contentious debates in Congress, the United States finally adjusted laws pertaining to belligerents in the war. As noted earlier, in the 1939 revision of the Neutrality Act, cash-and-carry remained in effect (so Britain would still have to provide cash for merchandise—in the form of dollars or gold) but the prohibition on arms sales was eliminated.[58] Writing in *Foreign Affairs* shortly after the revision was passed, Dulles commented, "Public opinion was unanimous in the desire to do nothing which might involve us in war; but there was reluctance to assume the responsibility of withholding aid which could properly be given to the democracies."[59] With the ban on weapons sales lifted, Britain anticipated placing many large orders. To pay for those orders, Britain began in earnest to plan more "special shipments" to North America.

Consistent with the prevailing mood of isolationism, the amended Neutrality Act banned American merchant vessels from traveling in the broadly defined danger zone of Atlantic sea-lanes to avoid an incident that might trigger U.S. involvement in the war.[60] Churchill responded favorably to these changes—despite their restrictions. "Deepest gratitude for your wonderful neutrality [b]ill," he wrote in the *Evening Standard*. It "certainly has the merit of rendering to superior sea power its full desserts [*sic*]. . . . It may be rather chilling comfort, but it is comfort none the less."[61]

The "comfort" allowed Britain, as well as France, to proceed with heavy expenditures for military and civilian goods from America. After the latest version of the Neutrality Act was passed, an Anglo-French Purchasing Board was established in Washington. With the goal of pooling resources, the British and French agreed to coordinate most of their economic activities, including shipping, airplane production, and the purchase of munitions, food, and oil.[62] The Purchasing Board was led by Arthur Purvis, a Scottish-born Canadian industrialist with extensive connections on both sides of the Atlantic. He had served in a similar capacity in World War I, during which he was in charge of buying up stocks of acetone (a key ingredient in the manufacture of explosives) in the United States.[63] Purvis played an instrumental role over the coming months as Britain and France sought to convert their nations' gold into weapons and other goods.

President Roosevelt was a strong supporter of Britain. As historian Martin Gilbert explained, "With the knowledge that Roosevelt himself was not only responsive but also inventive in regard to Britain's needs, the British government could pursue the war with a confidence far greater than if Britain had been truly 'alone.'"[64] Treasury Secretary Morgenthau also worked tirelessly to help the British and the French obtain as much weaponry from the United States as possible. After Morgenthau persuaded the president to allow the sale of airplanes, for example, FDR in turn told a reluctant Secretary of War Harry Woodring to accept the Allies' purchase order or resign. Woodring relented, and on April

10, 1940, Purvis and his colleagues from the Anglo-French Purchasing Mission signed contracts for 2,400 fighters and 2,160 bombers.[65] A month later, Purvis secured even more supplies, many on favorable terms. At the end of May 1940, the British acquired 500 mortars, 500 field guns, "some thousands" of antiaircraft guns, 10,000 machine guns, 25,000 automatic rifles, 500,000 Lee-Enfield rifles, and 100 million rounds of machine-gun and rifle ammunition. Purvis also relayed to his superiors in London that the United States could supply Britain with large quantities of "surplus" munitions.[66]

On a popular level, the British had considerable support in the United States, especially as the situation in Europe worsened. According to a British visitor to the American West Coast on May 14, 1940,

> San Francisco, as you know, is the 2nd most cosmopolitan city in the USA. Today, I sat in a news theater and was amazed at what I saw & heard. Many notables were screened. Mussolini was hissed. The Norwegian King got a mild hand. President Roosevelt got quite a generous applause, but when a picture of Rt. Honorable Winston Churchill reviewing the troops in France was shown, the house went frenzied & applauded until the last scene in it. There is no question that "Winnie", with his frankness & his action, appeals tremendously to American audiences.[67]

Nevertheless, stubborn isolationist sentiment in the United States directly and indirectly affected Britain's treasure shipments throughout the remainder of 1939 and into 1940. At the start of World War II, Britain's finances were in poor shape given the prospects of a lengthy war with Germany. Less than a week into the war, British Cabinet officials knew that their gold reserves were unlikely to hold out. According to secret minutes from a meeting on September 8, 1939,

> It is obvious that we are in grave danger of our gold reserves being exhausted at a rate that will render us incapable of waging war if war is prolonged. I propose that the War Cabinet should issue directions immediately calling for:
>
> (1) the maximum possible restriction of unnecessary imports involving payments in these currencies and early action as regards rationing schemes for home consumption of commodities needing to be bought with such currencies
>
> (2) the greatest possible encouragement to export trade. In this connection steps should be taken to restrict consumption at home of goods

which might be marketed abroad and to expand as much as possible the production of export goods available in this country and particularly of coal which seems likely to be almost as valuable to us as gold;

(3) the restriction of payments by the Defence Services particularly in North America to the absolute minimum of essential and speedily available services.[68]

In short, if the goods purchased in the United States could have been bought on credit, the need to make risky gold shipments would have been significantly reduced. But with war in Europe gaining momentum, the demands upon British treasure would grow—slowly at first and then at an astounding pace.

4

Gold and the Phony War

Adolf Hitler convened his military chiefs on October 10, 1939, to refine Germany's strategy for controlling western Europe. According to Hitler's Directive Number 6, the Germans planned to seize Belgium, the Netherlands, and France and use bases in northern France to wage an air and sea war against Britain.[1] On October 15, a lengthy German study on the direction of the war noted, "The chief opponent of Germany in this war is England. Her most vulnerable point is commerce at sea. The war at sea against England, militarily, is therefore to be conducted as an economic war with the aim to destroy in the shortest time England's will to resist and force her readiness for peace."[2] Hitler expected Britain to initiate a naval blockade of Germany after the start of the war, which it did, but the German leader sloughed off concern about it. "We need not be afraid of a blockade," he told his commanders. "I am only afraid that at the last minute some Schweinhund will make a proposal for mediation."[3] Hitler was committed to all-out war, blockade or not.

Hitler's optimism about the war at sea was boosted by some early naval reports. In mid-October, Kapitänleutnant Günther Prien's U-47 submarine executed a daring raid into the very heart of the Scapa Flow naval base in Scotland's Orkney Islands. In what Karl Dönitz called "the boldest of bold enterprises," Prien managed to evade both enemy ships and submerged obstacles to sink the battleship *Royal Oak*. Of the 1,200 sailors on board the ship, 833 perished.[4]

While the Battle of the Atlantic raged on, the stewards of Britain's finances were busy analyzing how the country could afford to pay for the war. Months into the war, the status of Britain's gold reserves was unsettling, a situation that had been anticipated before the war had even begun. According to secret Cabinet minutes from July 3, 1939, Britain's £500 million stock of gold was "rapidly diminishing." In a "Most Secret" memorandum from the Office of the Chancellor of the Exchequer, John Simon indicated that at the start of the war, Britain's gold reserves were just 45 percent of what they had been only eighteen months earlier.[5] As the financial demands of the war grew week by week, the situation was going from bad to worse. Given Britain's large but declining gold reserves, the Treasury initiated plans to requisition gold from other parts of the Commonwealth, notably Australia, India, and especially South Africa. In due course, the Treasury and the Bank of England arranged shipments to North America from Sydney, Bombay, Cape Town, and Hong Kong. In all, approximately 11 percent of the gold shipped to North America originated in these cities.[6]

Some of the shipments did not go unnoticed in the American press. The *Wall Street Journal* could identify neither ship nor cargo value, but it did report a major increase in gold imports to the United States from throughout the British Empire via Canada: "While the upturn in [British] gold imports from Canada has been the most marked recent change in the flow of the metal to this country, other regions in the British Empire also have been shipping relatively substantial amounts here over the past five or six weeks. In the week ended December 6, net imports from the United Kingdom, the Union of South Africa, Australia, and British India amounted to only $4.5 million, but in November these sources shipped about $53.5 million to this country."[7]

Meanwhile, Sir Frederick Phillips at the Treasury delivered more bad news about Britain's money troubles. He warned that a

> mere repeal of the Johnson Act to enable us to borrow in the New York market would be useless. We cannot borrow on our own credit in the United States sums sufficiently large to finance our war effort for more than a brief period. . . . What we want, if it can be obtained, is a direct grant from the United States government, and we can plead in support that we are the advanced defense line of the United States, which they would have to arm and man *themselves* if we were not there.[8]

Phillips noted a hypothetical "large loan" of roughly £2 billion, which Britain would be "physically incapable" of repaying. Of course, such a loan or direct grant was a nonstarter given the isolationist mood in the United States in 1939 and 1940.

At the same time, the British Treasury and the Foreign Office studied how—as well as how many—dollar-based securities held by British citizens could be sold in the United States. Holders of the securities would be paid in pounds sterling while the government retained the dollars—the only currency the United States would accept. By October 1939, the Treasury estimated that of all foreign securities, about $600 million worth could be "reasonably marketable" in the United States. In addition, roughly 150 million Canadian dollars' worth of securities were reasonably marketable in Canada.[9]

In October 1939, Phillips told U.S. ambassador Joseph Kennedy that Britain preferred money derived from securities in order to reduce the amount of gold that had to be shipped.[10] The escalating financial demands of war, however, meant that even greater quantities of both gold and securities would have to be sent across the world's oceans in the months ahead.

In the midst of the gloomy political and financial news, the Chamberlain government authorized shipments of more treasure to North America, in spite of the U-boat dangers in the Atlantic. In early September 1939, two ships carrying a combined $28 million in gold made it safely to Canada. A third gold shipment worth $13.2 million was most likely sent to Canada initially and then "diverted" to New York.[11]

Among the ships sent in October 1939 were the cruisers HMS *Enterprise*, HMS *Emerald*, and HMS *Caradoc*. The *Enterprise*'s motto seemed quite fitting for the voyage: *Spes aspera levat* (hope lightens difficulties). From the huge and forbidding Scapa Flow naval base in Scotland, the captains of the three ships were given orders to set sail for Plymouth, England, "with all dispatch." The Admiralty's orders for the impending mission were not initially disclosed even to the captains. Within thirty-six hours of their arrival at Plymouth, the ships were loaded up with ammunition, oil, and miscellaneous stores.

In the middle of the night of October 6, recalled Capt. Augustus Agar of the *Emerald*, "a small railway truck was placed alongside the ship with cases of special secret explosives which had to be handled carefully, and placed in one of the ship's magazines. . . . I summoned six sailors to manhandle these packages from the railway truck in barrows down two ladders into the 'small arm magazine,' after which I had it locked up

FIG. 4.1. One of the fastest ships in the British Royal Navy, HMS *Emerald* carried gold and securities from Britain to Canada on six occasions in 1939 and 1940. *Courtesy of the Imperial War Museum*

and kept the key myself. Each package contained a dozen smaller ones, the size of bricks and weighed about 130 pounds." Since thousands of explosives packages had already been handled that day, no one was particularly interested in the contents of the boxes. When all of the loading was completed, the *Emerald* received two civilians in bowler hats who proceeded to the captain's cabin for a confidential discussion.[12] Capt. Henry Jack Egerton watched over a similar operation on his ship, the *Enterprise*, as did Capt. Eric Longley-Cook on board the *Caradoc*.

To throw off any spies who might be watching, the ships' crews were given tropical clothing. So the "mess deck buzz" suggested that the ships were heading for the warm waters of the East Indies or perhaps Freetown in Sierra Leone. Just short of midnight, the captains were finally given their destination and told what the boxes of special explosives really contained. Each captain read this message from the commander in chief of the Western Approaches to Britain:

To: The commanding officers, HM Ships, *Emerald, Enterprise* and *Caradoc*: Two million pounds in gold bars is to be embarked in each ship for transit to Halifax. A railway truck is expected to be placed alongside each ship about 0100/7th October. Each truck is expected to contain 148 boxes each weighing 130 lbs. The total number of boxes is numbered from Z.298 to Z.741 inclusive. Guards are to be put on each truck on arrival at the ship. Embarkation is to commence about 0630, or as soon as daylight permits. Adequate steps are to be taken for supervision of each box from unloading from truck to stowage in ship. Finally a receipt is to be forwarded to Commander-in-Chief, Western Approaches on the attached Form. 2351/6th October 1939.[13]

The value of the cargo heading west was significantly enhanced by crates that did *not* contain gold. Agar reported that his ship was also carrying four boxes of financial securities from the Bank of England, which he estimated to be worth ten times the value of the gold. The battleships HMS *Revenge* and HMS *Resolution* accompanied the three ships across the Atlantic, and each of these ships carried £2 million in gold as well.

The convoy faced weather conditions so poor that the crews got little sleep.[14] Looking back on events, Wally Devine, a young steward, wrote a poem about his experiences on board the *Emerald* in bad weather:

There came a time when we could not relax,
Carrying Britain's gold to Halifax;
You were chosen for the task, for indeed
They wanted a ship that had the speed.
Thirty knots was nothing new to you,
Plus a few more if you so had to do;
You did the job without delay,
And we liked you better every day.
At times the trips and weather were rough
And life below decks was pretty tough;
Going from the galley with food in my grip,
You threw me down the ladder, arse over tip.
The Chief Cook shouted "Grab hold of that sling.
One hand for yourself, and one for the King!"
Our thoughts of you then were very blue,
You *three funneled bastard*, we hated you![15]

By October 16, the convoy had completed the journey undisturbed by any elements of the German navy. But the horrendous weather during the trans-Atlantic crossing had taken its toll on the *Emerald*. In Halifax, Rear Adm. L. E. Holland of the *Revenge* told Captain Agar, "You may not know it, but [the *Emerald* looks] like a Surrealist drawing."[16]

In order to maintain the treasure's secrecy in Halifax, the one hundred or so RCMP officers who stood guard were told that they were protecting secret explosives. Sailors from other ships in the harbor wondered why so much security was required for the transfer of explosives, but all they could see were sailors unloading wooden boxes. The gold was transferred from the ships to special railcars. The manager of the Bank of Canada officially received the gold and handed the ship captains written receipts for the goods.[17]

As was typical with other "special shipments" at the time, the ships' logs contained no references to the unusual cargo. Admiralty records indicate how mundane ship's logs could be. Following is an example from the *Emerald* in October 1939:[18]

> 1 October 1939 (Sunday) Secured ship (at Scapa) for sea 0600.
>
> 4 October 1939 Secured alongside Enterprise at No. 6 Wharf. "Hands employed ammunitioning." 1050 also 1315. Hands employed stowing ship at various times 5 and 6 October 1939.
>
> 7 October 1939 Left for Halifax. In company with *Caradoc* and *Enterprise*. Took station with *Resolution* and *Revenge*.
>
> 8 October 1939 1500 put clocks back 1 hour.
>
> 9 October 1939 Lost overboard in heavy weather: 2 Brass boat locks, 3 oars, 2 brass crutches, 1 towing ballard. 1 tiller, 1 grapnel, 1 anchor, 4 lifebelts, 5 set oilskin jackets, 5 set oilskin trousers . . .
>
> 16 October 1939 gets to Halifax No. 23 wharf, Canadian National Railway terminus (at 0910) starboard side.
>
> 17 October 1939 1315 Hands employed painting ship.
>
> 18 October 1939 Left Halifax for Plymouth.

The tropical clothing that had been issued to the crew upon departure from England was, of course, thoroughly inappropriate for the North Atlantic. Once in Halifax, Captain Agar discussed the problem with a representative of the Bank of Canada who, in turn, spoke with Canadian Red Cross representatives. Within forty-eight hours, a grateful Agar could report, cases were arriving on board containing "those warm horsehide gloves used by Canadian lumbermen, lovely woolen scarves and sea boot stockings, leather headgear lined with wool and fur outside for ear protection; and to cap everything, woolen underwear of long pants and vests with enough for every man in the ship. . . . No sailor who served in our ships during those early days at Halifax will ever forget the Canadian Red Cross."[19]

That same month, the British dispatched half a dozen other ships to Halifax, each carrying £2 million in gold.[20] Meanwhile, the War Cabinet met to discuss ways of preventing Belgian and Dutch gold and securities from falling into German hands. Unlike Britain, at least for the time being, Belgium and the Netherlands were less interested in using gold to buy war matériel than in evacuating it to safety. As secret British Cabinet documents reveal, "It will be for the Treasury in collaboration with the Bank of England, and the Foreign Office, to examine the possible means of getting the bullion and negotiable securities into some place of safety. The transport of many hundreds of tons of bullion presents a difficult problem and the loading would take a long time." It was proposed that the roughly £70 million in Belgian gold and £110 million in Dutch gold be transferred to Britain or the United States.[21] Amazingly, the two countries managed to evacuate most of their gold to Britain with the help of the Royal Navy.

For the crews responsible for moving the gold from bank vault to truck or from ship to shore, the special consignments represented wealth beyond their comprehension. Yet many of their descriptions of the treasure were, ironically, quite dull. Leading Seaman Bob Smith of the *Emerald* said that the ship's sailors were dying to know what was in the boxes, "so we dropped one down a hatch and it split open." Some of the crew initially thought the bars were soap, but they quickly realized what had caused all the fuss. "After that," Smith recalled, "the subject was never mentioned again. As a matter of fact, we got rather blasé about loading and unloading gold. As far as we were concerned it was just the same as handling any other stores."[22] Cdr. Humphrey L. Jenkins of the *Revenge* recalled after the war that transporting bullion "became quite humdrum after a while. We just had to muck along and get on with it. You had to get the ship there. It didn't matter what or who was on board."[23]

T. W. Pope, an officer on HMS *Royal Sovereign*, reacted to the gold in the same way. For one of the ship's special trips from Britain to Canada, "[t]he gold arrived, and just before we sailed from Portsmouth, in an unmarked lorry, no escort of any kind, but when we unloaded in Halifax the ship and pier was surrounded with Royal Mounted Police, all carrying guns." Pope's account of the voyage, however, included no further mention of the gold: "Our convoy duties took us from Halifax to a point 300 miles off the coast of Ireland, where we handed over the convoy to other H.M. ships and took over the return convoy for Halifax."[24]

For others who were handling the gold, however, thrill and amazement accompanied the realization that the cargo was gold and not just any stores. This account of Terry Hulbert, an eighteen-year-old crewman on board HMS *Drake*, was typical. While the ship was anchored in Plymouth, England, Hulbert recalled,

> One morning, I was marched down to the docks with about thirty other matlots [sailors]; it was swarming with pongos [soldiers]. They were all armed with Thompson sub machine guns. We marched towards a Warship tied up along side the jetty. We went up the gang plank to a hatch on the quarter-deck, up came a hoist with some small box's on it, both the officer, and petty-officer were both armed with .45 Webley revolvers and clipboards with numbers on. A rating picked up and handed me a box, about the size of a house brick, which I nearly dropped owing to the weight of it. I suddenly realized we were unloading GOLD BULLION, every box was checked every 100 yards, we walked between two rows of Tommy guns, to a train about 300 yards away where it was finally checked against a clip board. The gold had come from South Africa to pay for the war. Somebody said each box was worth about £5,000, I worked it out that I unloaded around £40,000 [in] gold bars that day, and did not even get a thank you. I could do with one of them box's now, to supplement my pension. Still, as Frank Sinatra would say, THAT'S LIFE![25]

As another sailor would say about his role in humping gold from one place to the next, "The site of such wealth was something which we could only dream about and would never ever see again in our lifetime."[26]

———

Crossing the North Atlantic Ocean posed challenges to all who sailed it in 1939 and 1940. In addition to the immediate dangers of attack, the routine of life at sea was often horrible for both predator and prey. Historians Douglas and Greenhous provide this image of conditions for Canadian corvettes escorting convoys on the western side of the North Atlantic:

> Corvettes were what is known as wet ships. Seas breaking over them would result in salt water seeping in through hatches, ventilators, and leaky seams. For weeks on end their crews lived in a state of continual dampness, usually having to tolerate sea water mixed with food and sometimes vomit sloshing about on the deck.[27]

According to John Adams, first lieutenant on the convoy escort ship HMS *Cleveland*, the weather could wreak havoc for the escorts waiting to meet the eastbound ships near Britain: "If the convoy hadn't had a good sun sight crossing the Atlantic because of foul weather, they could be 50 miles out of place. . . . I can remember looking for a convoy for four days once."[28] Canadian sailor Barney Roberge remembers that three gales had actually pushed one of his convoys backward, doubling the length of the trip from Canada to Britain.[29] The bad weather did offer some consolation to Allied crews since it altered the dynamics of battle. Heavy seas made it much harder for U-boats to attack on the surface or fire torpedoes with precision.

Gerald R. Bowen, a telegrapher on a Royal Canadian Navy frigate on convoy duty in the North Atlantic, thought that everyone who sailed the North Atlantic probably had a favorite storm story. During one storm, he recalled, waves crested at fifty to sixty feet. His ship would

> chug up the side of one of them over the crest and then you'd drop into the trough with a crash and a bang. And the next wave then would wash over you. And you had a great fear because the convoy would break up under these circumstances and the ships would be up, they wouldn't have any more control than we did. And we always feared one of them coming over a crest and falling on top of you, you know. [We lost] all our boats, our Carli floats, everybody on the crew was cut and bruised, broken arms, banged heads, etc. Anybody on the bridge, the upper deck, lashed themselves to something. And the cooks couldn't cook of course, they couldn't have a galley stove so there was nothing to eat or nothing to drink, in the way of hot tea or anything. And this just prevailed and went on I guess for a day or two. It was horrible and I still remember that so well. In fact later, I was ashore in Newfoundland on a course and I was in my hammock in the barracks and there was a big storm blowing outside and I felt guilty

because I was warm and snug but I knew what was happening out on the sea, you know. And I still think of that when there's a bad storm nowadays. You know, here I am safe and sound. After the storm, then it took us a day or two to find all the ships and get them all in line again and off we went. Oh, it was brutal. And that's just one of the Atlantic storms.

I presume we were scared stiff. I don't really remember now but you know you had to work, you had to do your job, so that kept everything under control. We used to have a saying during the war, you know, particularly when nauseous things would happen. Keep laughing, because if you ever start to cry, you'll never stop.[30]

For ships operating in the North Atlantic—be they Axis or Allied vessels—the weather was often atrocious. The winter of 1939–40 was one of the worst in living memory. On February 12, 1940, *Time* magazine reported that it was so cold that the pipes at Buckingham Palace no longer worked and that "for a whole day His Majesty King George VI had to forgo a bath."[31] Historians Manchester and Reid described that winter as a "white horror, Europe's cruelest since 1895."[32] The foul weather at least had the positive effect of forcing Germany to postpone torpedo and diving exercises owing to freezing dry and floating docks.[33]

When enemy torpedoes struck ships, it was not uncommon for them to sink so quickly that the crew had no chance for survival. In wintertime, some succumbed to the waves while being dragged down by heavy, waterlogged winter clothing. Many who survived the sinking were never rescued because of the immense emptiness of the Atlantic or because escort ships were preoccupied protecting other ships from U-boat attacks.[34]

Many of the ship captains sailing in convoy also had to learn a new discipline. Captain Agar described it as follows: Rule No. 1 was to keep your place in the convoy. This was not an easy task with rough seas or when visibility was impaired by fog. Mistakes happened often as well. Agar said he could "imagine much swearing on the bridge of a few freighters when someone in the next column turned to port instead of to starboard, necessitating drastic action by helm and engines in both ships." Rule No. 2 was to make as little smoke as possible. This rule posed a problem for some ships because, according to Agar, the stingy owners of merchant ships "provided only the cheapest coal and the boilers are old, worn, and in urgent need of repair."[35]

Life on board the U-boats was often equaling grueling. The air in a World War II–era submarine, for example, typically went foul when the sub was underwater for long periods. The smell of various body fluids only made things worse. In order to prevent being spotted by the enemy, U-boats would avoid discharging feces because they are less dense than seawater. (Surfaced feces discharge would make it easier to spot the U-boat.) If depth charges rocked the German submarines, buckets or other containers holding human waste could spill, making the situation even worse.[36] What often kept morale high, as Volkmar König of U-99 put it, was that "somehow you felt engulfed by comradeship."[37] For the first year of the war, Karl Dönitz did a masterful job of maintaining a solid esprit de corps among the captains and crews of the U-boat fleet despite the dangers and inconveniences of submarine life.

In the distressing first months of the war, the British received a few pieces of good news. On Friday, October 13—while the *Emerald, Enterprise, Caradoc,* and their escorts were still at sea—Chamberlain and Churchill were given some very welcome and unexpected information while having dinner with their wives. "During the dinner," Churchill recounted, "the war went on and things happened. With the soup, an officer came up from the War Room to report a U-boat had been sunk. With the sweet [dessert] he came again and reported that a second U-boat had been sunk; and just before the ladies left the dining room, he came a third time reporting that a third U-boat had been sunk. Nothing like that had ever happened before on a single day, and it was more than a year before such a record was repeated." The BBC reported that Friday the thirteenth had been an unlucky day for the Germans.[38]

More good news came in November and December 1939 as Britain's westward gold shipments were becoming almost routine. Sir John Gilmour at the Admiralty reported to Sigismund Waley at the Treasury on November 6, "we anticipate no difficulty under existing conditions in moving sufficient gold from the United Kingdom."[39] In December, Gilmour reported that no troubles were expected regarding further gold shipments: "We never anticipated that the outflow of gold would be so absolutely regular. . . . [W]e anticipate that a deficit one month will be made good the next. . . . The total for the four months October

[1939]–January [1940] should therefore amount to £49 million (we actually sent £25 million up to the end of November)."[40]

The British also received good news out of South Africa. The Treasury noted that South Africa had roughly £40 million in gold and the capacity to increase its stocks by an average of at least £1 million a week.[41] After some discussion, the British decided to ship South African gold east to Sydney, Australia. From Sydney, the gold was shipped to Vancouver on the west coast of Canada.[42] Gold shipments from Cape Town included a November 18 consignment worth £1.75 million and another worth £4 million in December. From Bombay, £1 million in gold was shipped on November 17, and another £2 million in gold was shipped on December 6. Happily, all of these shipments went off without a hitch.[43]

By now, the special shipments to North America were becoming a permanent feature of the war. As Dean Marble, secretary of the Bank of Canada, put it to Rear Adm. Percy W. Nelles of the Royal Canadian Navy, "We have been asked by the Bank of England to make arrangement of a permanent nature at Halifax to take care of surprise shipments of gold."[44]

Would these many shipments be enough for Britain's war needs? It was highly unlikely given the growing financial demands of war. In October, Chancellor of the Exchequer John Simon wrote to Churchill at the Admiralty about the need to ship as much as £200 million in gold within a year. Simon then asked if £2 million represented the maximum amount that could be carried per ship. Churchill replied that if His Majesty's ships were used, larger sums could be carried. Simon added that the Treasury's immediate needs would be relieved if as much as £15 million in gold could travel in a single battleship.[45] Over the next several months, the Treasury would have to content itself with numerous but modest shipments. Most ships continued to ferry £5 million or less of the precious cargo.

═══════════

As 1939 came to an end, an unusual quiet settled across much of Europe. The Germans referred to this phase of the war as *Sitzkrieg;* the French called it the *drôle de guerre.* In the English-speaking world, it would come to be called the Phony War, although the British preferred Bore War or Twilight War.[46] As the Italian ambassador in Paris

FIG. 4.2. Reflecting the technology of the day, both Britain and Canada used large wall maps, and comparably large ladders, to plot convoy routes. *Courtesy of the Imperial War Museum*

put it, "I have seen several wars waged without being declared; but this is the first I have seen declared without being waged."[47]

American journalist Leland Stowe, who was in London at the time, observed during the Phony War that "Newsmen soon began to ask themselves; What's the matter with this war anyway? In those early days there was little in the demeanor of the average Londoner to indicate a recognition of the fact that the British Empire had become involved in a life-or-death struggle." He also recalled that a "Britisher of importance" confessed in the early weeks of the war, "I wish Hitler would bomb London. It would be one of the best things that could happen to us."[48]

Canada, which had declared war on Germany on September 10, 1939, also seemed relatively untouched by the war. Lord Tweedsmuir, wrote to Prime Minister Chamberlain, "I have just been spending a week in Halifax, which is the only part of Canada which may be said to be in the war zone."[49] A more common view of wartime conditions in Canada came from economist A. F. W. Plumptre. As he put it, "we were fighting a relatively leisurely war behind the Maginot Line and Mr. Chamberlain's umbrella."[50] From the western province of British Columbia, Canadian journalist Peter Stursberg wrote that the war amounted to a humdrum experience.[51]

During the Phony War, the Bank of Canada found itself in almost uncharted territory, having been established just four years earlier. As political tensions mounted in Europe in the 1930s, the Bank received more and more requests to earmark foreign gold in its vaults. Britain, France, Switzerland, Belgium, the Netherlands, and other states opened gold accounts in Ottawa.[52] Working closely with the Bank of England, the Bank of Canada seamlessly arranged to safeguard more than one hundred thousand gold bars and thousands upon thousands of valuable coins.[53]

The Bank of Canada's staff also refined procedures for dealing with foreign exchange and the transfer of British gold.[54] For gold shipments, the relevant parties settled on the following procedures: when a "surprise shipment" was scheduled to arrive in Halifax within twenty-four hours, the Bank of England would ask the Admiralty to notify the Canadian chief of Naval Staff in Ottawa. The latter would then inform the Bank of Canada about the arrival date and other relevant information.[55]

The relative calm of the Phony War led some to believe that the coming year's hostilities might also be limited. British general Edmund

Ironside confidently asserted that "Hitler had missed the bus" in December 1939.[56] Hitler's chance for taking more territory had passed, Ironside believed. British civilians were also affected by the lack of drama. By Christmas 1939, more than half of the 750,000 people who had evacuated London in the first days of the war had returned.[57] Rumors about the war were rife throughout London, perhaps because of its strangeness so far. For example, *Time* magazine reported one rumor that gold reserves of the Bank of England were being hidden in vaults distributed in the tunnels of the London subways.[58]

As Britain's leader, Prime Minister Neville Chamberlain knew that the real horrors of war would inevitably burst the calm of the Phony War. He felt that one of Britain's "greatest dangers through the coming winter [was] growing apathy."[59] Chamberlain told the House of Commons that Great Britain was ready and waiting for sudden military developments. "At the moment there is a lull in the operations of the war, but at any time that lull may be sharply broken and events may occur within a few weeks or even a few hours which will reshape the history of the world."[60] For his part, George Orwell said that he was "stunned" to find how many people showed no interest in the news on the radio.[61]

Those suspicious of the Phony War were right to look beyond the peculiar wartime conditions; there was still plenty of bad news. There was nothing phony about the conflicts at sea, where the Allies suffered significant damage. In the first four months of the war, the Germans sank two of Britain's largest warships and more than two hundred and fifteen merchant ships (amounting to 780,000 tons of shipping).[62] The heavy losses at sea presaged a long and bloody conflict.

In December 1939, German propaganda minister Joseph Goebbels initiated a propaganda offensive whose aim was to publicize Britain's vulnerability at sea. It included repeated broadcasts of Rudyard Kipling's poem "Big Steamers," familiar to many English listeners. The poem ends with this refrain:

> For the bread that you eat and the biscuits you nibble,
> The sweets that you suck and the joints that you carve,
> They are brought to you daily by all us big steamers,
> And if anyone hinders our way then you'll starve![63]

In fact, ham, bacon, butter, eggs, and sugar were already being rationed at four ounces per adult per week. Britain was also rationing coffee, clothes, soap, boots, and shoes.[64] Chamberlain wrote to his sister, Ida, about the "problematic" food situation facing the country: "We are already subsidizing food to the tune of about £50 millions a year to keep down cost of living and shall have to do more, but we shall get no credit for it."[65]

Morale in Britain was, nevertheless, holding up, and most citizens wanted to do their part to help the government get by financially. According to *Time* magazine,

> Prosperous Britons were pelting the Treasury last week with a patriotic shower of valuables to help win the war. Voluntarily they sent silver heirlooms, wedding and engagement rings, gold coins and even historic strings of family pearls. This mood of sacrifice was die-hard Britain at her best, but Chancellor of the Exchequer Sir John Simon, while giving thanks, was obliged to announce that Britain can meet the mounting cost of World War II only if the whole population submits to "the most fearful sacrifices, some of which we have hardly begun to dream of."[66]

Simon estimated that if the war expanded, Britain's military expenditures would amount to half the national income. As a result, he concluded, "We must face the fact that there will be a great fall in the standard of living, that we shall not be able to obtain luxuries and even supplies to which we are used, [and] that wages will not be able to rise in proportion to prices."[67] A government memo from December 29, 1939, stated that Britain's stocks of gold and foreign currency were "insufficient for our needs and the strictest economy is essential."[68]

At the end of 1939, the stress of war had taken its toll on most political leaders in Britain, including Winston Churchill. According to Scotland Yard inspector Walter H. Thompson, Churchill's personal guard for more than nineteen years, doctors ordered Churchill to have Christmas dinner with his own family, "even if the Germans were on their way to London."[69]

On Christmas day, nineteen-year-old Sydney Davies of the British merchant ship *Lissa* celebrated the holiday in neutral Portugal. While the ship was birthed in Lisbon, he could hear the crew of a nearby German merchant ship shouting, "England is Kaput! England is Kaput!"[70] In Germany, meanwhile, Adolf Hitler delivered a New Year's message to the German people, making the audacious claim that the "Jewish-capitalist world will not survive the Twentieth Century."[71]

5

Thin Armor

At the start of 1940 the Allies were on the defensive. The Nazi government had territorial ambitions for much of continental Europe; and if successful there, it could either initiate a full-scale invasion of the British Isles or simply force Britain to sue for peace.[1] Many in Britain even worried that their government might prematurely accept peace terms with the Nazis. Austrian economist Gustav Stolper sent a memo to the British Foreign Office to explain that European stock markets had recently gone through a "peace scare." Detailed reports in the United States, according to Stolper, were rife with "peace terms submitted by Hitler . . . and they found credence not only here but all over the world." Stolper added that "uninformed people" were even more prone to believe such fantastic notions and that the White House did little to discourage them.[2] The mounting sense of doom was palpable in Britain.

Britain's chances of surviving the chaos created by the German war machine depended directly on each side's naval capabilities. How many U-boats could Germany muster to sink Allied ships? How many escorts could the Royal Navy commit to the convoys trying to deliver British wealth to North America and vital goods to the British Isles? England had not been successfully invaded since the Norman invasion of 1066; would the English Channel continue to protect the country as a moat protected a castle? Would the enormity of the Atlantic Ocean strain the capabilities of the German U-boat fleet? The answers to these questions pivoted on the Allied and Axis naval resources committed to the Battle of the Atlantic.

"If we lose the war at sea, we lose the war." Adm. Sir Dudley Pound's assessment encapsulated Britain's strategic position for the war.[3] Germany's commander in chief of the Navy, Grand Adm. Erich Raeder, came to the same conclusion. Raeder told Hitler that if the Nazis wanted to establish a new order for Europe, British naval strength would have to be dramatically reduced.[4] The fate of Britain's "special shipments" consequently hinged on what happened at sea.

Germany based its political strategy on maintaining a quiet eastern front after taking Austria, Czechoslovakia, and Poland, so that its military could focus its energies on the west. To this end, Hitler achieved a compliant relationship with the Soviet Union with the signing of the Molotov-Ribbentrop Pact a week before the start of the war. The agreement was a mutual nonaggression pact designed, at least on paper, to last for ten years. The Soviet Union, of course, would eventually become a valuable ally of Britain and the United States against Germany. But for the crucial early part of the war, the Soviet-German pact allowed Hitler to concentrate his aggression primarily on the western European countries.

Germany hoped at first to seize Norway and Denmark to tighten the German navy's grip on sea routes to and from the North Atlantic. Next, Germany sought to gain control of Belgium, the Netherlands, and much of France.[5] German planners felt that if they could seize the military-industrial facilities there—including ports and airfields—they could then more effectively launch naval and air attacks on Allied shipping and on the British Isles themselves.[6]

Hitler, Raeder, and other leaders planned the naval war around two basic facts. First, the Kriegsmarine was far too small to compete ship by ship with the Royal Navy. Second, Britain's greatest vulnerability to its military and to the civilian economy lay in its dependence on the flow of goods, especially from North America. Thus, instead of challenging the Royal Navy head on, Germany concentrated its forces on disrupting the shipping lanes in the North Atlantic.

The shipping lanes to the west of Britain constituted the Kriegsmarine's most active target zone. These were the Western Approaches, or part of what Adm. Karl Dönitz, head of the U-boat fleet, described as Britain's vital arteries.[7] The Nazi effort to starve Britain of civilian and military resources was a global operation, however, and German warships menaced Allied shipping at many key points around the world. A German naval squadron, for example, patrolled off the broad estuary between Uruguay and Argentina looking for supply ships heading to Britain.[8] The Kriegsmarine's efforts were enhanced by the German

FIG. 5.1. Hitler and Grand Admiral Raeder discuss war plans at the Berghof in July 1940. Also present, from left to right, are Field Marshal Walther von Brauchitsch, Gen. Alfred Jodl, Field Marshal Wilhelm Keitel, and an unidentified Kriegsmarine staff officer. *Courtesy of the Imperial War Museum*

interception and code-breaking service, B-Dienst, which often broke British codes dealing with convoy routing.[9]

The pivotal decisions affecting Germany's naval preparations for war were made in 1938 and early 1939. After months of deliberation, Hitler decided in January 1939 to execute aspects of the Kriegsmarine's Z Plan. This construction program anticipated an aggressive expansion of the navy, organized around groups of ships designed to overwhelm the British escort ships protecting merchant convoys. Over the next several weeks, the particulars of the Z Plan evolved, leading to the February projections that envisioned the construction of 6 battleships, 8 heavy cruisers, 17 light cruisers, 4 aircraft carriers, 221 U-boats, and perhaps as many as 68 destroyers.[10] The Z Plan was unknowingly preparing Germany to put tremendous naval assets in the path of Britain's clandestine gold shipments to North America.

A most curious feature of the Z Plan in early 1939 was its timetable. The plan was expected to be completed by 1943 at the earliest but was more likely take two or three years more than that.[11] At the start of 1939, as the Kriegsmarine was determining its procurement needs for war, German military leaders assumed that a war would not occur for four to six years. Hitler repeatedly assured Kriegsmarine planners that a political accommodation with Britain and France would postpone a major military confrontation until 1944 or 1945.[12] To the surprise of Germany's military leaders, in late 1939 Hitler launched what became World War II much sooner than any of them had anticipated. Hitler insisted that rearmament of Britain and the other democracies was outpacing Germany's own efforts and believed that Germany had to strike soon.[13] The Führer's timing would have profound implications for the Kriegsmarine's capacity to seek out and capture or destroy the British warships and merchant ships carrying Britain's wealth to North America.

In the time frame spelled out by the Z Plan, Germany was expected to have a vastly larger naval fleet than what was available in September 1939. The four aircraft carriers envisioned by the Z Plan, for example, never materialized, and Germany's lone carrier, the *Graf Zeppelin*, made no impact on the war; work on the vessel was halted in early 1943. The Z Plan of early 1939 included six super-battleships (each displacing 56,200 tons and carrying 16-inch guns); none existed in the crucial month of September 1939. The Z Plan also called for twelve small battleships (20,000 tons each), but none of these existed at the start of the war either. Instead of sixty-eight destroyers, Germany had only twenty-one.[14]

Probably the most important gap between the Z Plan's ambitions and the reality of September 1939 was the U-boat fleet. The building program, when completed, envisioned a fleet of approximately 250 submarines. (Dönitz had actually hoped to have three hundred.) With that many U-boats, Germany could have committed up to ninety at a time to the North Atlantic.[15] Such a fleet, Dönitz reasonably assumed, could decimate Allied shipping and force Britain to accept peace terms favorable to Germany or suffer the consequences. Nevertheless, Dönitz had only fifty-seven U-boats at his disposal at the start of the war.[16]

Even this relatively small number of U-boats exaggerates their relevance to hunts in the North Atlantic because only about half these subs were capable of deployment there.[17] The number of U-boats designated for operations in the Atlantic was reduced further because of the need for regular maintenance and training.[18] From November 1939 to January 1940, the Germans managed to put, on average, only four to six U-boats on patrol in the North Atlantic. Through the first year of the war, Germany only once managed to have twenty-one operational U-boats capable of locating the Allied ships ferrying gold and securities to North America.[19] At times, Germany had less than a handful of operational U-boats. On October 1, 1939, Germany had only one U-boat in the Atlantic and one in the North Sea. Making matters even more complicated for Dönitz was the fact that his U-boats were falling victim to Britain's defenses. By March 1940, Germany had counted eighteen U-boats sunk. New construction was slow, and the U-boat fleet's total strength had fallen to fifty-two.[20] For almost three months in early 1940, Germany could not muster a single U-boat for duty in the Atlantic.[21]

At this point in the war, the British Admiralty remained in the dark about Germany's submarine strength. In fact, the British significantly overestimated the number of U-boats and, hence, overestimated the risk of sending Britain's wealth across the Atlantic. In correspondence with Chamberlain, Churchill wrote that Britain "may have to face an attack by 200 or 300 U-boats in the summer of 1940. Remember they will be building them day and night."[22] Churchill was so nervous about the potential loss of merchant shipping to U-boats that he even explored the potential of using concrete ships, which could relieve the strain on British steel production.[23] The anticipated shipping losses led Churchill to recall after the war, "The only thing that ever really frightened me during the war was the U-boat peril."[24]

Despite their small number, German U-boats still posed deadly challenges to the merchant ships and warships sailing to and from Britain. In February 1940, for example, a quarter of a million tons of Allied shipping was lost, two-thirds of which had been sunk by only ten U-boats.[25]

Allied shipping losses in the North Atlantic might have been even worse if Germany had been able to overcome technological problems with its torpedoes. On September 14, 1939, the submarine U-39 had the British aircraft carrier *Ark Royal* in its sights and fired three torpedoes. Each one of them exploded, but they did so about eighty yards short of the target. The U-boat was subsequently attacked and the crew captured. A similar failure resulted on October 30, when U-56 attacked the battleship HMS *Nelson*. The U-boat had maneuvered its way through a screen of destroyers before firing three torpedoes at the target. The torpedoes hit the *Nelson*, but none of them exploded, and the ship proceeded to its base at Loch Ewe, Scotland. The next day, coincidentally, Churchill and Adm. Dudley Pound boarded the *Nelson* to discuss the future disposition of British naval bases.[26]

The torpedo problem was a constant source of frustration for Dönitz and every member of the U-boat crews. According to Dönitz's war diary, in the early phases of the war, he lamented that "at least 30 percent of torpedoes are duds. They do not detonate or they detonate in the wrong place."[27] Some believed that the problem was crew nervousness, inexperience, or incompetence, but an inquiry in 1940 determined that the detonator "pistol" was unreliable.[28] Thus, unbeknownst to the British Admiralty, during the critical months when the most valuable shipments of British wealth were on the high seas, Germany's small number of U-boats were armed with unreliable torpedoes.[29]

The British were also deeply concerned about U-boat tactics.[30] A consequence of the prevailing submarine design was that speeds achieved below water were slower than those when the sub was cruising on the surface. At top speed, depending on the type of sub, U-boats could travel at 17 to 18 knots on the surface compared with 7 to 8 submerged.[31] In World War I, the Germans exploited the speeds afforded by surfaced U-boats to devastating effect. In the closing months of the war, for example, roughly two-thirds of U-boat attacks were carried out on the surface and at night. In World War II, Germany continued these tactics and also discovered that surface attacks neutralized British ASDIC technology.[32] The only way of detecting a surfaced U-boat was by sight, and spotting a U-boat was extremely difficult because of its low, lean silhouette. Helping Germany's U-boats further, Britain's antisubmarine aircraft were designed to locate and attack relatively slow-moving *submerged* U-boats.[33]

The tactic that instilled perhaps the most fear among those sailing on Allied ships during the war was an attack involving a group of U-boats. Based on his experiences in World War I, Dönitz assumed that "wolf-pack" tactics would prove to be invaluable in the next great war. The general procedures were clearly defined. Once an Allied convoy was spotted, U-boat command headquarters would be notified. It would in turn direct other U-boats to the area. While waiting for the pack to form, the initial U-boat would shadow the convoy, providing German headquarters with updates on the convoy's bearings. Once the pack of U-boats was in place, the attack would begin. One objective in the initial attack was to cause confusion and scatter the ships of the convoy, splitting its defenses.[34]

Thanks to Lt. Otto Kretschmer, the Germans developed a further innovation for nighttime wolf-pack attacks. The U-boat would surface, break through the ring of escorting vessels under cover of the darkness, and slip into the middle of the convoy. While it was on the inside, other U-boats would attack from the outside. So confident of this maneuver was Kretschmer that his motto became "one ship one torpedo."[35]

It is a common misperception—at the time and since—that U-boat wolf packs were used extensively throughout the war with consistently high rates of success.[36] In fact, the records show that for at least the first year of the war U-boats rarely operated in packs. Several factors confounded German efforts, but they all related to the small number of operational oceangoing subs. In addition, the Atlantic Ocean was a huge expanse for the mere dozen or so U-boats on patrol at any given time. Finding a large convoy of Allied ships on the open ocean proved to be only slightly less difficult than locating a small convoy.[37]

Organizing wolf packs proved to be extremely complicated as well. Timing and luck—good for Britain, bad for Germany—played important roles in the Battle of the Atlantic and the transfer of British wealth during the first year of the war. When Dönitz authorized the use of wolf-pack tactics for the first time in mid-October 1939, two U-boats (U-34 and U-25) could not participate because of delays in repairing mechanical problems, U-47 was reassigned for another mission, and U-40, U-42, and U-45 were sunk before they could form up with the pack. The three remaining U-boats (U-46, U-48, and U-37) did manage a coordinated attack but with limited success.[38] Another joint attack was attempted in November 1939, but it encountered similar problems and yielded similar results.

Foul weather frequently prevented any U-boat attack at all, whether the sub was operating alone or in a wolf pack. As Dönitz himself described in his memoirs, "With the U-boat twisting, rolling, and plunging any attack was quite often out of the question. In storms like these, the sea broke clear over the conning-tower. The bridge watch, consisting of an officer and three petty officers or ratings as lookouts, had to lash themselves fast to the bridge to prevent the foaming, boiling breakers from tearing them from their posts and hurling them overboard."[39]

In late 1940 wolf packs would grow to become a serious problem, but for the time being, Allied ships delivering British wealth to North America were threatened primarily by lone wolves, not packs. Of course, if British leaders had known these facts, they would have been much more confident about sending British wealth across the North Atlantic.

Germany's surface fleet paled in comparison to the Royal Navy's, but fear of the Kriegsmarine forced Britain to devote considerable financial, naval, and administrative resources to blunting its effectiveness. In the first four months of the war, for example, the German pocket battleship *Graf Spee* and its crew of over a thousand counted the following ships among their victims:[40]

September 30, 1939: *Clement*
October 5, 1939: *Newton Beach* boarded, then sunk on October 7
October 7, 1939: *Ashlea*
October 10, 1939: *Huntsman* boarded, then sunk October 17
October 22, 1939: *Trevanion*
November 15, 1939: *Africa Shell*
December 2, 1939: *Doric Star*
December 3, 1939: *Tairoa*
December 7, 1939: *Steonshalh*

According to historian Barrie Pitt, at one point early in the war, twenty-two British cruisers, carriers, and battleships formed nine separate hunting parties to pursue the *Graf Spee* and the pocket battleship *Deutschland*. The British carriers *Hermes* and *Ark Royal* were also among those involved in hunting parties.[41] Much to the disappointment of the Admiralty, none of these ventures proved particularly successful. Since resources were limited, these hunts diverted ships away from more constructive duties—such as protecting convoys and ships carrying gold and securities to North America.

The dangers posed by Germany's surface fleet were in some ways matched by that of the sea mine—an unglamorous weapon vital to so many militaries. In conjunction with the U-boat, Germany hoped that the destructive and disruptive capability of mines would discourage neutral countries from shipping to Britain.[42] German mines posed two serious challenges for the Allies. First, and most obviously, mines threatened ship safety. Second, mines compelled the Admiralty to alter ship routing and commit scarce resources to minesweeping. Early in the war, Germany laid mines off the eastern and southern coasts of Britain. These and other mines—deposited in the water by aircraft, submarines, and S-boats (Schnellboote in German, similar to American patrol torpedo boats and the British motor torpedo boats)—were responsible for the loss of twenty-seven Allied ships (121,000 tons) in November 1939. They were so effective that they actually sank more ships in November and December 1939 than did U-boats.[43]

The threat posed by German mines forced the Admiralty to temporarily close the Port of Liverpool and nearly forced the closure of the Port of London in the main channel of the Thames Estuary. As one young sailor on board a British warship described it, "The whole of the Thames Estuary and way up the east coast was soon littered with the protruding masts and funnels of ships sunk by [magnetic mines]."[44] Incensed by the German mines, Churchill accused the Germans of committing "an outrage upon the accepted international law" and called the German maneuver "the acme of villainy."[45]

German mines would have inflicted much more damage had it not been for technological developments in Britain. By early 1940, the Admiralty had learned how to demagnetize, or degausse, a ship by wrapping a cable around it and then running an electric current through the cable. Once the procedure was introduced on a large scale, Germany's stock of some twenty-two thousand magnetic mines proved much less lethal than Germany had hoped.[46]

Thanks in part to British antimining efforts, there is only one known case of a mine affecting a British gold shipment during the war. In April 1940, the British dispatched the Royal Mail Steamer *Niagara* with approximately £2 million in gold from Sydney, Australia, to Canada. The *Niagara* was at first expected to arrive in Vancouver on May 1. Rear Adm. P. W. Nelles of the Royal Canadian Navy, who routinely kept the Bank of Canada informed about British gold shipments, cabled Dean Marble at the Bank: "I expect to advise you later regarding [the] expected arrival date when her recent movements are ascertained." Two days later, Nelles reported to Marble that the *Niagara* was due on May 3. Nelles then cabled Marble to say that the ship was "reported sinking," and later he concluded that the ship was a "total loss." The *Niagara* had hit mines laid by the German ship *Orion* off the coast of New Zealand. Fortunately, most of the *Niagara*'s 555 bars of gold were

FIG. 5.2. The passenger ship *Niagara*, carrying roughly £2 million in gold, sank while en route to Vancouver after hitting mines off the coast of New Zealand in the spring of 1940. Most of the ship's gold was eventually recovered. *Courtesy of the W. A. Laxon Collection, Voyager New Zealand Maritime Museum*

recovered in 1941, and 30 of the remaining 35 gold bars were recovered in a 1953 salvage operation.[47]

Standing in the way of further losses was the Royal Navy. If Britain could keep the shipping lanes open for the goods flowing in from North America—made possible thanks to many of the gold and securities shipments—then Britain's economy and military could hold out until, perhaps, the United States decided to enter the war.

In 1940 no other country in the world could match the size and scope of British maritime capacity. Ship to ship, the Royal Navy easily outnumbered the Kriegsmarine, but the types of demands asked of Britain's ships mattered significantly. Britain had to import food, raw materials, oil, machine tools for its factories, and manufactured goods for both military and civilian purposes. If imports of wheat from North America were cut off, for example, Britain's strategic reserves would have been depleted in just a few months. In all, at the end of the 1930s, Britain was importing more than 55 million tons of goods by sea a year, including all of its oil. Most of the imports came across the North Atlantic.[48]

To deliver these goods, Britain had some three thousand deep-sea, dry cargo merchant ships and tankers and one thousand coastal ships. The Allies contributed an additional three thousand or so merchant ships. On any given day, at any given time around the world, roughly twenty-five hundred merchant ships, and 160,000 men, were at sea.[49]

The Royal Navy's capabilities were enhanced by the French navy (for the time being) and with resources from throughout the Commonwealth. The Royal Canadian Navy contributed seven destroyers and five minesweepers to the cause at the beginning of the war.[50] Additional contributions were made by the Royal Australian Navy (six cruisers, five destroyers, and two sloops) and the Royal Indian Navy (six escort and patrol vessels), and two cruisers and two sloops were received from the New Zealand Division of the Royal Navy (later the Royal New Zealand Navy).

Despite advantages in warships and its extensive merchant marine, Britain suffered from important weaknesses that put the treasure shipments heading to North America at risk. The most important weakness was a shortage of warships to escort the merchant ship convoys across the Atlantic. For example, when war broke out, Britain possessed over 150 destroyers, but as James B. Reston of the *New York Times* reported in 1940, Britain's complement of destroyers in the fall of 1939 was far below the 527 destroyers it had at the start of World War I.[51] This deficiency explains in part King George VI's desire to complete the "destroyers for bases" deal with President Roosevelt before the war.

Neglect on the part of the Admiralty since World War I left Britain scrambling to find enough escorts for the first two years of the war. In addition, much of the knowledge and experience gained in World War I related to the defense of merchant shipping was lost because the Admiralty had eliminated the Trade and Anti-Submarine Divisions during the interwar years; they were not reconstituted until 1939.[52] Through mid-1940, most convoys—including some with thirty ships or more—rarely had more than one Royal Navy escort.[53] The same was true for most of the treasure ships.

The dearth of escort ships was sorely felt by British banking and political leaders. In late January 1940, John Gilmour, a civilian advisor to the Admiralty, notified Sigismund Waley at the British Treasury that few warships were available for their needs: "To meet this situation we are proposing: (i) to increase the amounts carried in such warships as still are available, and (ii) to commence sending smallish consignments in fast, unescorted liners."[54]

In addition to having too few escorts on hand, some ships that could have been employed as escorts were operating elsewhere—sometimes for good reason, sometimes not. Some naval vessels, for example, were assigned to the protection of Britain for fear of an invasion. Germany indeed had developed plans, called Operation Sea Lion, to invade the British Isles. (The British code word "Cromwell" referred to an imminent invasion by Germany.)

Some British warships were also distracted during the first several months of the war by concerted hunts for U-boats. As early as June 1938, the Tactical Division of the Admiralty had proposed establishing nineteen hunter-killer groups, each with five ships and supporting aircraft. The proposal was dropped because it left too few ships available for convoy escort duty, but the desire to use groups of ships to search for U-boats remained.[55] Like similar pursuits of German surface ships in World War I and in early World War II, these hunts proved fruitless and drained resources away from where they could have been employed.[56] Historian V. E. Tarrant found that during the first six months of the war, convoy escorts actually had a higher U-boat kill rate than did hunting groups.[57]

Another challenge facing the British was a shortage of aircraft for escort duty. When the war started, the Royal Air Force's Coastal Command had neither aircraft nor trained crews for antisubmarine duty. Resources had instead been devoted to reconnaissance against surface ships.[58] The Royal Navy's historian S. W. Roskill later wrote that in the twenty years of peace between the wars, not one exercise was undertaken in the protection of a slow-moving convoy of merchant ships from submarine or air attack.[59]

In the struggle to nullify the U-boat threat to Allied ships, Britain was hampered by an important technological weakness. In the interwar period, Britain planned on neutralizing the U-boat with ASDIC.[60] Ships equipped with ASDIC technology could emit high-frequency sound waves that would pass through the water and echo back as a "ping" from any metal structure. The average range of ASDIC was 1,500 yards, with an extreme range of 2,500 yards.[61] At the start of the war, the Royal Navy had 180 ASDIC-fitted ships, so the Admiralty's hopes that U-boats would play only a minimal role were high.[62]

ASDIC, however, suffered from several important weaknesses. First, it could not provide information about the depth of the target. This drawback was particularly relevant when an Allied ship attacked U-boats with depth charges—explosives that are triggered by water-pressure fuses. According to historian Bernard Ireland, the average depth charge was dropped to five hundred feet. Since ASDIC could not determine depth, "it was customary to lay patterns of 10 or even 14 charged sets for two levels. Three such patterns could exhaust the depth charge capacity of a small escort."[63]

Second, and more important, ASDIC proved ineffective against U-boats on the surface.[64] As we've seen, German U-boat commanders did not take long to realize that riding on the surface afforded U-boats both speed and an antidote to ASDIC. At night, surfaced U-boats were particularly dangerous.

Before the war, as Germany prepared for battle against the British, intelligence reports could not determine the extent of ASDIC's capabilities. As naval historian Jochen Brennecke explained, some in the Kriegsmarine thought that ASDIC might have actually neutralized U-boats. Others weren't so sure. Grand Admiral Raeder described it as "just a typical bit of British bluff." But he added that "we don't know the apparatus, and so, if bluff it is, we can't call it. We're groping in the dark." This explains, at least in part, why Raeder may have been reluctant to commit too many resources to the U-boat arm.[65]

The stewards of Britain's finances had no choice but to accept the naval situation as it was. As Gilmour put it to Waley in early February 1940, "As regards the risk involved, all ships going to sea necessarily incur an appreciable risk, but the Admiralty's arrangements for their protection are (we believe) the best that can be devised with existing resources."[66]

In January and February 1940, while the Kriegsmarine sought to disrupt the shipping lanes between Britain and North America, the Bank of England and the British Treasury secretly authorized more than a dozen gold shipments to North America. All of the ships arrived safely. Hitler's hasty decision to begin the war in 1939—and the corresponding shortage in Kriegsmarine resources—was certainly handicapping the Germans' capacity to intercept the treasure ships.

Britain was fortunate as well in that its gold stocks were being partially replenished from newly mined gold from throughout the Empire. The greatest source of new gold (some 40 percent of the world's total output) was South Africa. In March, South African gold mines produced a record 1,147,382 fine ounces. The *Wall Street Journal* estimated that March's output could "buy a fleet of about 535 American pursuit planes." Even more gold was extracted in April 1940. In all, the newspaper estimated that Britain gained an average of $26.3 million a month in gold from throughout its empire.[67]

The amount of British gold carried in each ship in early 1940 varied depending on financial conditions and the type of the ship available. At this point in the war, most shipments consisted of about £1 million in gold.[68] A few exceeded this average significantly. HMS *Ascania*, a passenger ship requisitioned by the Admiralty on the second day of the war and converted into an armed merchant cruiser, carried £3 million in gold to Canada in February. The most valuable consignments to date were carried by HMS *Malaya* and HMS *Revenge*, each transporting £10 million in gold.[69]

Most of the shipments originated in Britain, but by the end of February 1940, gold was reaching North America from other parts of the Empire as well.[70] Up to this point—with the exception of the *Niagara*—none of the ships had been attacked by the Kriegsmarine.

Several ships were called upon to make multiple gold runs. One such ship, HMS *Emerald*, played a pivotal role in the operation from nearly start to finish. Completed in 1926, the *Emerald* spent most of its prewar service in tropical climates. In late 1939 and early 1940, however, its duties usually kept it in the frigid waters of the Atlantic. By April 1940, the ship had made four gold runs from Britain to Halifax.

Capt. Augustus Agar described his ship as "the one I loved best in the whole of my service career." In the tradition of referring to vessels in feminine terms, Agar said, "She really was a lovely ship with beautiful lines. She had three funnels and an ever-so slight rake on her masts, like the tilt of Beatty's cap."[71] When he took command of the ship in 1937, Agar appreciated the fact that, despite being seventeen years old, the *Emerald* and her sister ship, HMS *Enterprise*, were the fastest ships in the Royal Navy, capable of 35 knots.[72] Such speed was invaluable against the U-boat threat. On a good day, the fastest U-boats could travel on the surface at only half that speed.

Like many of the ships Britain relied on to ferry gold from Britain to North America, the *Emerald* was not perfect. It had a low freeboard and no turrets; thus there was no protection against the bitter cold weather for the sailors who had to stand by their guns, often "wet to the skin."[73] The *Emerald* was outfitted with a Sea Fox plane, described by Agar as the poorest performing aircraft ever built: "who ever heard of a seafox, anyway?"[74] Because the ship had spent its prewar life in the tropics, it had no heating system at all, making it poorly suited to the North Atlantic. Before the ship's trip to Halifax in November 1939, however, the crew managed to install a rudimentary steam heating system.

Weather was a concern for Agar as it was for every other ship captain traveling across the North Atlantic. Fog, wrote Agar, was a

> bugbear with which we had to contend as Masters of ships know so well on the North Atlantic run. We had it sometimes for days on end during which, in a slow convoy, ships easily lose touch with each other, the Commodore with the ships and the Ocean Escort with the Commodore. Once in a slow convoy we had fog over half the distance travelled and, at the end of the fifth day when it lifted for a few hours, there was hardly a ship of the convoy in sight out of a total of forty. I couldn't help laughing on the bridge when our situation was revealed, for it looked so comic. Here in the middle of the Atlantic we were like a broody hen who has lost temporarily all her chicks. One by one, however, they turned up, so that by the time we had reached the limit of the western rendezvous for the destroyer escort, they were all there barring two French fish carriers who had joined us off Newfoundland and had decided to go to Bordeaux on their own.[75]

What seemed to distress the captain even more was the fact that the *Emerald*'s 650 officers and sailors had to cope with the "worst and most antiquated cooking arrangement" he had ever seen. For Agar, "the preparation and cooking of the men's food should come before modernization of anything else in the ship, including guns and armor. How else could we expect the men to be happy and efficient?"[76]

By February 1940, the ship was designated for a proper refit. The taxing journeys across the Atlantic had left the ship's decks buckled and strained. The engines and boilers needed serious attention after having worked for 140 days at sea. The ship was also fitted with a degaussing apparatus. That month, Francis Cyril Flynn became the ship's new captain. The *Emerald*'s next convoy work began in April 1940, and the ship settled into a routine of escorting convoys while periodically delivering consignments of gold and securities to Canada.[77]

═══════════

The vast quantities of wealth delivered to North America on board the *Emerald* and every other Allied merchant ship and warship involved in the operation was beginning to unnerve financial observers on both sides of the Atlantic. Their main concern was whether American markets could absorb this magnitude of gold and financial securities.

From the start of the war to February 1940, Britain was able to raise £30 million through the sale of securities.[78] That month, the Bank of England warned the British ambassador to the United States, Lord Lothian, that transferred British assets risked flooding U.S. markets. U.S. ambassador to Britain Joseph Kennedy warned FDR that "the sale of British securities to raise dollars would have a 'disastrous' effect on American markets."[79] In actuality, the sales were proceeding cautiously, and American markets were not disrupted.[80] By mid-December 1939, sales, which had initially peaked at $1.4 million a day, were now rarely above $300,000 a day.[81]

The steady liquidation of British-owned American stocks caught the attention of the *Wall Street Journal*, which seemed quite impressed with how well the British were managing the task. "Well informed quarters," the newspaper reported, "state that the selling of American stocks which the British government obtained through nationalization of privately owned foreign assets is being carried out in a masterful fashion. Apparently it is being conducted by a small group of expert market operators centered in London, possibly at the Bank of England."[82]

The British Treasury had envisioned the need to requisition privately held securities before the start of the war. On August 25, 1939, private owners of securities denominated in certain currencies—and especially dollars—were required to register the securities with the Treasury, or the Bank of England as the agent of the Treasury. Supervising the monthlong process, and head of the newly established Securities Registration Office, was Alexander Craig of the Bank of England. Craig's work with the securities would continue for much of the war from a facility not in London but in Montréal.

Having taken a solemn pledge of secrecy, the staff from fifty major banks and hundreds of smaller branches around Britain labored around the clock to catalog the securities before they were sent to special regional collection centers.[83] According to Bank historian Elizabeth Hennessy, Alexander Craig's office eventually received truckloads of more than a million registration forms relating to some two thousand different securities.[84]

By February 1940, the Bank of England recommended the sale of Britain's dollar-based securities at a rate of $1 million to $1.5 million a day. "It would suit neither [the United States] nor us to break the market by unduly forcing the pace," the cipher telegram to Lothian read.[85] The same month, the British Cabinet discussed the possibility of persuading U.S. companies to buy back securities that were owned by the British. Minutes of the February 13 Cabinet meeting note, however, that Henry Morgenthau Jr., the U.S. treasury secretary, found the idea "impracticable."[86]

The status of gold in the United States posed greater risks for the capitalist world. In February, the United States held roughly 60 percent of the world's gold. The imbalance grew even more lopsided in the coming months. In April, Kennedy advised FDR to curtail British gold sales "before the Treasury was overrun with gold it did not need and could not exchange."[87] In May, John Balfour of the Foreign Office estimated that, in two or three years, the United States was likely to possess between 80 and 90 percent of the world's gold. Balfour was particularly concerned that if the United States held too much of the precious metal, gold would actually cease to be a medium of exchange, its value dropping to the point of being even less valuable than lead.[88]

Economist John Maynard Keynes came to a similar conclusion claiming that, by international convention, gold was of value so long as all of the gold was not "in one hand."[89] Back in January 1940, Winthrop Aldrich, chairman of Chase National Bank, even suggested that the United States should take its gold, some $17.8 billion or two-thirds of the world's visible supply, "and put it back in public circulation, in order to preserve its monetary value 'for ourselves and for the world.'"[90] Rumors sprouted in Washington that the U.S. Treasury would halt its gold-buying policy altogether in order to avoid such an eventuality.[91]

The worldwide gold imbalance continued throughout 1940. According to a "Very Secret" Bank of England document of November 1,

1940, the United States "already possesses by far the greater part of the world's gold which will become a meaningless hoard if no other major country possesses any, and the disappearance of gold as an international medium of exchange would suit neither the United States nor ourselves."[92]

The steady flow of gold to North America was also affecting U.S. estimates of Britain's staying power. According to Lord Halifax, Britain's secretary of state for foreign affairs, "It has come to our notice from various unofficial sources that [Ambassador] Kennedy has been adopting a most defeatist attitude in his talks with a number of private individuals. The general line which he takes in these conversations as reported to us is that Great Britain is certain to be defeated in the war, particularly on account of her financial weakness."[93] Kennedy's defeatist inclination notwithstanding, Britain's financial situation was quite precarious whether or not all of the treasure shipments made it safely to North America. In early 1940, Montagu Norman, governor of the Bank of England, considered Britain's financial situation to be "worse than tragic."[94]

Britain's financial, and hence political, survival would be determined by a myriad of economic developments throughout the war, but also by the ability of Britain to safeguard further gold shipments to North America. Could Britain's naval assets continue to withstand the Kriegsmarine's efforts to intercept Allied shipping—carrying British treasure or not? As spring approached, Germany was preparing to launch major campaigns in the west, forcing Britain to take even greater risks in transferring its wealth to North America.

6

Into the Furnace of the War

The Phony War, that peculiar calm that settled over most of Europe at the end of 1939, persisted through early 1940. As the winter days gradually lengthened, the British wondered what the Germans were planning next. Prime Minister Neville Chamberlain speculated about Hitler's intent in a letter to his sister Hilda on April 6, 1940:

> There is a curious and some would say ominous lull in war activities. Do you realize that not a single ship has been torpedoed since the 4th of March, and recent sinkings having been due to mines or aircraft[?] As far as we know there are at the moment no U-boats at sea, and one wonders what the Boche is up to. Is he fitting them all out with some new weapon or having them up for some new adventure? We can only wait and see. We are getting the naval information from "reliable sources" that something prodigious is imminent but I remain skeptical as I can't think any offensive on a large scale would pay the Boche as well as keeping quiet and developing relations with Russia.[1]

Chamberlain, at least for the time being, was apparently not influenced by the words of the American undersecretary of state Sumner Wells, who had told him several weeks earlier that Germany intended "to launch a tremendous offensive" against Britain in the near future.[2]

Hitler would eventually show his hand, as Chamberlain and the other Allied leaders knew, and the next phase of the war would be anything but phony. And what happened over the next several months would determine the course of the war. For representatives of the British Treasury and the Bank of England, the coming months would impact their lives far more deeply than they could have imagined.

On February 7, 1940, the Bank of England sent a cipher telegram to

Lord Lothian, British ambassador to the United States, to explain that it was "futile" for the British to think that they "could meet demands without heavy shipments of gold."[3] So far, Britain had shipped roughly £50 million in gold and was spending roughly £2.25 million (or $9 million) a week in the United States for military supplies.[4] The special shipments they had authorized were relatively modest and had been dispatched at somewhat routine intervals—and without loss. However, before the summer of 1940 was over, near panic would grip the stewards of Britain's finances as they rushed to relocate Britain's liquid assets as quickly as possible.

The end of the Phony War came when Hitler authorized the invasions of Norway and Denmark and then France. The fall of Norway in particular would transform the political leadership of Britain. These campaigns would eventually alter the naval calculation in the Atlantic and profoundly affect Britain's treasure shipments to North America. By June 1940, the purpose for shipping gold and securities to the New World changed seemingly overnight. No longer were the special shipments designed merely to buy war matériel and civilian goods. Suddenly, Britain's gold and securities had to be *evacuated* in order to prevent them from falling into German hands.

The value of Denmark and Norway to Germany hinged on the Nordic countries' geographic location. Control of Norway in particular meant greater control of the North Atlantic sea routes, giving the Kriegsmarine a more commanding position from which to attack merchant ships and lay siege to France and, if necessary, Britain. Norway was also attractive to the Germans because it was the most important supply route for Sweden's high-grade iron ore, crucial for satisfying Germany's steel demands.[5]

In preparation for Germany's campaign to the north, U-Boat Command issued the following orders on March 4, 1940: "All further sailings of U-boats to be stopped forthwith. U-boats already at sea will refrain from any operations in the vicinity of the Norwegian coast. All ships will be made ready for action as soon as possible."[6] The lack of U-boat activity that Chamberlain had described to his sister was linked to Germany's preparations for this campaign. The German military took the rest of the month to put its offensive assets in place, and on

April 9, Hitler gave the order to initiate the invasion and occupation of Denmark and Norway.[7] Within hours, Denmark capitulated. Norway now faced Germany's focused attention.

Germany's offensive demonstrated that through conquest, it could use the gold reserves of a captured nation to fuel Nazi ambitions. Minutes from the British War Cabinet meeting of April 13 reveal that Denmark's gold—some £12 million to £18 million—was expected to form "part of the German booty" and that Norway's gold was believed to be the next target.[8] The minutes also reveal that with the eventual acquisition of Sweden's £41–42 million in gold, Germany would more easily be able to pay for essential imports.[9] There is no record of Cabinet members expressing a concern about British gold, but Germany's financial problems would have been significantly relieved if Britain's gold fell into German hands during an invasion of Britain or if some of the large gold shipments were apprehended on the high seas.

The War Cabinet minutes also expressed Britain's ongoing structural financial problems. Britain was already using up its reserves of gold and foreign exchange "at a very alarming rate."[10] Yet, by the standards of the upcoming summer months, what now seemed alarming would soon be considered unexceptional.

Britain's troubled financial situation did not go unnoticed in the American press. Samuel Grafton of the *New York Post*, for example, focused on Britain's securities:

> The British Empire is rendering its own fat. It has put out a list of 117 American stocks and bond issues and has ordered Englishmen who own securities on this list to turn them over to the British Treasury. The former owners will be paid off in English pounds, and the Treasury will sell the securities here for dollars with which to buy airplanes.

This sensational and underexplored development, Grafton wrote, demonstrated that Britain's "stocks and bonds have been her food and drink. They, more than lands, have meant England, Seat of Empire. Now she is shoving these investments into the furnace of the war."[11]

In the days following Germany's offensive in Norway, the Allies struggled to slow German momentum. Their efforts were generally unsuccessful, and on April 23, the Allies began their withdrawal.[12] By the night of April 29–30, the British dispatched HMS *Glasgow* to evacuate the King of Norway, the Crown Prince, members of the Norwegian government, British and French ministers and their wives, and twenty-three tons of gold.[13] The ship, its passengers, and the gold eventually made it safely to Britain.

While the Admiralty had its hands full trying—unsuccessfully—to expel Germany from Norway, it could at least appreciate the effect the battle was having on Allied shipping in the North Atlantic. With most operational U-boats deployed in the North Sea, German preoccupation with Norway created a breathing space for Allied shipping in the Atlantic. Between April and May, U-boats sank only twenty ships in the North Atlantic—a relatively small number in the context of all-out war.[14] In April, the British sent more than a dozen gold-laden ships to North America. Several of those shipments originated in South Africa, Australia, India, and Hong Kong, sailing routes that avoided the strongest of Germany's naval assets. Other ships embarked from British ports and crossed the Atlantic undisturbed to Halifax and New York.

Meanwhile, Allied forces suffered significant losses in the Norway campaign. The Royal Navy lost the aircraft carrier HMS *Glorious* and six destroyers, and Germany eventually gained air superiority in the region. On May 3, 1940, the Allies were forced to evacuate the rest of their troops through Namsos on the west coast of Norway.[15] Norway eventually fell to the Germans. Shortly thereafter, Grand Adm. Erich Raeder proudly exclaimed, "The portal to the ocean has been broken open!"[16]

The jubilation in Berlin translated into mounting fears of invasion in Britain. Member of Parliament Col. Josiah Clement Wedgewood postulated that if the Royal Navy was incapable of preventing a landing in Norway, it did not seem up to the task of preventing an invasion of Britain.[17] Britons also began to wonder if sea power—Britain's historic strength—would eventually lose out to Germany's airpower and lead to the invasion of the British Isles. The lessons of Germany's campaign against Norway would weigh on the minds of British leaders months later as they considered evacuating their own government along with the national larder.

For Germany, the Norway campaign proved to be a short-term success with adverse medium-term consequences. British Cabinet minutes from April 30, 1940, indicated that the known losses to the German war fleet included the following:[18]

Capital ships damaged: 2

Cruisers sunk: 4

Destroyers sunk: 11

U-boats sunk: 5

The U-boat losses, at least for the time being, hindered Germany's ability to sweep the Atlantic for ships carrying British wealth to North America. For Germany, then, the newly acquired geographic advantages of controlling Denmark and Norway came at a heavy price, and the British Cabinet took at least some comfort in this fact. Crossing the Atlantic was still precarious for the Allied merchant vessels and warships, but the loss of life and cargo would have been much worse if the Kriegsmarine had not been so weakened by the offensives in Norway.

━━━━━━━━━

In the midst of the battles in northern Europe, tectonic shifts were altering Britain's political landscape. Heated debates took place in the House of Commons on May 7 as Neville Chamberlain sought to defend both his appeasement policies and his prosecution of the war so far. Winston Churchill, too, came under attack for his Admiralty's role in the loss of Norway, but unlike the prime minister, Churchill did not suffer from a perception of having made a long string of foreign policy mistakes. Member of Parliament Leo Amery was so incensed by Chamberlain's record that he repeated the words of Oliver Cromwell in 1653, ordering the prime minister to "Depart, I say, and let us have done with you. In the name of God, go!"[19]

By May 10, Chamberlain was not quite gone, but he was no longer prime minister. For a time, King George VI and many in the House of Commons considered granting the premiership to Foreign Secretary Lord Halifax (Edward Frederick Lindley Wood). Even Churchill was prepared to accept the decision in part because Halifax had the backing of a majority of Conservatives. But Halifax declined the promotion. Instead, in one of the twentieth century's biggest what-ifs, Winston Churchill became Britain's next prime minister. How Britain's conduct of the war would have been different under the leadership of a Prime Minister Halifax is hard to say, but the general consensus is that Churchill was the right man at the right place at the right time.

From the start, the new Churchill government seemed infused with both purpose and vitality. As Cabinet Secretary Lord Bridges put it, "Within a very few days of his becoming Prime Minister, the whole machinery of government was working at a pace, and with an intensity of purpose, quite unlike anything which had gone before."[20] This new mood in London was essential—Hitler's armed forces were making their first major steps to gain control of western Europe.

Churchill saw that Germany's best chance for victory was to break British national unity.[21] To prevent this, he crafted a war government that included not only the opposition Labour Party but also competing factions within his own Conservative Party. Chamberlain remained the leader of the Conservatives and took the post of Lord Presidency with a seat in the five-member War Cabinet.[22] Thus, the Cabinet consisted of Churchill and Chamberlain, as well as Clement Attlee (Lord Privy Seal), Lord Halifax (Secretary of State for Foreign Affairs), and Arthur Greenwood (Minister without Portfolio). Several key officials who were not in the War Cabinet remained in the government, including A. V. Alexander (First Lord of Admiralty), Anthony Eden (Secretary of State for War), Sir Archibald Sinclair (Secretary of State for Air), Sir John Simon (Lord Chancellor), and Sir Kingsley Wood (Chancellor of the Exchequer).[23]

The relationship between the incoming and outgoing prime ministers was, naturally, complex. John Colville wrote in his diary that he believed that the two men "got on admirably" and that Churchill professed "absolute loyalty" to Chamberlain.[24] In keeping with Chamberlain, Churchill magnanimously told *Daily Mirror* publisher Cecil King that if he (Churchill) were dependent on people who had been right in the past few years, it would be a very small group.[25]

Walter H. Thompson of Scotland Yard, Churchill's personal guard, believed that "Winston retained Chamberlain in his own Cabinet . . . to keep the old gentleman, who was very ill by then, from dying a few weeks prematurely from a broken heart. Winston never said anything unkind about Chamberlain though I know there were many times when it was nothing but nobility of self-control that kept Churchill from exploding and foaming at his colleague's exacerbating lack of realism."[26]

Chamberlain's view of Churchill was less conflicted. The day after his ouster, Chamberlain wrote to his sister that he "remained in both a formal and a very real sense the leader of a Conservative party which was largely appalled by the idea of a Churchillian regime surrounded by unscrupulous hangers on and disreputable jackals."[27]

In Washington, FDR's initial reaction to Churchill's appointment did not contribute to the diplomacy expected among close allies. Roosevelt told members of his cabinet that he thought "Churchill was the best man England had even if he was drunk half the time."[28] Yet FDR quickly threw his weight behind a campaign to energize American support for Britain. In a May 10 speech at the Pan-American Scientific Congress in Washington, FDR said, "In modern times it is a shorter distance from Europe to San Francisco, California, than it was for the ships and legions of Julius Caesar to move from Rome to Spain. . . . I am a pacifist, but I believe that by overwhelming majorities . . . you and I, in the long run if it be necessary, will act together to protect and defend by every means at our command our science, our culture, our American freedom and our civilization."[29]

The president put these broad statements to practical use several days later in his May 16 address to a joint session of Congress during which he called for an increase in aircraft production from the current level of 2,100 to 50,000 planes. The planes would serve the U.S. military but would also be useful to British pilots. U.S. leaders also hoped that the creation of tens of thousands of new planes might deter Italy from entering the war. The president later wrote that the request "seemed at first like an utterly impossible goal, but it caught the imagination of the Americans, who have always believed they could accomplish the impossible."[30]

Over time, the relationship between the president and the new prime minister became both constructive and cordial. They had first met in London in 1917, when Roosevelt was assistant secretary of the Navy. FDR remembered the meeting, but Churchill did not. In 1939 FDR told Ambassador Kennedy that he had disliked Churchill since that meeting in England. "At a dinner I attended," FDR said, "he acted like a stinker." But Roosevelt added, "I'm giving him attention now because of the possibility of his being PM, and wanting to keep my hand in."[31] In wartime, Roosevelt and Churchill would go on to exchange roughly 1,800 messages and telegrams. While Churchill was First Lord of the Admiralty, Chamberlain granted him permission to begin correspondence with the president. Churchill replied to FDR's letters by signing himself simply as "Naval Person." Later, when Churchill became prime minister, he signed his letters to FDR "Former Naval Person."[32]

From the very start, the new British prime minister made it clear that he needed support from his American counterpart. Churchill's first secret message to FDR addressed Britain's fear of a German invasion. It was also the first of many letters in which Churchill alluded to the fact that without American political, military, and financial help, the Allied cause would be lost:

> We expect to be attacked here ourselves, both from the air and by parachute and air-borne troops in the near future. . . . You may have a completely subjugated, Nazified Europe established with astonishing swiftness, and the weight may be more than we can bear. All I ask you now is that you should proclaim non-belligerency, which would mean that you would help us with everything short of actually engaging armed forces.[33]

Churchill also took the opportunity to mention that a shortage of dollars could spell the end for Britain. Anticipating the worst financially, he argued that even after his country was broke, the United States should still give Britain what it needed.[34]

The same day that Churchill became prime minister, Germany began its invasion campaign of the Netherlands, Belgium, Luxembourg, and, most importantly, France. Conquering these countries would provide Germany geographic and industrial advantages resulting in a more favorable position with which to threaten Britain. Hitler expected Britain to sue for peace. If Britain failed to accept German terms, Hitler could invade Britain from occupied Western Europe.[35]

On May 13, the Germans crossed the Meuse River into France, and the Dutch Cabinet fled from advancing German forces. Churchill addressed the House of Commons and presented a much-needed, rousing speech for the benefit of both Parliament and the people of Britain:

> I have nothing to offer but blood, toil, tears, and sweat. You ask what is our policy? I will say: It is to wage war, by sea, land, and air, with all our might and with all the strength that God has given us, to wage war against a monstrous tyranny, never surpassed in the dark, lamentable catalog of human crime. You ask what is our aim? I can answer in one word. Victory, victory at all cost.[36]

The next day, Churchill received good news from his overtures to the Americans. Arthur Purvis, the head of the Anglo-French purchasing mission in Washington, informed the new prime minister that the Roosevelt administration would allow Britain to purchase 81 of 100 fighter planes then under construction as well as more than half of the 324 planes already on order over the next few months. Purvis noted that this channeling of aircraft to Britain represented "real sacrifices by United States Services"—sacrifices about which the chiefs of U.S. armed forces were none too happy. Army Chief of Staff George C. Marshall, who worried about having too few suitable aircraft for training American pilots, conceded that he did not think the United States could "afford to submit ourselves to the delay and consequences involved in accommodating the British Government."[37]

The positive news from the New World, however, was quickly overshadowed by the deteriorating situation in the Old World. On May 15, the Dutch Army surrendered to German forces. The same day, Churchill met with U.S. ambassador Kennedy to discuss, among other things, the possibility of the British government withdrawing to Canada. The subject had been broached two months earlier, when Churchill (then at the Admiralty) told the War Cabinet that if Britain "were beaten by the Germans, we might have to surrender our fleet, in which case Germany would at once have a fleet stronger than that of the United States."[38] Now as prime minister, Churchill told Kennedy that so long as he was prime minister, the government would continue, and, if necessary, move to Canada, along with the Royal Navy, and fight on from there.[39]

Coincidentally, on the same day, the Canadian newspaper Globe and Mail contemplated the possibility of accommodating not only the royal family but also "large numbers of British aristocracy and as many commoners as could come."[40] Similar discussions took place ten days later between FDR, Secretary of State Cordell Hull, and Hugh Llewellyn Keenleyside of Canada's Department of External Affairs. Keenleyside believed that Britain was unlikely to survive when up against Germany's five-to-one air superiority. Roosevelt feared that Britain would find German proposals for a "soft peace" irresistible. Roosevelt and Hull were anxious to ensure that if Britain reached terms with Germany, "the remnants of the British Fleet should be sent out to South Africa, Singapore, Australasia, the Caribbean and Canada."[41]

In discussions with British ambassador Lord Lothian, Roosevelt asked what would happen to the Royal Navy if Britain fell to Germany. Lothian said it would depend on whether the United States had entered the war. Lothian doubted that British public opinion would condone the transfer of the fleet to the United States without a declaration of war. Roosevelt seemed to concur.[42]

Less than a week later, on May 20, Lothian telegrammed London to explain how British diplomatic strategy with the United States should unfold:

> It is true that, in the event of our defeat, the future existence of the rest of the Empire as independent nations would probably depend largely on the combination of the United States and our fleet, and Mr. Roosevelt must know that we believe this to be so. But none the less we must continue to lay on the idea that unless the United States was a belligerent—and that too very soon—we should probably elect to send our fleet to Australia and New Zealand as being that part of the Empire where British ideals and ways of life would have the best chance of survival. This is rather like blackmail, and not very good blackmail at that, but I think we are justified in planting the idea rather more firmly in Mr. Roosevelt's mind.[43]

Later that month, Lothian spoke directly with Roosevelt about the fate of his government in the event of a German invasion of the British Isles. Roosevelt suggested that if the Royal Navy were to remain intact, the British government could carry on the war from across the Atlantic. Roosevelt, however, suggested that the seat of the British government should be in Bermuda and not Ottawa. The idea of a monarchy on the American continent, Roosevelt believed, was too disagreeable for the American public.[44]

Meanwhile, all through May, the British went to great lengths to impress upon the Americans how precarious Britain's situation had become. Churchill's diplomatic efforts with Kennedy and Roosevelt, however, did not translate into U.S. approval for the transfer of surplus American destroyers to the Royal Navy—nor was financial aid forthcoming. Isolationism continued to restrict U.S. maneuverability, and FDR did not think either form of assistance was politically possible.[45]

Canadian prime minister Mackenzie King stepped in to help alleviate some of the tension in U.S.-British relations. On the phone with the president on May 23, King told FDR that the impression in Britain was that the United States was "trying to save itself at the expense of Britain." King advised him to talk directly about this impression with Churchill. Roosevelt, in turn, told King that the Dominions (Australia, the Union of South Africa, New Zealand, and Canada) should press Churchill to send the British fleet across the Atlantic before Hitler's peace terms would include the surrender of the fleet.[46]

The fate of the Royal Navy and Britain itself took on greater urgency as 350,000 German troops advanced across the Netherlands and Belgium and eventually pinned down hundreds of thousands of Allied troops at Dunkirk on the northeastern coast of France. All hope seemed lost until the German High Command issued orders to halt its advance for reasons still being debated today.[47]

In Operation Dynamo, some 850 Allied vessels—warships, ferries, fishing boats, yachts, and other small vessels—carried troops from the beaches of Dunkirk to safety across the English Channel from May 26 to June 4. So many people had to be evacuated that British Cabinet Secretary Edward Bridges commented, "Evacuation is becoming our greatest national industry."[48] Churchill believed that the Allies would have been lucky if as few as twenty or thirty thousand soldiers made it to safety. The German letup allowed the rescue of more than 338,000 British, French, Canadian, and Belgian troops.[49]

However, the success of Operation Dynamo—commonly known as the "Miracle at Dunkirk"—could not mask the broader military failure of the Allied forces. On May 27, King Leopold and the Belgian army surrendered. The next day, French and British leaders discussed the merits and shortcomings of holding peace talks with Hitler. Despite the dire circumstances, the War Cabinet enthusiastically supported Churchill's impassioned argument: "I am convinced that every one of you would rise up and tear me down from my place if I were for one moment to contemplate parley or surrender. If this long island story of ours is to end at last, let it end only when each one of us lies choking in his own blood upon the ground."[50]

By June 4, the last troops were rescued from the beaches of Dunkirk, but tens of thousands of Allied soldiers had been captured. The departing Allies had also "left their luggage," as Churchill put it: forty-five thousand trucks and other vehicles, twenty-two thousand motorcycles, ninety thousand rifles, eleven thousand machine guns, seven hundred tanks, other weapons, and seven thousand tons of ammunition were abandoned at Dunkirk.[51] By the time the evacuation was over, the Royal Navy had suffered the loss of seven thousand troops and nine destroyers with another twelve destroyers temporarily forced out of action.[52]

The financial costs of the equipment lost at Dunkirk would strain Britain's resources further. Reequipping the evacuated soldiers meant additional demands for gear and weapons from North America. And to pay for everything, Britain would have to dip further into its war chest and hasten the transfer of its liquid assets to North America.

═══════════

A German invasion of Britain now seemed more likely than ever. Perhaps Josiah Clement Wedgewood had been right all along. If the British military could not prevent Germany from taking over Norway or from routing French and British forces in northern France, maybe it could not stop the Nazis from taking over Britain. As Churchill had recently stated, Britain "must expect that as soon as stability is reached on the Western Front [i.e., in Germany's favor], the bulk of that hideous apparatus of aggression which gashed Holland into ruin and slavery in a few days will be turned upon us."[53]

Britain's banking community responded swiftly to the deteriorating political situation. The Bank of England, for example, selected Martin's Bank of Liverpool as a major repository for British gold and securities in advance of the journey across the Atlantic. Like other facilities responsible for protecting extraordinarily large quantities of gold, the Liverpool bank had to cope with the challenges of security, storage, and weight.

According to the bank's internal magazine, near midnight on May 22, 1940, the first of three special trains arrived at No. 8 Platform at the Lime Street station.[54] It took nearly three hours to transfer the treasure, packed in 130-pound wooden boxes, from the train to the waiting trucks. The trucks then made their way to the bank's head office building, which offered an "admirable" storage facility. The vaults were built on rock and had steel-reinforced concrete walls and ceilings nearly a yard thick. The vaults were also protected by doors that weighed nine tons each.

The bank's "bullion lift" could not handle the magnitude of the job, so bank personnel borrowed a long wooden chute originally designed for transferring butter and cheese. The goal was to send the boxes down the chute to a large room near the vaults. Unfortunately, the box corners damaged the chute, causing several boxes to fall and spill their contents. "By a little coaxing of the contrivance," according to the bank's magazine, the chute was repaired and survived the night's operation. For the next consignment, the chute was disposed of, and the Bank

FIG. 6.1. Martin's Bank in Liverpool was one of several banks to serve as a temporary repository for gold and securities bound for the New World. Accounting for every gold bar was a laborious process. *From "Martin's Bank at War,"* Martin's Bank Magazine, *Autumn 1946*

of England supplied platform conveyors each capable of bearing one and a quarter tons.

The nighttime procedure was repeated forty-eight hours later, and then again on May 31. In all, Martin's Bank stored 4,719 boxes of gold weighing about 280 tons. With a rate of $35 an ounce, the haul was worth roughly £65 million ($264 million). The gold would be worth approximately $10 billion today. A month later, when the Bank of England hastily ordered the boxes be shipped to Canada, the gold had to make the more difficult journey out of the bank; gravity now served as a hindrance, not an aid. Martin's Bank reported that "all hands were required to load up the convoy of lorries to take it to the docks for shipment—this time in daylight." Security procedures were not recorded, but the gold apparently made it to the ships safely.[55]

Back in London, fears of invasion drove Sir Kenneth Clark, the director of the National Gallery, to arrange for the art in the National Gallery and royal collections to be sent to Canada. On June 1, Clark suggested this directly to Churchill, but the prime minister refused the request.

Putting on a brave face, Churchill said, "No. Bury them in caves and cellars. None must go. We are going to beat them."[56]

Despite Churchill's bravado with Clark, the prime minister took many precautions nonetheless. Just the day before, he had ordered that all signposts throughout Britain be taken down, all milestones be uprooted, and all names of streets, railway stations, and villages be obliterated.[57] In addition, several days later, members of Parliament were carrying gas masks, and government buildings had recently been protected by barbed wire and sandbags. *Time* magazine described many of the precautions now affecting most of Britain:

> Motorists were cautioned to remove spark plugs from their cars when parking so that Nazi invaders could not use them. An 8 p.m. to 6 a.m. curfew was imposed on all foreigners, Americans and Frenchmen included. Motor launches between 30 and 100 feet in length were requisitioned by the Admiralty for coastal patrol. Police swooped down on firearms dealers, gunsmiths and pawnbrokers throughout Britain and confiscated their guns and pistols. A new "treachery bill," designed to put teeth in the present treason law dating from the 14th Century, was rushed through Parliament, which voted dictatorial powers to the Government.[58]

France and Britain continued to pressure the United States for support. French prime minister Paul Reynaud told American ambassador to France William Bullitt on May 18 that he wanted Roosevelt to declare that the United States would not allow Britain and France to be defeated.[59] To the frustration of the French and the British, FDR never issued such a declaration—and it seemed that France would soon be lost. Lord Halifax wrote in his diary on May 25, 1940, "The mystery of what looks like the French failure is as great as ever. The one firm rock on which everyone was willing to build for the last two years was the French Army, and the Germans walked through it like they did the Poles."[60]

Irish writer George Bernard Shaw, who lived in England, took a detached but optimistic view of the deteriorating situation for both Britain and France: "Now that we're thoroughly frightened, we'll be all right. Until the British are frightened, they never do anything but play cricket, football, hopscotch and tennis."[61] And frightened they were as German forces thrust southward toward Paris with London, perhaps, as the next target. The Allies would now have to scramble to transfer ever larger portions of their wealth to North America.

7

Living from Hour to Hour

As British fears of a German invasion intensified, the Bank of England, the Treasury, and the Admiralty discussed how quickly gold and securities could be evacuated from the British Isles. On May 21, 1940, the Admiralty reported to the Bank that it was moving £30 million worth of gold and securities a month.[1] Days later, however, it had become readily apparent that the pace would have to be increased dramatically. Vastly more than £30 million now needed to be evacuated in a matter of weeks.

In late May, the Bank of England organized an extensive set of lower-value gold shipments (£1 to £2 million), while the Treasury prepared much larger shipments for the near future.[2] Eventually, the Admiralty convinced the select government officials and bankers involved that it could take on significantly larger consignments. In short order, the crew of HMS *Revenge* prepared for Britain's most valuable voyage of the war to date: £40 million in gold. This consignment represented more than triple the value of most other consignments previously considered "large," and it was worth almost the value of all British purchases in the United States during the first half of 1939.[3] With the invasion of Britain an increasing possibility, sending one ship with £40 million could help speed up the evacuation.

According to Midn. W. S. Crawford of the *Revenge*, on May 29 the last of the "gold which we have been loading for some days was struck below. . . . *Revenge* slipped her buoy this forenoon and proceeded on her degaussing trials. These took place just outside Greenock." Another midshipman on board the *Revenge*, R. Raban-Williams, noted that the ship would join a convoy consisting of the *Samaria*, the *Duchess of Atholl*, and the *Duchess of Bedford*—cruise ships requisitioned for service by the

Admiralty after the start of the war. The *Duchess of Bedford* "produced a brass band and gave us a cheering send-off and then followed us to sea." The two *Revenge* crewmates did not mention that each of these ships carried more than £5 million in gold.[4]

The trip across the Atlantic was uneventful for the *Revenge* and the other ships in the convoy—a great relief to all involved. Once in Halifax, Raban-Williams noted on June 7 that "all arrangements are being made to unload our special cargo of 'margarine' as soon as possible when we berth alongside."[5] The next day, Raban-Williams wrote that "our escort of Canadian destroyers joined us in the morning watch: we came alongside in No. 23 berth at 1000 and began to unload our special cargo as soon as possible. . . . All the bullion was unloaded by midnight."[6] It thus took the crew more than twelve hours to unload the nine tons of gold.

Upon arrival in Halifax, Crawford provided this interesting description of the wartime port:

> The city of Halifax turned out to be a rather incongruous combination of ambitious hotels and provincial mediocrity. It was obvious that its importance as an ocean and railway terminus surpassed its importance as a city. The predominance of wooden houses struck an unusual but pleasant chord in minds schooled in stone and brick. The eastern and western ends of the docks presented totally different aspects. While the eastern docks bristled with loading facilities and spacious warehouses, those to the west were little better than broken down wooden piers. The wharves and anchorages were crowded with shipping, both naval and merchant.[7]

In June 1940, Britain dispatched more than forty other gold-laden ships to North America. Some caught the attention of major media outlets in New York, much to the chagrin of those overseeing the operation. In early June, for example, the *Wall Street Journal* reported that the New York Federal Reserve Bank received enormous shipments of gold from Britain, France, and perhaps several other European countries. According to the newspaper's account, in a two-day period alone, the Fed received roughly $600 million worth of gold. Some of this gold may have come from the *Revenge* and the other ships in its convoy, but it may have simply been an amalgamation of prior gold shipments to Canada. With so much gold arriving in New York and especially Canada, it was hard to know.

FIG. 7.1. HMS *Revenge* delivered treasure from the Bank of England five times between 1939 and 1940. The warship also led the most valuable convoy of the war in July 1940. *Courtesy of the Imperial War Museum*

The *Wall Street Journal* also provided fascinating details about some of the shipments—a rare occurrence for the newspaper's war-related financial coverage. Early on Tuesday, June 4, the newspaper reported that "12 railroad cars rolled into a mid-town freight terminal where they were met by 100 special guards. By 11 a.m. armored trucks loaded down with the precious metal began to roll into the receiving entrance on Maiden Lane of the New York Federal Reserve Bank."[8] The bank could accommodate a dozen trucks at a time, the newspaper reported, and armed men were spaced apart so that every point in the room could be "swept by a deadly fire." Even at the end of the business day, trucks were still lined up in the streets waiting their turn to deliver their share of the gold. By the end of the evening, more than $286 million in gold had been unloaded at the Fed, roughly matching the amount that had been delivered the day before.

The detail in the *Wall Street Journal*'s story shocked some of the British officials working in the United States, and it was likely the impetus for a letter from Gerald Pinsent, a financial adviser at the British Embassy in Washington, to Sigismund Waley, assistant secretary at the Treasury, back in London. Pinsent wrote, "It came as a surprise to us—though a satisfactory one—that some £500 million worth of gold was delivered to the Federal Reserve in New York on the 3rd and 4th intact, to be earmarked for British and French accounts." Because of the secrecy surrounding the gold shipments, neither Pinsent nor the British ambassador to the United States had known of the gold transfers until they appeared in the American press.[9] (After the war, historian Alfred Draper asked Anthony Eden about the operation. Eden, who had been secretary of the war at the time, claimed he had no knowledge of it.[10] Eden was perhaps disingenuous about what he knew at the time and since.)

The newspaper account prompted a very concerned Pinsent to pose an insightful set of questions to the British Treasury. Pinsent asked Waley, "Are you planning any step (a) to vest all registered dollars or other securities, and any other securities in the Treasury? (b) to remove all dollars or other securities from the United Kingdom to Canada or the United States? (c) to destroy any securities in the United Kingdom after a record has been made and authenticated and sent to Canada or the United States?"[11] British leaders in the know were probably wondering whether German observers of American newspapers were asking the same questions. If Britain was indeed planning to move its marketable financial resources to North America, Germany could concentrate its naval resources to their capture at sea.

In the United States, even Germany's stunning successes against France in May and early June 1940 did not signal the end of isolationism. Back in 1939, after the collapse of Poland, 63 percent of Americans polled by the American Institute of Public Opinion were convinced that if Germany were victorious in Europe, it would eventually attack the United States. Roughly the same number of those polled believed that *after the fall of France*, Germany would make an immediate attempt to seize territory in the Western Hemisphere. Yet, fewer than 8 percent of those surveyed in a *Fortune* poll at the end of May 1940 actually favored an immediate American entry into the war. Only 19 percent of Americans believed that the United States should intervene to prevent the defeat of the Allies, and a full 40 percent opposed American intervention under any circumstances.[12]

Churchill proved unable to withhold criticism of Americans as he told

Canadian prime minister Mackenzie King to take a cautious approach with them. On June 5, Churchill wrote, "We must be careful not to let Americans view too complacently the prospect of a British collapse out of which they would get the British Fleet and guardianship of the British Empire minus Great Britain." Churchill also told King that even though "the President is our best friend, no practical help has been forthcoming from the United States yet."[13] John Colville seemed to sum up best the British view of the United States at this critical juncture of the war: "[T]he plain truth is that America has been caught napping, militarily and industrially. She may be really useful to us in a year; but we are living from hour to hour."[14]

The situation grew even worse starting on June 10. Sensing the direction the conflict was now taking, Italian leader Benito Mussolini declared war on the Allies. Two days later, German forces were within twelve miles of Paris. French officials made the painful but necessary decision to leave the city, ultimately declaring Paris an open city in order to spare it from German bombardment.

On June 14, French prime minister Paul Reynaud once again pleaded with Roosevelt for help: "France can continue the struggle only if America intervenes to reverse the situation, thus rending Allied victory certain." Without U.S. help, he warned, "you will see France go down like a drowning man and disappear, after having thrown a last look toward the land of liberty from which it expected salvation."[15] But the Americans disregarded the prime minister's last plea. Later that day, the German army entered Paris and raised the swastika from the Arc de Triomphe. Reynaud was quickly replaced as prime minister by Marshal Henri-Philippe Pétain, who facilitated France's surrender to Germany.

In the secret world of Britain's financial flight, June 14, 1940, proved to be a momentous day. The British government made the decision to ship its remaining marketable securities to Canada. According to a secret British Treasury document, the "securities were shipped in three consignments. The bulk of the American securities went first followed by the Canadian securities. The third shipment was comprised of U.S. and Canadian securities of lower value, along with Dutch, Belgian, Swiss, and Argentine holdings."[16]

There was little optimism for Europe's lot in the United States. On June 17, Gen. Raymond Lee, the American military attaché in London, recorded in his diary that he encountered nothing but defeatist

FIG. 7.2. The German military's success in France was swift. Hitler poses for a typical tourist photo opportunity in Paris on June 23, 1940. *Courtesy of the U.S. National Archives*

attitudes on a commercial flight from New York to Europe. He also described an "almost pathological assumption that it was all over but the shouting, that the French are going to give up, that it is too late for the United States to do anything."[17]

On June 22, 1940, France was formally finished. At Armistice ceremonies, Hitler spoke triumphantly of a war that was almost over:

> German People! In a short six weeks your soldiers have brought an end to the War in the West after an heroic battle against a brave foe. Their deeds

will be entered in history as the most glorious victory of all times. Humbly we thank the Lord for this blessing. I order the display of flags throughout the Reich for ten days and the ringing of bells for seven days.[18]

In New York, a group of pro-German industrialists and their sympathizers met at the Waldorf Astoria Hotel to celebrate Germany's victory over France.[19] In exile in the Netherlands, the old German kaiser Wilhelm II wired Hitler to congratulate him "on the mighty victory granted by God."[20]

Lord Lothian cabled London from Washington to explain that most Americans seemed to regard Britain's defeat as inevitable and that this belief hampered Roosevelt's ability to aid Britain.[21] Nonetheless, as before, the Roosevelt administration quietly worked around the isolationists as best it could. The United States maintained and gradually increased its patrols in the Atlantic, and FDR said that Britain could leave its Caribbean interests to the U.S. Navy.[22] According to British air chief marshal Hugh Dowding, if the Germans appeared in West Indian waters, the U.S. Navy would not hesitate to deal with them.[23]

Germany's victory over France had several deleterious effects on the Admiralty and the Allied ships rushing to evacuate Britain's wealth. First, the British took over French purchasing contracts in North America—valued at more than $500 million.[24] In addition to Britain's need to replenish military stocks from the evacuation of Dunkirk, this placed acute financial strains on Britain's diminishing war chest.

Britain sought financial relief by acquiring France's substantial gold reserves held in Canada. The Churchill government's logic seemed sound and beyond question: with the French government now under Nazi control, French gold in Canada should be made available to serve the Allied war effort and to expedite France's return to freedom.[25] At stake was approximately £37 million, or almost $150 million.

The Canadians, however, had very different ideas about the role of the French gold, and for the next several months, it remained in legal limbo. British Treasury official Sir Frederick Phillips was sent to Ottawa to make Britain's case before the Canadian government and Graham Towers, the governor of the Bank of Canada. Prime Minister King and his foreign policy aide, Oskar D. Skelton, balked at the British proposal. Both hoped to maintain foreign policy autonomy vis-à-vis Britain. In addition, King's political health depended on votes from Québec, the

French-speaking province that was likely to react negatively to the liquidation of French assets in favor of Britain.[26]

The fall of France also rendered the protection of the gold shipments even more challenging. Fears of a German invasion forced the Royal Navy to devote the already scarce resources to home defense, weakening convoy defense. Making matters worse, U-boats damaged by the Norway campaign had been repaired by June 1940.[27] Karl Dönitz's submarine fleet also now had access to French submarine bases at Lorient, Brest, Saint-Nazaire, La Rochelle, and Bordeaux. Before the fall of France, U-boats had to make the long haul from bases at Hamburg, Wilhelmshaven, and Kiel through the North Sea and over the top of the Orkney Islands in northern Scotland. These long routes greatly restricted the time that could be spent on patrol in the Atlantic.[28] The recently acquired French bases afforded U-boats the ability to carry out more patrols in the Atlantic and stay in the hunt longer—granting them some 22 percent greater endurance.[29] It was clear that the longer Britain delayed the evacuation of its wealth, the more likely the Germans would be able to sink or capture the treasure ships.[30]

The paramount issue now facing Britain was Germany's next move. Was a German invasion on, and if so, when and where would it begin? The intelligence available offered no definitive answers, but many indicators signaled that an invasion was imminent. Under the assumption that Germany would in fact begin an invasion of Britain in the coming days or weeks, the Bank of England, the Treasury, and the Admiralty again stepped up the pace of the evacuation of British wealth.

The invasion scare in Britain also generated a panic of sorts in Canada. In late June 1940, Québec suffered from a paranoia that German spies were everywhere. Contributing to the climate of fear was a German radio broadcast directed at a French Canadian audience. German propagandists sought to exploit the long-running political and linguistic divide within Canada. The German radio broadcast sent the message that Hitler was offering Québec "plain and complete independence" from Canada.[31]

═══════════

As the situation in France worsened, the beleaguered custodians of the British Empire were forced to contemplate a variety of fantastic scenarios. British leaders were still wondering if they would be forced

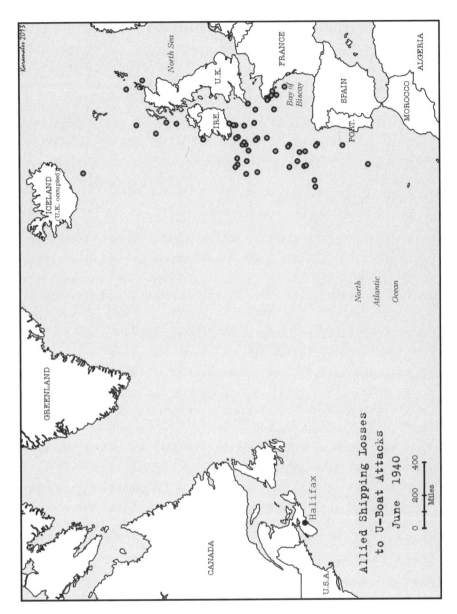

FIG. 7.3. June 1940 proved to be an especially dangerous time for Allied ships sailing in the waters to the west and south of the British Isles. Each dot represents the loss of an Allied ship. Adapted from "Ship Losses by Month: June 1940," www.uboat .net, by Jay Karamales

to evacuate their government and the Royal Navy along with the treasure. On June 19, Lord Lothian told a gathering of Yale alumni what Churchill had already told Roosevelt in private. The Allies' strategic picture was shattered with the fall of France. "Let me be blunt," the British ambassador told the audience. "Many people in the United States believe that somehow or other, even if Great Britain is invaded and overrun, the British Navy will cross the Atlantic and will still be available through Canada or otherwise as part of your own defensive system. I hope you are not building on that expectation. If you are, you are building on an illusion."[32]

On June 24, the British Cabinet evaluated Mackenzie King's suggestion that the British fleet be sent to North America "if the situation deteriorated" further. Churchill, however, told the Cabinet that he was confident in "the final outcome of the war and that there was no reason to fear that the Royal Navy would have to be transferred to American waters."[33] The same day, Churchill told the Canadian prime minister, "I shall myself never enter into any peace negotiations with Hitler, but obviously I cannot bind a future Government, which, if we were deserted by the United States and beaten down here, might easily be a kind of Quisling affair ready to accept German overlordship and protection."[34] Churchill, it seems, could not help but make another appeal to the conscience of his American allies for not doing enough for Britain. Churchill was probably hoping King would relay this sentiment to Roosevelt in the coming days.

The relocation of the Royal Navy and the British government to Canada represented but one of many seemingly fanciful scenarios under consideration in those harrowing days. On June 13, Jean Monnet, the chairman of the Anglo-French Coordinating Committee, and René Preven, a member of the French Economic Mission in London, proposed an Anglo-French union. In essence, citizens of the two countries would be joined into one. When Charles de Gaulle, representing the Free French, presented the plan to British political leaders, Churchill and the Cabinet accepted it. But when the proposal was presented to French government ministers, it was rejected in the belief that "in three weeks England will have her neck rung like a chicken." Marshal Pétain allegedly claimed that union with Britain would be like a "fusion with a corpse." French minister of family and veterans Michel Ybarnegaray also argued that it would be better for France to become a Nazi province than a British dominion.[35]

Another startling proposal surfaced on June 16, when Arthur Greenwood, Britain's minister without portfolio, delivered a memo to the Cabinet titled "Economic Aid from the New World to the Old." The seventeen-page document highlighted many drastic measures to be taken in the event of a German invasion. Perhaps its most astounding feature was the idea of evacuating millions of women and children to North America to minimize the chances of famine in Britain. "A reduction of each 1 million in the number to be fed," Greenwood calculated, "would reduce by about ½ million tons the necessary volume of imports. It is for consideration whether within the limits of outgoing shipping capacity it would not be of advantage to encourage the transfer for the time being of women and children to the American continent. . . . Our power to survive the period until the assistance of the United States can become fully effective will depend largely on our power to import. The smaller the population to be fed, the less will our difficulties be."[36]

This cold calculation about evacuating British civilians took place amid the rapid evacuation of British wealth. Dozens of ships from throughout the British Empire were preparing to sail for North America or were already on their way. How would these ships fare against the resurgent German naval vessels plying the waters of the North Atlantic? The capture of any of the larger consignments would simultaneously cripple Britain's ability to pay for the war and extend Germany's staying power at this most crucial stage of the war.

8

Keeping Mum

Maintaining operational secrecy of the treasure shipments posed a daunting challenge for British and Canadian leaders. With over 180 ships making some 340 separate shipments of gold and securities, vital details about consignments, ports, and ships could have leaked out and found their way to the German naval staff in innumerable ways. Obviously, it was imperative that Germany not discover the location of the valuable consignments at any stage of their preparation in Britain, Bombay, Sydney, or Cape Town, or along their subsequent transfer by ship, rail, or truck. Every aspect of the evacuation had to be as hush-hush as possible.

It was just as important to keep the British public in the dark about the special shipments. The financial demands of the young war were draining Britain's reserves—a fact that the British government tried to hide from its own citizens as much as from the Germans. Back in late December 1939, Sir John Simon, Britain's chancellor of the exchequer, expected the war to take a heavy toll on the country's economic situation, and he linked the economic situation to the fragility of the national will: "The question is whether the morale of the home front is good enough to bear" the war's economic hardships. He added, "Judging from the raucous criticism of hitherto minor inconveniences, I am inclined to doubt this, unless the public's enthusiasm and determination is increased by sensational events in the war. . . . From this angle Germany, and any totalitarian Government, is in a better position to wage war than we are."[1]

Concerns about British morale persisted throughout the first year of the war. In early July 1940, the status of Britain's confidence weighed heavily on the mind of Air Chief Marshal Hugh Dowding, whose leadership would subsequently prove invaluable in the Battle of Britain. Dowding thought that sooner or later Britain and Germany would have to begin bombing raids to destroy each other's aircraft industries. Of course, Dowding said, this "will imply bombing the civilian population. Then the real test will begin: have we or the Germans the sterner civilian morale?"[2]

Under the leadership of Winston Churchill after May 10, 1940, the government's message to its people was that the country could weather the Nazi storm. In reality, many political leaders on both sides of the Atlantic had serious doubts about Britain's chances of survival. In the United States, occasional disclosure of the now-massive treasure shipments could have been interpreted as a sign that the British government was not prepared to fight to the bitter end. For those holding this perspective, what was the point of giving aid to Britain if the Churchill government was preparing to move to Canada and cede all of Europe to the Nazis? As Edward Bridges, a military adviser to Churchill and a former Treasury official, put it, "nothing is more helpful to Hitler than to say we must start thinking about preparing skeleton Government departments in Canada."[3] Just days after taking leadership of his government in May 1940, Churchill told American ambassador Joseph Kennedy that his government would continue "even if England were burnt to the ground."[4] As it turned out, Britain sent its wealth to North America but not its government. Safeguarding the treasury was critical to keeping the government in place in London.

―――――――――――

Documents related to the transfer of British wealth invariably included restrictions such as "Secret," "Most Secret," "Highly Secret," and "To be kept under lock and key." Many of the British War Cabinet documents asked that "special care" be taken to ensure the documents' safety. Communications sent back and forth between Britain, its Empire, and the United States were coded cables that had to be deciphered.

On occasion, Bank of England officials used the code word "fish" to refer to gold and securities. Journalist and war veteran Alfred Draper later dubbed the fight to save Allied gold during the war "Operation Fish." However, as even Draper states in his book by the same name, no such code name was used at the secret meetings held in Allied political, banking, and military circles.[5] In Winston Churchill's book

Their Finest Hour, appendix E lists sixteen operational code names for the years 1940–41, but Operation Fish is not one of them.[6] Thus the removal of the Empire's treasury was so secret that the operation never even had a formal name. (See appendix I for a discussion of code names and nicknames.)

Even important agencies were sometimes deliberately left out of the loop. The War Risk Insurance Office (WRIO) was one such government bureau. "As far as we know," a secret June 17, 1940, Bank of England memo stated, "the W.R.I.O. have no knowledge of our 'special' shipments, [and] it is not proposed to enlighten them now."[7]

British and Canadian authorities took many measures to ensure the secrecy of the treasure shipments. For example, at the crucial meetings held at the Bank of England, no minutes were taken and no secretaries were allowed to attend.[8] An additional example can be seen in the explanation of George Bolton of the Bank of England to his colleague D. K. Cherry: "We have arranged with the shipping companies that one man in each company is detailed to prepare documents and arrange shipments. Further, no cables or letters may be sent referring to gold and no telephone calls are to be made."[9] (Bolton exaggerated the point a bit; ciphered cables of a general nature were sometimes allowed.)

Those highest up understood the urgent need for secrecy. There was no need for the mottoes designed for the general public, such as "Be Like Dad and Keep Mum," "Keep Mum She's Not So Dumb!" "Tittle Tattle Will Lose the Battle," or "Careless Words Cost Lives."[10] The greatest concern for British officials was the thousands of bank employees, deck hands, railroad employees, truck drivers, and guards who would play a role in moving billions of pounds in gold and securities across thousands of miles. For example, according to historian William Breuer, when the gold and securities in Britain were sent by rail to the ports, guards were sworn to secrecy under penalty of long prison terms.[11]

Many other precautions were taken to prevent anyone from piecing together details of the complex operation. Though the vast majority of shipments were destined for safekeeping at the Bank of Canada, Bank of England officials kept their Canadian counterparts in the dark about ship arrival times until late in each voyage. On October 11, 1939, for example, the Bank of England notified the Bank of Canada by letter that £10 million worth of gold was on its way and would arrive at some unspecified time: "Last week we sent off to Halifax, through the Admiralty, five separate shipments of gold to the value of £2 million each. We have no idea when this gold will arrive at Halifax and we are prohibited from cabling or telephoning to you any details of the movement."[12]

The Canadians took special precautions as well. On occasion, coded messages were used to acknowledge the arrival of a gold ship. Bank of Canada secretary Dean Marble requested that he be notified, if necessary, at his home. As Marble explained to the Bank's agent in Halifax, "Will you please telegraph the word 'completed' to me at my home address . . . [in] Ottawa, when the shipment has been transferred to the Express Company [railroad]? If there should be any unfavorable developments, please telephone to me."[13] In the case of a May 1940 gold shipment, Marble did indeed receive a cryptic telegram on the 16th, which simply read, "Completed."[14]

The Bank of Canada also made special arrangements with the Canadian Customs Department. As Marble explained in February 1940, "no customs documents are required for gold shipments arriving at the ports of Vancouver, Saint John and Halifax. The Chief of the Currency Division, however, is required to make a monthly confidential report to Mr. Scully, Commissioner of Customs, Ottawa, showing the origin and amounts of shipments received."[15] As the first consignments from Sydney, Australia, were making their way to Vancouver on Canada's west coast, Marble provided similar guidelines to Walter Winsby, the Bank's agent in Vancouver. To reassure the Bank of England that appropriate measures were being taken in Canada, Marble also sent the following message to Bolton in London: "While the newspapers in Canada are already forbidden to carry any news with respect to the arrivals and departures of ships, we thought it well to ask the Director of Censorship to prohibit publication of any nature of items respecting movements of gold into, out of or within Canada."[16]

The security precautions taken in Britain and Canada were of course imperative, but they created sizable gaps in the historical record. Naval regulations forbade most officers from keeping a private diary on active service ashore or afloat.[17] Government officials were also forbidden from keeping diaries, although the rule was often violated. Unfortunately, two diaries that could have yielded valuable nuggets of information come up empty—those of John Colville (assistant private secretary to both Neville Chamberlain and Winston Churchill) and Alexander Cadogan (permanent undersecretary at the Foreign Office).[18]

Sometimes a paper trail was created only to disappear later under mysterious circumstances. One of the Bank of England's key archival folders for 1940 happens to be missing every page for June, July, and August—the months when the largest consignments of British treasure were prepared and sent to North America. In a recent inquiry, the archivists at the Bank could only speculate as to the fate of the missing documents. Perhaps the contents were believed to be too secret to be stored among the Bank's records. Perhaps the documents were taken home by a Bank governor and never returned. We may never know.

<hr>

The press played an unexpected role in the British and Canadian efforts to keep a lid on the operation's particulars. Leland Stowe, the journalist who first broke the story of Britain's financial flight, wrote that "Perhaps never before have so many kept so great a secret so incredibly well."[19] According to historian Duncan McDowall, the Bank of Canada "did its best to appear shy" about press inquiries. In one case, Bank governor Graham Towers simply told the Montréal *Gazette* that "quite a bit" of gold had been sent to Ottawa.[20] Towers might have provided this morsel of information because it could not be directly linked to specific British activities. For several years, the Bank of Canada had been receiving earmarked gold from many European countries, so the Bank's message was probably perceived as nothing out of the ordinary.

However, in light of newspaper accounts, notably in the United States, Stowe's assessment needs reevaluating. When the war began, press restrictions went into effect in Britain and Canada. In Canada, for example, censorship laws prevented newspapers from printing anything related to gold shipments to or within the country.[21] In the United States, however, newspapers were much freer because it was still a neutral country from 1939 to late 1941. In general, simple statements about gold and security movements occurred in all three countries from time to time.[22] Specific information occasionally appeared, but only in the United States, and its disclosure must have caused some sleepless nights for British and Canadian authorities both before and during the war.

In April 1939, for example, the *Wall Street Journal* reported that a shipment of £2 million in gold would be leaving Britain for New York on board the Cunard liner *Antonia* on the 26th.[23] Several months later, the newspaper provided some very revealing details about gold that had arrived and even gold that was still on the high seas heading for New York. On July 3, it reported, "Including the gold *which is now en route* from the United Kingdom to Canada, it is estimated that there is about $323.4 million gold held under earmark for foreign account. Of this amount, about $159 million has been shipped from the United Kingdom in the past month [emphasis added]."[24]

Coverage of gold shipments from the other great New York newspaper, the *New York Times*, was far from thorough but occasionally included some whoppers. Its coverage of the *Britannic*'s arrival in New York was typical. On January 10, 1940, the newspaper reported that in addition to the *Britannic*'s 180 passengers were eight racing horses, "five of which were from the stables of the Aga Khan." Two of the horses were bought by Charles S. Howard, owner of the famed racehorse Seabiscuit, and four were bought by the motion-picture executive Louis B. Mayer.[25] However, the *Times* made no mention of the *Britannic*'s consignment of £5 million in gold. A month later, the *Times* also failed to mention the £48,000 in gold carried on board the British ocean liner *Cameronia*, but it did mention that the ship carried 123,000 cases of Scotch whisky, which was "the largest such load ever carried on one ship."[26]

The *Times*, however, sporadically informed its readers of British gold on board inbound ships. On February 12, 1940, for example, the *New York Times* brazenly used the headline "$3,000,000 Gold Arrives." The article made note of the fact that the gold arrived in twenty-five cases, "which will be guarded in the specie room until tomorrow morning when the New York Federal Reserve Bank opens."[27] About a week later, the same newspaper reported that the *Britannic* had again arrived in New York with 375 passengers, including the wife (Kathleen Belcher) and children of C. S. Forester, author of the Horatio Hornblower series of sea stories. The *Times* also mentioned that the ship had brought with it $3 million in gold.[28]

As a result of such revealing press accounts, Britain introduced tighter regulations to limit the potential damage of news leaks, including those derived from civilians on board passenger ships. According to the *New York Times*, in April 1940, passengers on the *Britannic* and *Cameronia*, which had recently reached New York, were "markedly more silent about their crossings than passengers have been previously."[29]

BEWARE

HE WANTS TO KNOW YOUR UNIT'S NAME.
WHERE YOU'RE GOING, WHENCE YOU CAME.
EVEN ALONE OR IN A CROWD
NEVER MENTION THESE OUT LOUD.

FIG. 8.1. In the wake of unwanted leaks of information regarding gold and other vital topics, the British government used posters to discourage civilians from revealing military secrets. *Courtesy of the University of Minnesota Library*

Both ships carried new posters warning civilians to keep quiet about any information that could have military relevance. One such poster warned the passengers, "Beware: Above all, never give away the movements of His Majesty's ships." Other posters carried this verse:

> Whether alone or in a crowd
> Never write or say aloud
> What you're loading, whence you hail,
> Where you're bound for, when you sail.[30]

In spite of Britain's attempt to make its citizens more circumspect, and, indirectly, to encourage more discretion among the American press corps, gold stories continued to surface in the United States. On May 12, the *New York Times* reported that the *Britannic,* in yet another trans-Atlantic trip, carried 733 passengers and that the ship brought $4.5 million in gold from the Bank of England.[31] The *Britannic* got the attention of the *New York Times* again in June. Apparently unconcerned about Britain's desire for secrecy, the paper ran a headline reading "$39,444,000 of Gold Discharged Here." It reported that the gold was stored in 704 boxes and that eight "armored cars were waiting on the lower level of the dock to convoy the bullion to the Federal Reserve Bank of New York."[32]

The most astounding newspaper account of a gold shipment appeared on July 17, 1940, when the British passenger liner *Eastern Prince* delivered a reported $52 million in British gold to New York. In this particular case, the *New York Times* article raises two perplexing issues. First, the newspaper had no qualms about announcing the arrival of so much gold—even at this crucial time in the war and even after it was clear that Britain wanted to suppress such vital information. Second, and more puzzling, is how the newspaper chose to deliver this sensitive information: it was buried in a thicket of information about Britain's child evacuees.

> Altogether the ship brought ninety passengers across the Atlantic. All but one of the ten adults who remained on board after leaving Halifax were women attending the children. They included mothers, governesses and two grandmothers. In addition to the passengers the vessel also brought in $52,000,000 in gold. The children, like those who have preceded them here in the last two weeks, were all brought over privately with their parents paying for their passage.[33]

The article made no other reference to the gold. One can only speculate as to why the *Times* editorial board felt the need to print the information about the gold but in such an indirect and cursory way.[34]

A few days later, on July 30, the *New York Times* provided another fascinating account—but this time uninformative regarding gold—of the arrival of the *Britannic* and *Cameronia* in New York. Two articles that day mention that the ships "delivered supplies of woolen goods, cotton textiles, linens and laces, as well as a wide variety of other merchandise." The *Times* also noted that playwright Noel Coward was a passenger, as was Geneviève Tabouis, the foreign news editor of *L'Oeuvre* of Paris, who was sailing to the United States to escape the Nazis. J. P. Morgan was at the port in person to meet family members of bank employees working in London. In addition, because of the hundreds of children on board the *Britannic*, the newspaper quoted a member of the crew who said that "the youngsters had taken possession of the ship and that the deck stewards had a hard time keeping them out of mischief." The articles failed to mention that each ship carried £6 million worth of gold.[35]

———

With thousands of valuable crates being loaded and unloaded from truck or railcar to ship, from ship to truck or railcar, and so on, accidents were bound to occur. Almost any accident could have undermined aspects of the operation's secrecy. In one instance in December 1939, a railcar carrying £2 million in gold from HMS *Letitia* was inadvertently unhitched at Eastleigh near Southampton in southern England. A party of bank officials traveling with the shipment, but in a different car, had no idea what had happened until the train arrived at Southampton without the gold. After panicked inquiries, the gold was found and the mistake quickly corrected.[36]

Other mishaps threatened to expose operational details over the next several months. In Canada in December 1939, the wrong person received and opened a letter marked "Urgent and Confidential." The letter contained information about 101 boxes of gold delivered from Bombay (Mumbai) on board the British merchant ship *Alipore*. Walter Winsby wrote to his colleague Dean Marble at the Bank of Canada to explain the mistake: "[T]he Post Office wrongly delivered the registered letter to the Royal Bank, where it was opened and after being opened, was found to be for the Bank of Canada, Vancouver." The letter was quickly forwarded to its proper destination. Banking representatives and members of the Post Office Department fired off a series of letters to determine the extent of the breach. F. T. Palfrey, manager of the postal service, concluded that the individual at fault had misdelivered the confidential letter. Trying to calm the nerves of everyone involved, Palfrey explained that the guilty party had been in a rush and was confused by similar-looking envelopes. Palfrey reassured the Bank of Canada that the "officer in question is thoroughly reliable, with many years' experience, and we wish to assure you that had he read the contents of the letter he would not divulge the information contained therein."

Nevertheless, the person in question was removed from his post "and assigned to other duties."[37]

Accidents involving the special crates sometimes occurred because gold is such a heavy metal. The average gold bar weighs 27.5 pounds, and thus, even in small quantities, bullion is difficult to pack and move. Poorly prepared crates were sometimes the result of shoddy workmanship, sometimes the result of unavoidable haste.[38] Internal documents of the Bank of Canada revealed the nature of the problem involving 347 boxes of gold bullion delivered on June 8, 1940:

> I was informed by the Commander of the ship that it was received by them in [very bad condition], as it was a very rush job in loading and the authorities in England had found it impossible to properly pack this shipment. You will notice that the majority of the boxes were neither banded nor sealed, and some had been repaired by the ship's crew previously to being handed to us.[39]

The weight of gold was responsible for an incident on February 5, 1940. As Winsby reported, "Box #230 was cracked but seals are intact; accidentally dropped on wharf while loading truck for this Office." A similar accident occurred in October when gold was being unloaded from the New Zealand steamship *Waiotapu* in Vancouver.[40]

On occasion, the potential security breach proved to be quite comical. While gold was being unloaded from a ship in Halifax, a crate broke open. As Dean Marble put it, a sailor or longshoreman tried "to repair the box by using a gold bar as a hammer with chips of gold flying all around. This was quickly stopped."[41]

On November 10, 1939, when HMS *Emerald* was preparing to make a gold run to Halifax, Capt. Augustus Agar reported, "Nobody in the dockyard took the slightest notice and everything went without a hitch, until at a late hour, when the Admiral Superintendent of the Dockyard somehow got wind of what was going on and was extremely irate with me on the telephone. 'Who was responsible should the truck disappear,' he asked, 'he or I?' [He] was soon mollified, especially when I promised to bring back for him a frozen salmon on my next return journey."[42]

In October 1940, a shipment of £2 million in gold from Sydney typified how easy it was for minor accidents to occur and for sailors to learn of the contents of the crates. Winsby informed the Bank's headquarters in Ottawa of the incident:

FIG. 8.2. The Vancouver Agency staff at the Bank of Canada, 330 W. Pender Street. Although the photograph was taken in 1935, two figures played important roles in the gold operation in 1940. Walter Winsby helped coordinate gold shipments arriving at the west coast of Canada. K. C. MacLean worked with Sidney Perkins in processing, at very short notice, some of the biggest treasure shipments of the war as they arrived in eastern Canada. From left to right, front row: K. C. MacLean, F. J. Wilks, Walter Winsby, G. Watts, G. H. Llewllyn. From left to right, back row: A. Goodson, C. Malcolm, A. W. Webb, Constable Clearwater. *Courtesy of the Bank of Canada Archives, BCP.205-1, Staff at Vancouver Agency, June 1935*

I have to report that the metal seal on box Number 2745 was broken by accident when the box was taken from storage in the ship early this morning. The ship's strongbox was jammed tight with [gold] boxes, and in attempting to pry loose the first box, a longshoreman used his steel hook on the iron band containing the seal instead of the box, thus the seal came apart. However, I saw the occurrence and together with the [rail] Express Company, have re-sealed the box, which of course, shows no other marks of having been tampered with.[43]

On at least one occasion, the loading of gold took place with neither a police nor military security detail.[44] On two occasions, accidents actually led to the loss of gold. George Bolton of the Bank of England recalled after the war that £500,000 in gold was lost in a ship in a convoy off

Newfoundland when it "zigged instead of zagged." He also noted the loss of one third of a gold shipment valued at £750,000 after an explosion in Bombay scattered the gold over the harbor area.[45]

Despite all of the press leaks, paperwork mishaps, and accidents, by the spring of 1940, even otherwise well-informed British citizens remained in the dark about the operation. Chamberlain received a curious letter in June 1940 from D. M. Mason, former member of Parliament for East Edinburgh and a man generally well versed in financial matters. Mason was, nevertheless, clearly unaware of the special shipments. He offered to lead a mission to the United States with experts from the British and French Treasuries in order to generate financial support for the war. Mason finished his letter with this interesting piece of advice: "As a cautionary measure, if this has not already been done, the gold reserve of France and Great Britain should be sent to America for safe custody."[46]

The operation also remained safely under wraps from many high-level American officials who could have known otherwise. In May 1940, for example, Secretary of State Cordell Hull instructed American ambassador Kennedy to speak with Kingsley Wood at the British Treasury and Montagu Norman at the Bank of England about taking the prudent course of sending gold and securities to Canada. Wood told Kennedy that he would raise the issue with Churchill, whose response was only partly truthful. Churchill said that he would not agree to ship Britain's valuables to Canada because the move might make the public think that the government was panicking.[47] While the fear of domestic panic was authentic, Churchill and Wood were clearly choosing to leave Kennedy and Hull in the dark. One, or both, of the men apparently could not be trusted with the sensitive information.

The Germans should also have been thinking about the role of gold in the war. Britain's financial experience in the first year of the war shared striking parallels with its experience in World War I. As the *New York Times* wrote on August 10, 1915, a "rumored sum" of $100 million in gold had just been carried on British warships to Halifax. The newspaper reported that Britain and Canada were running short of gold and surmised that Britain had sent the gold to pay for munitions and to bolster the value of its currency. The *New York Times* article also added that the German espionage system, "it was thought, would be very quick to learn of the shipment and give opportunity to the German submarines to waylay such a shipment."[48]

To prevent the Kriegsmarine from learning about specific shipments, Allied officials on both sides of the Atlantic had to keep a close eye on German spies operating in Canada, Britain, and the United States. In January 1940, an agent working for German naval intelligence, Marie Koedel, reported almost daily to her superiors about shipping news in New York. Marie was the foster daughter of Simon Emil Koedel, a successful German spy operating in the United States under cover of the American Ordnance Association, an organization of weapons manufacturers with strong ties to the War Department. Marie's beat included frequenting saloons "in dresses that left little to the imagination." The willowy brunette, as historian William Breuer described her, succeeded in extracting information about ship sailing schedules, routes, ship armaments, and cargoes.[49]

At one point, Marie Koedel managed to enlist the help of Duncan Scott-Ford, a British sailor she had met in a waterfront bar. According to historian David Kahn, information supplied by Scott-Ford led to one of her father's most important documents: "Report on the Conduct of Enemy Ships in Convoy at Sea in the Atlantic, Based on Conversations with British Seamen."[50] Nevertheless, the Koedels' intelligence provided no information related to gold or securities on the inbound ships from Britain. Scott-Ford later spied for Germany in Lisbon but was caught by the British and hanged in November 1942. Koedel and her father were eventually arrested in 1944 and convicted of espionage in 1945.[51]

German naval intelligence does not appear to have acquired any specific information about Britain's treasure shipments. If excitement can be conveyed through the logs of a rear admiral, it may be perceived in a few of Karl Dönitz's remarks about the prospects of attacking several convoys in 1940. Some of his notes are quite detailed, such as his criticism of German torpedoes or the haste with which U-boats should sail to a specific area where the hunting was expected to be good. But his logs make no mention of British ships carrying gold or securities. There is also no description of the potential capture of a great prize or the disappointment in missing a golden opportunity.[52]

An authoritative postwar assessment of U-boat activities, written by Günter Hessler on behalf of the British Admiralty and U.S. Navy, made no mention of British gold or securities either. Hessler commanded U-107 in 1940 and 1941 and was later a staff officer (Operations) to the flag officer commanding U-boats. He was also a son-in-law of Dönitz. Hessler's study describes, among other things, German naval strategies as well as U-boat capabilities and tactics. The report rarely included particulars about the types of cargo aboard Allied ships. Usually, the hunting was considered good simply if enemy ships were in a target zone. One exception is a section devoted not to British treasure but to "The Timber and Ore Traffic to Britain" from northern Russian ports.[53] If timber and ore merited the attention of the German naval staff (and Hessler's study), one would expect something to have been included about British treasure had, indeed, anything important been known about it. As for German espionage in the United States, historian Hans Trefousse put it succinctly: "the vaunted Nazi secret service was singularly inefficient."[54]

━━━━━━━━━━

What worried the British public and government officials the most were fifth columnists, or "traitors" as Deputy Prime Minister Clement Attlee preferred to call them.[55] In contrast to German spies, the fifth column represented a potentially more pervasive danger.[56] Before the start of the war, but especially in mid-1940, it was widely assumed that Britons favorable to Germany would assist the Nazis in taking over the country. Alarming rumors circulated that a fifth column would carry out sabotage and otherwise undermine the government.

Fears of a fifth column were widespread at both the mass and elite levels of society. Gen. Sir Edmund Ironside warned that there were "people quite definitely preparing aerodromes in this country" for use by the German air force.[57] Sir Nevile Bland, the British minister in the Netherlands, reported that a German-born maid was responsible for leading German paratroopers to one of their targets in that country and warned that Britain would face a similar challenge. "Every German or Austrian servant, however superficially charming and devoted, is a real and grave menace," he wrote. When Bland presented his report to the War Cabinet on May 15, 1940, Churchill said that "urgent action" was needed to combat the threat.[58]

Rumors of a fifth column in Britain were fanned by Joseph Goebbels's propaganda machine. The Luftwaffe (the German air force) made drops over England that included fake maps, air photographs of landing fields and beach defenses, paratrooper radio gear, and instructions to agents and supposed fifth columnists.[59] Four German radio stations broadcast messages to Britain of an imminent invasion and of the need for "loyal" Britons to undermine Churchill's defiance. Lending credence to the existence of a fifth column, the Right Club, a pro-German group, distributed stickers, leaflets, and posters supportive of the fascist cause.[60]

In the spring of 1940, concerns over fifth-column activities were magnified by the discovery of a spy, American Tyler Kent, working as a cipher clerk in the U.S. Embassy in London. For years, Kent passed secret documents to Nazi sympathizers. On May 20, 1940, Britain's Special Branch raided Kent's apartment and found, among other things, copies of more than fifteen hundred classified documents, including secret correspondence between Churchill and Roosevelt and duplicate keys to the U.S. Embassy code room. Kent was motivated in part by the desire to keep the United States out of the war, and that year his main goal seemed to be preventing the reelection of Roosevelt. In addition to information sent to the Nazis, Kent hoped to pass on damaging documents to the AFC and sympathetic members of the Senate Foreign Relations Committee so as to ensure both public and congressional support for the impeachment of the president.[61]

When Kent was captured, British authorities found a ledger belonging to the Conservative member of Parliament and German sympathizer Archibald Ramsay. Among those listed in the red-leather-bound book, commonly referred to as the Red Book, were Arthur Wellesley (the Duke of Wellington), three other peers (members of the nobility), three sons of peers, and twenty members of Parliament. The Red Book also included Sir Alexander Walker (head of the Johnnie Walker whiskey dynasty), and fifty-four members of the pro-Nazi Nordic League.

In addition, the Duke of Wellington chaired a committee that coordinated the activities of three pro-German, anticommunist, and anti-Semitic groups: the Right Club, the Link, and the Anglo-German Fellowship. As the war began, the Link and the Anglo-German Fellowship disbanded, but the Right Club's activities continued underground. The Right Club was "harmless enough, even slightly ridiculous," according to historians Ray Bearse and Anthony Read, but Britain's security services took the group seriously.[62]

The Red Book also included Adm. Sir Barry Domvile, a former director of British naval intelligence and founder of the Link. Domvile had visited Nazi Germany several times and was a guest of the German ambassador Joachim von Ribbentrop at the Nuremberg Rally in 1936. Also on the list was Right Club founding member William Joyce, an American-born Irishman who later broadcast Nazi propaganda messages during the war. (He was known to the British as "Lord Haw Haw."[63]) A report to the Home Office described Joyce as anti-Catholic, anti-Semitic, and someone whose mental balance was "not equal to his intellectual capacity."[64]

Tyler Kent was eventually convicted under Britain's Official Secrets Act and the Larceny Act and sentenced to seven years.[65] The day after Kent's apartment was raided, Sir Oswald Mosley, head of the British Union of Fascists, was sent to prison. He did not help his case by saying, "I know I can save this country and that no one else can." As part of wider antifascist sweeps, nearly four hundred other British fascists were also incarcerated within a week.[66]

With fear of invasion gripping Britain, the government and much of the public increasingly focused attention on the many foreigners in their midst. On May 16, 1940, the government interned Grade "B" aliens—those whose absolute reliability was uncertain. On the same day, a headline from the *Daily Herald* read, "Country Saved from Fifth Column Stab."[67] On June 24, 1940, at Churchill's direction, police carried out a program to "collar the lot." More than fifteen thousand Grade "C" foreigners living in London were rounded up and interned. Grade "C" cases represented most of the recent immigrants to Britain who were initially deemed *not* to pose a serious threat to the country. Unfortunately, many of those interned were Jews who had escaped from Germany and Austria. Ultimately, some eleven thousand aliens were deported to Canada and Australia.[68]

Eventually, however, the British government realized that fifth-column fears were reaching unhealthy proportions.[69] Top officials also developed serious doubts about the veracity of the many stories about fifth columnists.[70] In short, according to historian Christopher Andrews, none of the reports about fifth columnists sent to Britain's counterintelligence agency MI5 "led to the discovery of any real fifth column."[71]

In the United States, meanwhile, concerns of a fifth column grew feverish in the late spring of 1940. *Time* magazine reported on June

3, 1940, that from Louisiana to New York, rumors were circulating "wraithlike" about German sympathizers. In Atlanta,

> a 54-year-old German-American was questioned about his sketches of high-ways, railroads, and gas lines; in Rochester, N. Y., two young Germans pad-dling kayaks in Lake Ontario were questioned by immigration authorities because of their photographs of bridge abutments, spans and industrial plants along the Hudson River and the Barge Canal. The bag of suspects was small compared to the rumors. It was smaller still compared to the organizations which, formed to combat the fifth column, seemed adequate to suppress a revolution. In Pennsylvania it was announced that 2,500 vol-untary agents, mostly American Legionnaires, were on guard at industrial plants to prevent sabotage; in many a county, aliens were dropped from relief rolls; the House of Representatives banned WPA to Communists and Bundsmen.[72]

George Britt's 1940 book, *The Fifth Column Is Here*, became a big seller in the United States. The journalist claimed that there were 10,000 "Hitler-heiling Germans in the U.S.," that 100,000 communists were actively collaborating with the Nazis and Italian fascists, and that, over-all, the number of fifth-column members in the United States reached one million.[73] *Harper's* magazine reported, "Every home with a foreign-born head is believed to be the nucleus of a fifth column, and a hue and cry is aroused about the alien which is amounting to proportions unheard of since World War One."[74]

In July, Frank Knox, U.S. secretary of the Navy, took to the news media to express his own concerns in an introduction to a series of articles appearing in U.S. newspapers.[75] Partly as a result of such fears, Congress passed a law requiring aliens to be fingerprinted. Out of fear of fifth columnists from Mexico, the mayor of San Antonio, Maury Maverick, equipped the police with submachine guns.[76]

At least for a time, President Roosevelt himself believed that Nazi fifth-column activities jeopardized American security. He was worried that pro-Germans might be in the ranks of the officers of the Army and Navy. In a fireside chat on May 26, 1940, FDR told the public: "Today's threat to our national security is not a matter of military weapons alone. We know of new methods of attack. The Trojan Horse. The Fifth Col-umn that betrays a nation unprepared for treachery. Spies, saboteurs and traitors are the actors in this new tragedy. With all of this, we must and will deal vigorously."[77] To combat pro-German infiltration, FDR ordered the Federal Bureau of Investigation (FBI), Army Intelligence (G-2), and the Office of Naval Intelligence to coordinate their activities.[78]

In 1939 the FBI investigated 1,600 cases of reported espionage. In the month of May 1940 alone, it investigated 2,900.[79] Symptomatic of the fears about the alien within, Hollywood released seventy films from 1940 to 1942 dealing with fifth columnists. FBI director J. Edgar Hoover believed that German spies had infiltrated every layer of American society. As early as January 1940, Hoover's concerns about German subterfuge were evident in the arrest of seventeen members of a pro-Nazi and anti-Roosevelt organization called the "Christian Front." Hoover charged the group with planning to "knock off about a dozen congressmen" and "blow up the goddamed [New York City] police department." Hoover, however, offered little proof, and a jury refused to convict the accused.[80]

Despite the uproar over German-directed subversion, an exhaustive study by the FBI found no evidence after looking at some 20,000 cases.[81] Hitler actually ridiculed American fears of a fifth column. In May 1940, Hitler, with the support of Ribbentrop (by then Germany's foreign minister), ordered that there be no attempts at sabotage in the United States. The German leadership did not want to risk precipitating an unnecessary American declaration of war.[82] Hitler believed that the downfall of the United States would result from something other than sabotage by Nazi sympathizers in America. "It is not because of 'Fifth Columnists' in their midst that our enemies will lose this war, but because their politicians are corrupt, unscrupulous, [and] mentally limited men. They will lose it because their military organization is bad, and because their strategy is truly miserable."[83]

There also appears to have been no effective fifth column in Canada, but like Britain and the United States, Canada assumed that it had to exist and that it posed a serious threat to national security.[84] By late spring 1940, the same hysteria that took hold of Britain and the United States gripped Canada as well. In April, for example, the RCMP issued an internal report, a section of which included the heading "Guarding against a Canada 'Blitzkrieg'" of industrial sabotage. On May 13, another RCMP report noted that 500,000 people of German birth or origin lived in Canada and that of these only a few hundred had been interned and only a few thousand "investigated," despite the fact that a "very large number are known to be in entire sympathy with Nazi aims and conquests." The same report also listed potential fifth-column threats in the United States, South Africa, Hungary, Norway, Romania, Turkey, and Yugoslavia. There was so much concern about German and Italian fascists in Canada that a group of World War I veterans in British Columbia organized a "Sixth Column" to counter the alleged activities of fifth columnists.[85]

A month later, however, the RCMP was beginning to acknowledge the feeble nature of the threat, particularly from pro-German Canadians. According to the agency's secret June 10 Intelligence Bulletin,

> Police forces are swamped with a flood of complaints regarding alleged subversive activities. Switch-boards are jammed with messages to the same effect. A well meaning but ill-informed public, particularly veterans and their organizations, are letting their imagination run riot. Old incidents, second-hand gossip, a German-sounding name, a Teutonic haircut, almost anything now assumes a sinister aspect and immediate and drastic action is demanded by the police.[86]

The report also noted that the Canadian minister of justice and senior police officers felt compelled to issue statements to the press, "pointing out to the public that all this is merely hampering the police and is in fact liable to create the very effect desired by the enemy—confusion."[87]

Despite a few cases of sabotage, Canada was not significantly affected by the activities of the "enemy within." Prewar preparations, for instance, helped reduce the potential harm from pro-fascist organizations. By 1938 the RCMP had infiltrated such groups, and within two days of the start of the war with Germany, several hundred Nazi sympathizers from around Canada were placed under arrest. More suspects, from the Canada Fascist Party, were arrested a few months later.[88] Canadian authorities actually spent most of their time worrying about communists of all stripes—not pro-Hitler fascists.

The absence of a serious fifth-column threat to the operation that transferred Britain's gold and securities to North America may feel anti-climactic in hindsight. However, the fear that pro-Nazi forces existed, especially in Britain, certainly contributed to the overall sense among political and financial leaders that special precautions were required to protect the transfer of Britain's wealth.

One of the enduring questions about the greatest transfer of wealth in history was how Britain and its Commonwealth partners could have succeeded in wartime conditions. The answer rests partly on the extraordinary security measures, especially those taken by British and Canadian authorities. It also rests partly on the weakness of Germany's intelligence capability, especially in exploiting the leaks that did occasionally occur. The German intelligence community was often bureaucratic, competitive, and inefficient. As a U.S. Naval Intelligence report concluded, for example, in the United States both before and during the war, German spies did obtain useful information from time to time, but "it was almost always too late, too inaccurate, or too generalized to be of direct military value."[89] These weaknesses explain in part why the German naval staff never appeared to have had information about the treasure shipments.

The thousands of people involved in transporting the gold and securities must also be credited with the vital task of keeping mum. Hundreds of people, mostly women, helped process the financial securities in Montréal, and they too kept quiet. Luck played its part in the drama as well. Leaks and accidents occurred, but fortunately none of them seem to have found their way to the leaders of the Kriegsmarine, the branch of the German military capable of intercepting Britain's treasure ships.

9

Taking Fearful Risks

"The disastrous military events which have happened during the past fortnight have not come to me with any sense of surprise." Thus rang Prime Minister Winston Churchill's voice in the House of Commons on the fateful day of June 18, 1940. Churchill was calling to put aside domestic battles in order to confront the Nazi foe that would soon direct its war machine at the British Isles. Churchill aimed his speech as much at the American government as at his own Parliament, and it could just as easily have been addressed to members of the Bank of England, the British Treasury, and their counterparts in Canada. Churchill concluded his speech with these inspiring words:

> What General Weygand called the Battle of France is over. I expect that the Battle of Britain is about to begin. Upon this battle depends the survival of Christian civilization. Upon it depends our own British life, and the long continuity of our institutions and our Empire. The whole fury and might of the enemy must very soon be turned on us. Hitler knows that he will have to break us on this Island or lose the war. If we can stand up to him, all Europe may be free and the life of the world may move forward into broad, sunlit uplands. But if we fail, then the whole world, including the United States, including all that we have known and cared for, will sink into the abyss of a new Dark Age made more sinister, and perhaps more protracted, by the lights of perverted science. Let us therefore brace ourselves to our duties, and so bear ourselves that if the British Empire and its Commonwealth last for a thousand years, men will still say, "This was their finest hour."[1]

If this were to be *their* finest hour, those planning and implementing the transfer of British wealth to North America would have to surmount huge challenges. Their task so far had been to ensure the steady flow of relatively modest amounts of mostly gold to ports on the coasts of Canada and the United States. But now they needed to ramp up the pace—dramatically. The threat of a German invasion meant that, under immense time pressure, thousands of tons of gold and financial securities had to be collected from hundreds of banks throughout the realm. The loot then had to be delivered to docks, loaded onto ships, ferried across the Atlantic, unloaded at docks in North America, and transported by rail or truck to secure vaults—all without security breaches, tragic accidents, or theft. Given the magnitude of the task ahead, British and Canadian organizations were about to be tested as they never had been before.

Ensuring the success of this massive transfer of wealth required extraordinary organizational effectiveness, secrecy, and trust. For each transfer from bank vault to dock, British planners had to requisition the correct number of trucks and coordinate their deliveries with train routing. The Admiralty chose appropriate ships to ferry the treasure and selected other vessels to escort the treasure ships at the start of their westbound journey. The large number of ships involved complicated ship routing, which had to be effectively coordinated with bank deliveries to the appropriate ports and the correct berths.

The vast quantities of gold often required ample cargo space on board the vessels—not so much for its volume as for its weight. Gold bars weighed roughly 400 troy ounces or about 27.5 pounds each. The magnitude of this operation is exemplified by a typical shipment. A large, but by no means the largest, consignment worth £14 million (more than $55 million) came in the form of 3,550 bars weighing roughly 50 tons. This heavy load took up 440 cubic feet of space.[2] Depending on packing considerations, a fleet of at least 10 five-ton trucks would have been required to transport the gold from bank to port or vice versa.

American and especially Canadian naval and banking authorities responsible for receiving the special deliveries made comparable arrangements. They ensured that proper security procedures were in place and that berths were available for the incoming ships in a timely manner. As in Britain, transportation officials coordinated the ground transfers from the docks to the receiving banks. The intermittent shipments of the previous months would seem like dress rehearsals for the big show that was about to take place.

New and vexing problems emerged during this phase of the operation. If Germany invaded, for example, what was to be done with Britain's paper currency? Was there a way to dispose of the money before the Germans could get their hands on it? British banknotes were spread across the country's banks. The Newcastle branch, for example, held £3.7 million in small notes. The Leeds branch held £14.1 million, the Manchester headquarters had £35.3 million, and so on. In practical terms, all of this money added up to a lot of paper. According to calculations in a secret British Treasury document of May 25, 1940, new banknotes in London alone weighed approximately 115 tons. Treasury records indicated how massive sums of paper currency could be accumulated and delivered at short notice. The Treasury estimated that it "could be removed from the vaults and loaded into lorries in about 15 hours. . . . If 5 ton lorries were available, 23 would be required, while the number of vans on the railway, which take up to 10 tons, would be 12."[3]

Basil Catterns, deputy governor of the Bank of England, was tasked with exploring procedures for disposing of the currency at short notice. Catterns reported to the Treasury that newly printed banknotes were tightly packed and thus "terribly hard to destroy in a hurry." Even burning the paper money was deemed infeasible. So, Catterns advised that the notes be put "on board a boat under military guard and kept either in dry dock or, say, somewhere in the Mersey [near Liverpool on England's west coast] so that, if necessary, the boat could be taken out to sea and sunk."[4] The Bank of England suggested alternatively that the merchant ship SS *Cressado* "could be easily disguised as a naval Armament Store Ship." The banknotes would be concealed in ammunition boxes, and the ship would fly the "red for danger" flag to keep other ships away. If the Germans got close, the ship could be sailed out to sea and scuttled.[5]

———

When Churchill's wife asked if he thought the Nazis would "get aboard the Island," he quickly responded, "No. But they'll make a mighty try. At least I would if I were Hitler."[6] Germany's anticipated invasion meant that Britain's special shipments would no longer merely serve to help finance the war. The imperative now was to evacuate the liquid assets off the British Isles lest they fall into German hands. Starting in May 1940, the previously slow but steady flow of British wealth to North America became a deluge.

Sir Kingsley Wood, the new chancellor of the exchequer, laid out Britain's financial strategy in this new, more dangerous environment. In a memorandum stamped "Highly Secret," Wood wrote,

> All the gold in the Bank of England is being packed and this process will be completed in a week. . . . We can send £300 million to Canada by the end of June and no doubt could break the banks of the whole job by end-July. This involves taking fearful risks which we would not anticipate for a moment in normal times. We will for instance be sending £50 million on one battleship. . . . We must assume also I think that the risks will increase as time goes on.[7]

Allied ships heading into and out of Britain would also be at greater risk because Germany's Norway campaign was over and repairs had been completed; the German submarine fleet was again ready for action in the Atlantic. In June alone, U-boats sank more than a quarter of a million tons of Allied shipping, presaging more trouble in the weeks ahead.[8]

Invasion fears affected nearly all aspects of British military and civilian life. Preparation strategies included the Royal Navy laying minefields and reassigning ships to protect the British Isles. The Royal Air Force attacked German airfields hoping to weaken the Luftwaffe's ability to bomb Britain or provide air support for amphibious landings on British shores. More than 150,000 full-time (and thousands more part-time) civilian workers helped the Army place barbed wire on strategic beaches and cliffs. Throughout much of the country, the British government ordered tank traps dug and pillboxes built. Arrangements were even put in place to set fire to stretches of shoreline and roads in case the Germans appeared. The government instituted certain minor measures that nonetheless penetrated British society, including a ban on ringing church bells except in the case of a German landing, and housewives were called upon to turn in their aluminum saucepans for recycling.[9]

Invasion fears also led to many unhelpful political distractions, including a rumor that former prime minister Neville Chamberlain would replace Churchill and make peace with Germany. On June 26, 1940, the Associated Press reported, "Neville Chamberlain's foes are said to believe that if the Germans invade England and score early successes, Chamberlain could overthrow the fighting Churchill government and form a peace Cabinet which would not hesitate to deal with Germany."

Separately, Reuters ran a story about a London meeting of the British fascist organization the Link at which the question of peace terms under a sympathetic (pro-Hitler) government was discussed.[10] No such conspiracy was being hatched, but the sensational news stories contributed to the hysterical atmosphere gripping Britain.

For the British Treasury, the Bank of England, and the Admiralty, transporting one, two, five, or even ten million pounds sterling per ship was not enough. They now contemplated risking vastly greater portions of the Empire's wealth in a single consignment. On May 25, Basil Catterns wrote to Sir Frederick Phillips, "We have had a further discussion today with Gilmour of the Admiralty, from which it appears that it should be possible, given any sort of luck, to ship up to £50 million, but this would mean that there would be no hitch anywhere, which I feel is a bit unlikely."[11] For the time being, British banking and naval officials authorized a few large shipments for early June 1940, using the *Antonia* and *Duchess of Liverpool*, each of which carried gold valued at £10 million; HMS *Furious*, which carried £20 million in gold; and HMS *Revenge*, whose consignment was valued at a formidable £40 million.

In light of France's precarious situation in early June 1940, the Treasury's new estimates of how much gold should be shipped made the projections of just six months earlier look trifling. Back in December 1939, Sir John Gilmour at the Admiralty issued this report to the Treasury:

> We are keeping a careful watch on gold shipments from London to Ottawa with a view to taking suitable action if for any reason we look like [we are] falling behind [our goal] of £150,000,000 a year.[12]

The planned amount of £150 million for mid-1940, however, was dangerously low given the expected German invasion and the greater financial demands placed upon Britain with the loss of France.

Banking and naval authorities thus called upon several ships that had previously made gold runs to North America to make the trip again. The *Montclare*, for example, made prewar deliveries in April 1938 and again in May 1939, when war scares prompted the first gold trips to Canada. Called to service yet again, the *Montclare* left Greenock, Scotland, in June 1940 with a load worth £5 million destined for the Bank of Canada. The *Cameronia* had delivered gold in February, March, and April 1940. The Admiralty now instructed the ship to deliver £6.5 million in June and £6 million in July. Many more ships that had never carried British gold or securities were also now pressed into service. Between May and August 1940, for example, nine different ships from the Manchester line—including the *Manchester Brigade*, *Manchester Exporter*, and *Manchester Progress*—each carried consignments valued at between £1 and £3 million.

Most of the ships carrying British wealth that sailed in May, June, and July 1940 departed from Greenock in the north, Liverpool in the west, and Portsmouth and Southampton in the south. A few also embarked from Glasgow, Manchester, Bristol, and other British ports. These ships delivered their valuable cargo mostly to Halifax and Montréal in Canada and to New York in the United States.

So many ships were ferrying gold and securities that coded messages between British and Canadian officials were being churned out several times a day. At the center of many of these exchanges was Dean Marble, secretary of the Bank of Canada. Marble routinely corresponded with George Bolton at the Bank of England about the status of specific ships—their names, their ports of destination, and the value of their cargo. Marble also kept in constant contact with Percy Nelles, rear admiral and chief of naval staff of the Royal Canadian Navy. Nelles was the critical link between the British and Canadian naval authorities and the Bank of Canada. Regarding gold shipments from Australia, Singapore, and Hong Kong, coded messages were exchanged between Marble and Walter Winsby, the Bank of Canada agent in Vancouver, Canada. L. P. J. Roy, deputy secretary at the Bank of Canada, kept in constant contact with Kenneth Peppiatt, the chief cashier at the Bank of England. Within Canada, additional exchanges took place between various branches of the Bank of Canada for the overland gold transfers carried by the Canadian Pacific Express Company and, on occasion, the Railway Express Agency in the United States. Further exchanges occurred on a routine basis between Bank of Canada officials and those of the New York Federal Reserve Bank in Manhattan, thus linking some of the British shipments with their final destination in the United States.

This "Most Secret" message from Rear Adm. Percy W. Nelles to Dean Marble on June 4, 1940, was typical:[13]

> I have been informed the following ships carry Bullion up to the value of One Million Pounds each, but ports for disembarkation and estimated

arrivals are indefinite. I am indicating possible ports and arrival dates, but will confirm necessary information when received.

S. S. Manchester Brigade, Montreal 9th June

S. S. Aracataca, Boston 12th June

S. S. Northern Prince, New York 10th June

S. S. Cameronia, New York 8th June

S. S. Europa, New York 9th June

S. S. Port Hunter, Montreal 12th June

S. S. Gregalia, Montreal 12th June

Over the next few weeks, Nelles was sending Marble more than one such message a day. On June 20, for example, one of Nelles's messages read,[14]

The following ships carrying Bullion up to the value of One Million Pounds each, and expected arrivals are as indicated:

S. S. Newfoundland, St. John's 29th June (Probably proceed Halifax to arrive 3rd July)

S. S. Bayano, Montreal 27th June

S. S. Norwegian, Montreal 30th June

Another of Nelles's messages sent that day read,

The following ships carrying Bullion up to the value of One Million Pounds each, and expected arrivals are as indicated:

S. S. Delilian, Montreal 27th June

S. S. Manchester Division, Montreal 29th June

S. S. Kaituna, New York 28th June

S. S. Crispin, New York 29th June

Even these shipments, however, were not enough to guarantee that large quantities of Britain's wealth would be evacuated in time. As the days ticked by, pressure was building within Britain's military and financial institutions to evacuate nearly everything they had left.

━━━━━━━━

On June 23, 1940, the day after the fall of France, 2,229 boxes of gold and 448 boxes of securities arrived at Greenock to be loaded on the cruiser HMS *Emerald*. The gold was worth £30 million and the securities were worth approximately £200 million.[15] The *Emerald*'s consignment was formally escorted by Alexander S. Craig of the Bank of England and three of his colleagues, Harold C. Kent, Harold Forrest, and Leslie Phelps. Craig and the others were heading to Montréal to run a new banking facility whose sole purpose was to sell many of the securities being transported on board the *Emerald* and other Allied ships. After the war, Kent recalled the unusual meeting that had taken place with the four bankers only a few days earlier:

> On Wednesday, June 19th I was asked to go down to the parlors. That was our expression for the [Bank of England's] directors' room. I was given no indication of what it was about, but I had a perfectly good idea. When I got there I found the others who came to Canada with our group. We were told we were going to Canada (with the first big consignment of securities).[16]

The *Emerald* was joined by the same Royal Navy escort, HMS *Cossack*, that had accompanied it during a gold run to Canada in October 1939. Three other destroyers helped provide security at the start of the trip in case of any trouble with U-boats. Philip Vian, captain of the *Cossack*, was in charge of the convoy.

At 6 p.m. on June 24, 1940, loading was completed, and the ships set sail for Halifax. On board the *Emerald*, the special boxes were stashed away in every possible corner of the ship. According to journalist Leland Stowe, the *Emerald*'s "storage magazines were so heavy that before the voyage was over they bent the angle irons beneath the magazines' floors."[17] For want of space, one of the banking officials was forced to sleep on top of some of the boxes. Even though the bankers were expected to spend a considerable amount of time in Canada, they were allowed to carry only one suitcase apiece.[18] No record of the reasoning is available for the luggage quota or limitation, but it may have been because every foot of available space on board the ship was required for the boxes.

As the *Emerald* set sail, Dean Marble, in Ottawa, received a simple but "Most Secret" message from Rear Adm. Percy Nelles of the Canadian Royal Navy: "A large quantity of Bullion in one of H.M. Ships can be expected Halifax 30th June."[19] Two days later, Nelles sent another message, this time with a few more details: "With reference to my Most Secret Letter NS.1068-2-4 of 24th June, this ship carries Gold valued at Thirty Million Pounds and a large quantity of Securities."[20]

The *Emerald*'s paymaster found Alexander Craig on deck and passed along information that increased the bankers' anxiety: "The Skipper's just had a flash from the Admiralty. There's a couple of German subs waiting for us off the north of Ireland." Craig later recalled that he was not sure whether he was kidding, but, Craig added, "He seemed very serious."[21]

The journey across the Atlantic was far from ideal for the aging ship. The *Emerald* had a new but experienced captain, Francis Cyril Flynn, a stocky man of medium height with a ruddy complexion, steel blue eyes, and a firm voice.[22] Flynn recalled that the "seas whipped up as we rounded the north coast of Ireland next morning. When we turned out into the Atlantic we were punching into a heavy sea and rising gale." None of the Bank representatives had been on the North Atlantic before, and the stormy trip was quite an initiation. "Those first three days," Flynn recounted, "the going was such that many of our crew became seasick."[23]

The terrible weather conditions presented a mixed blessing for the crew and cargo. The *Emerald* was an old ship ill-suited to duty in the North Atlantic, but it was extremely fast. Captain Vian of the *Cossack* advised Flynn that the *Cossack* would hold a straight course through the rough seas and that the *Emerald* should zigzag behind the destroyers making it a more challenging target for U-boats.[24] Flynn later notified Vian that the *Emerald* would complete the journey on its own. The ship, traveling at 22 knots, could outrun any U-boats that might happen upon it in the Atlantic. And, thankfully, the rough seas would make it doubly hard for submarines to attack.

As Kent later recalled, he and the other bankers were given special dinners, and they often played whist with the crew: "We were not at all used to being aboard a cruiser & the pitch of waves—especially with the *Emerald* dashing near its top speed. When the petty officers took us on for a game of darts we couldn't even hit the dart board, let alone the target. . . . It was the craziest and funniest game of darts I ever saw."[25]

The weather eventually cleared, and as the *Emerald* approached Canada, two Canadian destroyers sighted the ship and escorted it for the remainder of the journey. Shortly after 5 a.m. on July 1, 1940, the crew could see for the first time the coast of Nova Scotia. The *Emerald* entered Halifax harbor at 7:35 a.m. Waiting at the dock was a train with twelve baggage cars—evidence of the well-coordinated effort to get the valuables to safety. Nearly twelve hours later, the boxes of gold and securities were safely stowed on railcars for the 840-mile trip to Montréal. The securities would remain there while the gold continued westward to Ottawa another 117 miles away.[26]

═══════════

Sidney Perkins was working long hours at Canada's Foreign Exchange Control Board on Sparks Street in Ottawa when he got an unusual call on July 2, 1940. Perkins was born in England but had been living in Canada since the age of eighteen. He believed in the old saying, "Many Canadians are only Englishmen who don't care how cold it gets." He was told to report to the office of David Mansur, the acting deputy governor of the Bank of Canada, whom Perkins described as a "tall, sedate, quiet-spoken" man with impeccable manners.[27] Mansur closed the office door, turned off the intercom system, and told Perkins that something big was up. Perkins was told to fly immediately to Halifax without telling a soul. He wasn't to change his clothes or pick anything up. Arrangements for him would be made in Halifax.

Mansur then informed Perkins that he was going to take charge of an "important shipment," adding coyly, "there may be some gold included." Perkins broke nearly all of the traffic laws to catch his flight in half an hour. He flew to Montréal and then boarded another plane for Halifax. But the flight was unnecessary because, as Perkins learned, the "stuff" had already left Halifax and had arrived in Montréal via a special train at the Bonaventure Station at about 5 p.m.

Eventually Perkins and Mansur boarded the train and were joined by the four men from the Bank of England who had sailed on the *Emerald*: Craig, Kent, Phelps, and Forrest. Craig, a small, gray-haired, bespectacled man of about fifty, then told his new Canadian colleagues,

> We're Bank of England people. We hope you won't mind us dropping in unexpectedly like this. The fact of the matter is, we brought along quite a large shipment of fish. The "fish" actually are a very large portion of the remaining liquid assets of Great Britain. We're cleaning out our vaults in case of invasion. The rest of the stuff—gold and securities—is on the way. . . . Afraid we're going to have to ask you boys for some help.

Craig then told Perkins and Mansur that the train carried between four hundred and five hundred boxes of securities.[28] The Canadians were speechless.

Time pressures in Britain were so acute that the planners—normally so effective in other aspects of the operation—could not attend to critical details regarding the securities. Most important, Craig notified the men that the securities needed a new home. Perkins knew of no vault available anywhere in Canada that was large enough for the securities and had the requisite banking staff and security detail. As Mansur was making calls to Ottawa, the police were closing off the streets around Bonaventure Station. They would eventually block off the streets between the station and the securities' new home: the Sun Life Assurance Building in Montréal's Dominion Square (now called Dorchester Square).

The securities, along with a certain amount of gold and valuable coins, constituted what became known as the United Kingdom Security Deposit (UKSD). The first few days of its existence were hectic but productive. However, on the first weekend after the arrival of the *Emerald*, a massive thunderstorm hit Montréal and became a serious threat to the operation. The boxes of securities rested on heavy planks, which were laid on struts two feet off the floor. The thunderstorm was so strong that it began flooding the Sun Life Building, and by the time it was discovered, three to four inches of water had already seeped into the securities room. Some confusion exists as to who first discovered the problem, but Edward Hanna, a stock expert at the Bank of Canada and a UKSD employee, appears to have been the first on the scene at 4 a.m. The Mounties protecting the vault called the nearby Hotel Windsor to get a hold of the Bank of England officials, but they had moved into more permanent accommodations the night before. Five irate American tourists were accidentally awakened instead.[29] Eventually, the bankers were located, and they dashed to the Sun Life Building to help prevent the securities from becoming stacks of useless, wet pulp. Meanwhile, Hanna and the other staffers rushed to get water pumps going. Fortunately, the pumps kept ahead of the water, and the securities were saved.[30]

British authorities were relieved to know that the *Emerald*'s consignment, as well as those from all of the other ships dispatched in May and June 1940, had reached their destinations safely. As important and as risky as these shipments had been, however, the biggest financial gamble of the war was still to come. Banking leaders such as Craig and Perkins were just beginning to realize the magnitude of their assignments.

10

Britain's Most Valuable Convoy

After Germany launched the invasion of France, nearly every day of the war exhibited momentous developments. On July 1, 1940, the day the *Emerald* safely docked in Halifax harbor, the Canadian magazine *Maclean's* reported that Ottawa was no longer the tranquil capital of a nation thousands of miles from the disaster unfolding in Europe:

> To tell that Ottawa . . . is in the midst of a crisis is to put it mildly. The "quietest war capital in Christendom" has become a cauldron of excitement . . . shocked from its complacency. Day by day, as the shadow of the Swastika lengthens across the English Channel, old shibboleths, old comfortable delusions, go overboard. Where once reigned smugness, self-satisfaction, there is now a wholesome fear; with it, fortunately, more of war stir and vigor.[1]

On the same day that workmen began the laborious task of disgorging the *Emerald* of its riches, intelligence about a German invasion was pouring into the offices of Britain's leaders. Alexander Cadogan, the permanent undersecretary at Britain's Foreign Office, wrote in his diary that this was "the zero hour for German invasion of England; tipsters say July 8."[2] The threat of invasion was so serious that Churchill instructed Gen. Hasting L. Ismay to review procedures for "drenching" with mustard gas the English beaches most likely to be used by German landing parties. Churchill's private secretary John Colville suspected that Churchill's interest in the use of mustard gas was likely prompted by reports that invading German forces would be using the chemical weapon.[3]

At the same time, 200,000 applications streamed in to Britain's Children's Overseas Reception Board (CORB) office, which was responsible for relocating children to Canada and the United States.[4] In the next few days, some of these children would sail to North America on ships carrying the riches of the Empire. Meanwhile, Karl Dönitz logged the status of Germany's U-boat fleet at the start of July as follows: six boats in the Wilhelmshaven and Kiel dockyards, five boats on return passage to Germany, and nine boats operating in the Atlantic operations area (UA, U-26, U-29, U-30, U-34, U-43, U-52, U-102, U-122), with another (U-47) outbound from Germany.[5]

July 2 was just as eventful as the day before. German field marshal Wilhelm Keitel signed orders for "The War against England." According to historian Peter Fleming, Hitler and Germany's Supreme Command decided that a landing in England was possible, "providing that air superiority can be attained and certain other necessary conditions fulfilled."[6] The same day in Vichy, Premier Marshal Henri-Philippe Pétain established the new pro-Nazi government in France.

On July 3, Britain initiated Operation Catapult. In order to prevent French ships from falling into German hands, Britain boldly seized all of the French ships it could in British ports. Doubts over the loyalty of French captains also compelled Britain to issue an ultimatum to the French naval fleet at Mers-el-Kebir, in Oran Bay, Algeria. The Royal Navy would attack if the French did not surrender their ships. Churchill was so concerned that Germany would gain possession of the French fleet that he ordered the ships belonging to their former allies to be sunk if the French did not transfer control to the Admiralty. Dissatisfied with the French response in Oran Bay, British warships attacked the French fleet killing nearly thirteen hundred French sailors. In addition, one French battleship was lost and several other ships were seriously damaged.[7] Given the fast pace of events, Colville wrote in his diaries a comment befitting much of the preceding few weeks: "War is said to be always full of surprises—but this is fantasy."[8]

Amid these historic developments, British bankers and naval personnel prepared to ship nearly all of Britain's remaining liquid assets to North America—more than £450 million ($1.75 billion) worth of gold and even more in securities.[9] The British chose five vessels to convey this vast stockpile of treasure to Canada: HMS *Revenge*, HMS *Bonaventure*, the liner *Monarch of Bermuda*, and the Polish ships *Batory* and *Sobieski*. In all, they carried roughly 9,000 boxes of gold and between 850 and 900 boxes of securities.[10]

Adm. Sir Ernest Russell Archer, on board the *Revenge*, took charge of the convoy. Under the command of Capt. H. J. Egerton, the cruiser *Bonaventure*, like the *Revenge*, carried gold and provided escort for the other ships. The Admiralty hoped that the two Royal Navy ships could provide the convoy with enough firepower to repel any U-boat attack, but everyone knew there was always a risk of a torpedo getting through. In the weeks leading up to this unique convoy, a single German submarine—U-37 under the command of Victor Oehrn—had sunk eleven ships in twenty-six days.[11] If a wolf pack sighted the five-ship convoy, the consequences would be catastrophic for this most valuable cargo in history.

Admiral Archer was a popular and respected leader.[12] Executive Officer, Cdr. Humphrey L. Jenkins said that Archer was "[a]n incredible man. Nothing worried him. Even when lifeboats were torn off by the waves, he just plugged on."[13] Despite Jenkins's assessment, Archer was anxious about this extraordinary mission. One big concern was that, according to the engineer, the gold stowed in a compartment above the propellers was making their bearings overheat. The propellers could have stopped functioning and the ship would have been vulnerable.[14]

Otto Niemeyer, deputy governor of the Bank of England, was the man directly in charge of the convoy's enormously valuable cargo.[15] Niemeyer had previously served in the Treasury and had joined the Bank of England in 1927. In the years leading up to the war, he had also been chairman of the Bank of International Settlements.[16] According to George Watts of the Bank of Canada, Niemeyer did not seem to have "much personal popularity" at the Bank, "and his colleagues apparently were never able to subdue a certain distrust of a former prominent Treasury official. On the other hand he seems to have been well thought of by Churchill with whom he had dealings in earlier years." In addition to overseeing the convoy's treasure, Niemeyer was heading to Canada to set up banking arrangements in Ottawa in case of invasion-related disruptions at the Bank of England in London. According to Watts, Niemeyer's presence in Ottawa would be kept "as secret as possible" to avoid unwanted speculation about the nature of his visit. To cover his tracks, Niemeyer used the nondescript language of "handling matters pertaining to British and Canadian foreign exchange control."[17]

Security was tight in Greenock, but astute deckhands suspected something important and unusual was going on. Commander Jenkins, in charge of stowing the gold and securities on board the *Revenge*, recalled how some of the special boxes had to be nailed together on the spot. Sometimes, Jenkins recalled, some of the gold sovereign coins got loose—temporarily. As Admiral Archer described it, "When a box of gold pieces broke, we'd go around looking for those blinking coins like a widow who had lost her earrings."[18]

In his midshipman's journal, W. S. Crawford described the gathering of the ships for this exceptional convoy: "This forenoon [July 8] we joined company with HMS *Bonaventure*, the *Monarch of Bermuda*, and the Polish ships *Batory* and *Sobieski*, at the entrance to the Clyde. We then proceeded into the Atlantic via the North Channel, passing in the course of the day, the Mull of Kintyre."[19]

The *Batory*, a Polish luxury liner converted to war duty by the British at the start of the war, was unique in the convoy. In addition to carrying a staggering £40 million in gold, its cargo included priceless historical artifacts and art treasures from Poland. The *Batory*'s consignment included the following:

> » Szczerbiec, the jeweled coronation sword of Polish Kings from 1320 to 1764
> » A Gutenberg Bible dating from 1453–1455
> » 136 Flemish tapestries, some of which had been commissioned by King Sigismund II Augustus between 1549 and 1572
> » The sword of the Order of the White Eagle and the Chain of the Order last used at the coronation of King Stanislaw Augustus Poniatowskii in 1764
> » A golden goblet with the image of King Jan Sobieski III, who was famous for breaking the Turkish siege of Vienna in 1683
> » A fourteenth century Florian Psalter containing the earliest translation of the psalms into Polish[20]

Also among the trunks, protective metal tubes, and crates packed inside the *Batory* were thirty-six original Frédéric Chopin compositions and thirteen pieces of the composer's correspondence, as well as silver cups, sabers, salvers, clocks, suits of armor from the seventeenth century, and hundreds of pieces of gold.[21] These and other Polish treasures had embarked on their dangerous and circuitous journey on September 3, 1939, from the Wawel Castle in Kraków. They journeyed to Bucharest, Romania, and then on to Istanbul, Athens, Malta, Genoa, Marseille, Bordeaux, Falmouth, London, and then Greenock, where they were loaded on board the *Batory* on July 3, 1940.[22]

The *Batory* and the four other treasure-laden ships were escorted by only four destroyers for the first two hundred miles, as was customary. Admiral Archer received the "usual Admiralty reports" of U-boats active in the vicinity. He recalled, "Whenever we knew they were near we'd do a few jinks [evasive maneuvers]. Enemy raiders were also active, but none showed up. Were we nervous? We knew what we had on board. You took the ships and did what you could."[23]

Weather conditions posed no real problems for the convoy, although, according to Crawford, "a number of the new boys had slight 'mal-de-mer' [seasickness]."[24] According to Commander Jenkins, "The gun crews were always at their stations. At night they slept beside their guns. Damage-control parties constantly inspected all parts of the ship for possible leaks or fire."[25]

The crews' fears were not unfounded. Jozef Polkowski, a senior staff member for the Wawel Castle in Kraków and a passenger on board the *Batory*, recalled a disturbing sight near the start of the voyage. According to Polkowski, the convoy passed through the same waters where the Germans had recently sunk two Allied ships that had been carrying twenty-five hundred German and Italian prisoners. As Polkowski explained,

> a large number of passengers who were not affected by sea sickness observed a great quantity of [what looked like] huge fish near the *Batory*. . . . Lieutenant Winkler told me that we were just passing near the place where two days before the ships with the prisoners of war had been sunk. And as usual on such occasions the sharks had gathered for a meal. This information was not too pleasant.[26]

On July 9, 1940, Crawford reported the sighting of a streak of light in the sky. Opinion was divided, but he surmised that the most likely cause was either a large meteor or a signal cartridge. The *Bonaventure* was dispatched to investigate the phenomenon, but nothing was concluded. The crews remained on edge.

Back in London, John Colville recorded in his diary on July 9 that, according to information circulating around the prime minister's office, "a great attack is now said to be due on Thursday [July 11]." That Thursday he wrote that Britain now had "definite evidence that the Germans are assembling a force in Norway which could be used for a descent on Scotland, the Orkneys, the Shetlands or the Faroes."[27]

On July 11, Basil Catterns of the Bank of England wrote to Richard Hopkins at the British Treasury for a status report about the consignments on board the five-ship *Revenge* convoy. "The present position," Catterns wrote, "is that by the end of this week, virtually the whole of [the] gold will be either in North America or on the way there."[28]

On the very same day, the *Batory*—the liner entrusted with Poland's treasures and British gold—suffered engine trouble three-fourths of the way across the Atlantic.[29] Admiral Archer believed that one damaged but capable ship should not endanger the rest, so he decided to divide the convoy in two. He ordered Captain Egerton of the *Bonaventure* to escort the *Batory* for the rest of the trip.[30] The two were ordered to proceed as best they could to St. John's, which was closer than Halifax by some four hundred miles. To make matters worse, once on their way, the *Bonaventure* and the *Batory* encountered "a most frightful peasouper, coupled with floating ice." For the next twelve hours, the two ships were forced to come to a dead stop. "Between us," Egerton recalled, "we carried some 60 million sterling in bullion and you couldn't see an iceberg until it was practically on top of you."[31]

———

With great relief, the *Revenge, Monarch of Bermuda,* and *Sobieski* finally arrived at Halifax on the afternoon of July 12. Surprisingly, the *Batory* and *Bonaventure* were not far behind. The Admiralty sent a coded message to London conveying the happy news that the ships had arrived safely. Two men at the center of the operation from the Bank of England—Cameron Cobbold and Basil Catterns—scrounged up a bottle of champagne and toasted the mission's success.[32] By the end of the day on July 13, the Polish treasure trove was loaded onto Canadian National Railway coaches and headed to the Polish consulate on Stewart Street in Ottawa.[33]

Compared to the Polish materials, the much more extensive cargo of gold and securities took longer to process. Responsibility for this important task now rested with three groups of men. One consisted of the crews of the arriving ships and local hands who helped move the heavy boxes from ship to dock. A second group of Canadian security personnel guarded against theft and unwarranted publicity. A third group of representatives from the Bank of Canada partnered with the representatives from the Bank of England to take on the herculean task of properly accounting for every box of securities and every single gold bar and coin.

―――――――――

The treasure on board the five ships of the *Revenge* convoy was still on the high seas when the *Wall Street Journal* ran a story that could have had dreadful repercussions. On July 9, 1940, the newspaper reported that "Official silence continued to shroud the English shipments, but the belief is growing in banking quarters here that the British government is transferring virtually its entire gold reserve to the New World and that most of it is finding its way to New York either by direct shipment or via Canada."[34] The newspaper account most likely ran too late for the Germans to mount a search for the convoy. However, other treasure ships were already sailing for North America, and some twenty more gold shipments were being prepared for August. British and Canadian authorities must have been infuriated, yet again, that the American press offered Germany blatant clues about the operation.

Movements of British wealth on the North Atlantic would remain precarious for the foreseeable future. On July 14, HMS *Esperance Bay* was voyaging to Canada with £10 million in gold when it was attacked by German planes (He-111s and Ju-86s) one hundred miles west of Land's End, England. In the fifty-five-minute attack, some forty to fifty bombs were dropped, damaging the ship and forcing it to limp back to Plymouth, England. Its cargo, however, remained intact.[35] Thus the *Esperance Bay* narrowly avoided sharing the fate of the *Niagara*, the only gold-laden ship to have been sunk by Germany during the war. As an indicator of how important timing was to the operation, if the *Revenge* convoy had left a week later, it might have been attacked as well.

In London, on the same day as the attack on the *Esperance Bay*, Churchill took to the airwaves to inspire the British people to stand firm against a possible invasion: "Bearing ourselves humbly before God, but conscious that we serve an unfolding purpose, we are ready to defend our native land against the invasion by which it is threatened. We fight *by* ourselves alone. But we do not fight *for* ourselves alone."[36]

The prime minister was also trying, yet again, to convince the United States to send aid in any form. Churchill claimed Britain's moral position as the defender of "Christian civilization" and a democratic Europe as well as the bulwark against Nazism that would help save the United

States. But the United States remained entrenched in isolationism, and it would be many months before it would grant financial help and almost a year and a half before a congressional declaration of war.

Meanwhile, there was no letup in the fighting. On July 16, Hitler issued Führer Directive Number 16, entitled "Preparations for a Landing Operation against England." The directive called on the Luftwaffe to "prevent all air attacks" on Germany, engage "approaching naval vessels," and "destroy coastal defenses . . . break the initial resistance of the enemy land forces and annihilate reserves behind the front." Luftwaffe leaders were surprised that Hitler wanted these missions completed before the German army and navy were prepared. Hermann Göring, air minister and chief of the Luftwaffe, however, was convinced that his air force was fully capable of fulfilling Hitler's wishes. "The Führer has ordered me to crush Britain with my Luftwaffe," said Göring. "By means of hard blows I plan to have this enemy, who has already suffered a crushing moral defeat, down on his knees in the nearest future, so that an occupation of the island by our troops can proceed without any risk!"[37] Göring's confidence was not completely unfounded. At the start of the Blitz in early September, Germany's 2,800 planes far outnumbered Britain's 700. Göring expected to destroy most of the Royal Air Force within a week and the rest of Britain's aircraft industry in about a month.[38]

11

Clearing the Decks in Halifax

An utterly transformed city of Halifax greeted crews of the Allied ships arriving in Canada. By the summer of 1940, the workaday Nova Scotia port, previously among the sleepier provincial capitals in Canada, was as involved in the war as any city in Britain. Its residents endured a host of security measures, including nighttime blackouts, searchlights, and air-raid sirens. A submarine net helped protect the extensive harbor. The city's Civil Defence force reminded citizens and soldiers alike that "danger and death lurk just beyond Chebucto Head at the mouth of the harbor—and perhaps much closer."[1]

Most of the gold arriving in Halifax was conveyed to the vaults of the Bank of Canada in Ottawa. By summer, the value of these transactions—and those elsewhere in North America—had already reached considerable figures. On July 17, 1940, George Bolton of the Bank of England wrote to Dean Marble at the Bank of Canada in Ottawa, asking him to release $50 million in gold to the Federal Reserve in New York. Even under the dire wartime circumstances, the bankers never failed to observe time-honored courtesies. This gold shipment, Bolton wrote, should be sent "at your convenience"; he also thoughtfully reminded his counterpart to charge the freight costs back to London.[2]

Shipping charges were significant owing to the cargo's weight and to the extraordinary security measures necessary to ensure its safe arrival. The cost of shipping the £40 million in gold carried by the *Sobieski* as part of the *Revenge* convoy, for example, amounted to more than $114,000.[3] Bolton's $50 million shipment from Ottawa to New York cost $70,000 to transport by rail.[4] Ground transportation was coordinated by the express agencies of the Canadian National Railway, the Canadian Pacific Railway, and in the United States, by the Railway Express

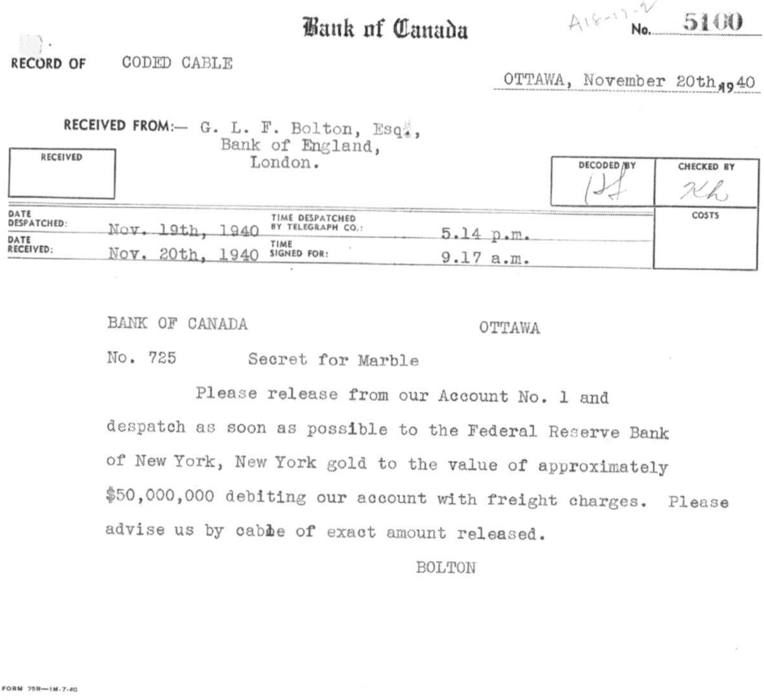

A18-17-2   No. 5100

RECORD OF   CODED CABLE

OTTAWA, November 20th, 19 40

RECEIVED FROM:— G. L. F. Bolton, Esq.,
Bank of England,
London.

RECEIVED		DECODED BY	CHECKED BY

| DATE DESPATCHED: | Nov. 19th, 1940 | TIME DESPATCHED BY TELEGRAPH CO.: | 5.14 p.m. | COSTS |
| DATE RECEIVED: | Nov. 20th, 1940 | TIME SIGNED FOR: | 9.17 a.m. | |

BANK OF CANADA   OTTAWA

No. 725   Secret for Marble

Please release from our Account No. 1 and
despatch as soon as possible to the Federal Reserve Bank
of New York, New York gold to the value of approximately
$50,000,000 debiting our account with freight charges. Please
advise us by cable of exact amount released.

BOLTON

FORM 75B—1M.7-40

FIG. 11.1. Much of Britain's gold shipped to Canada was eventually deposited in accounts at the New York Federal Reserve Bank. In this cable, George Bolton of the Bank of England has authorized the Bank of Canada to deposit $50 million into the Bank of England's account at the New York Fed. *Courtesy of the Bank of Canada Archives, Department of Banking Operations, A18-17-2.*

Agency. The steady arrival of gold from around the British Empire kept all of these companies busy conveying the precious metal from ports on both the east and west coasts of North America.

═══════

Of the five ships carrying the largest cache of British wealth (and Polish treasures), HMS *Revenge* was the first to arrive in Halifax. As the ship drew closer, a surface mist developed, obscuring nearly everything—one last obstacle to be overcome. Despite the impediment, the *Revenge* managed to dock safely along a pier usually reserved for large passenger liners.[5] Canadian rail authorities and representatives of the Bank of Canada were there to meet the battleship. Navigator and XO

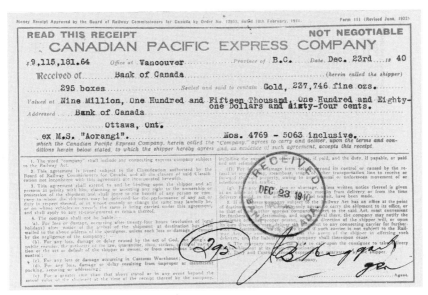

FIG. 11.2. This Canadian Pacific Express (railroad) receipt was typical of those used to acknowledge the transportation of British gold, in this case from the ship HMS *Aorangi*. At the time, the gold was worth roughly US$8.3 million or slightly more than £2 million. The notation "No.4769–5063 inclusive" refers to the crate numbers. *Courtesy of the Bank of Canada Archives, Department of Banking Operations, A18-17-2.*

Humphrey Jenkins, a burly man in his early forties, went ashore to meet the bankers. "I'm glad to get rid of this margarine," he quipped.[6]

Sidney Perkins of the Bank of Canada took charge of accounting for all the gold and securities and sending the precious cargo on its way to vaults in Montréal and Ottawa. Dawdling over drinks while Jenkins went to fetch a thick sheaf of papers from his safe, Perkins and his colleagues were unprepared for what they were about to find on the manifest. *Revenge* and its convoy, they learned to their amazement, had just delivered more than $500 million in gold. The metal was stored in approximately nine thousand boxes. In all, there were thirty-six thousand bars weighing roughly 450 tons. As if the gold were not enough, the bankers also learned that the five ships were delivering between 850 and 900 boxes of securities, worth at least another $500 million.[7] The quarter million residents of Halifax had no idea how much wealth had just arrived at their doorstep.

With the entire docking area near the *Revenge* fenced off, workers

R.M.S. " Talthybius " Blue Funnel Line. "

Received or discharged at Vancouver.B.C. *Date* May 9th 1940. *19*

by Dodwell &Co'y Limited. *Hold*

MARK	1	2	3	4	5	6	7	8	9	10	TOTAL
		462	463	464	465	466	467	468	469	470	
	471	472	473	474	475	476	477	478	479	480	
	481	482	483	484	485	486	487	488	489	490	
	491	492	493	494	495	496	497	498	499	500	
	501	502	503	504	505	506	507	508	509	510	
	511	512	513	514	515	516	517	518	519	520	
	521	522	523	524	525	526	527	528	529	530	
	531	532	533	534	535	536	537	538	539	540	
	541	542	543	544	545	546	547	548	549	550	
	551										

FIG. 11.3. Allied ships carried checklists indicating numbered crates of treasure. The surviving receipts exhibit signs of having been working documents; they are marked with checks or circles to indicate that an appropriate representative in North America had verified the presence of each crate. *Courtesy of the Bank of Canada Archives, Department of Banking Operations, A18-17-2.*

immediately began unloading the cargo. The job required a combination of hard, physical labor and astute attention to detail. As Perkins learned, the "bundles from Britain" on board the Revenge were stored anywhere space could be found: under bunks, in the sick bay, with engineers' stores, in latrines, and in the captain's cabin. Perkins also learned that the hatches in battleships were designed to avoid a straight line from the top deck to the engine room in case a bomb landed near a hatch. The ship's architecture thus forced the men unloading the heavy boxes to take "zig-zag routing" from the lower decks to the main deck.[8]

To speed things along, Perkins and his assistant, K. C. MacLean, pondered alternative unloading methods. Little could be done to speed up the extraction of the boxes from the belly of the ship, but gravity could be exploited for getting the boxes from the ship's deck to the dock. Perkins and MacLean eventually found a large signboard lined with heavy sheet metal. With help from some of the ship's sailors, they quickly created a chute for the boxes. It worked like a charm.[9]

From the dock, sailors dogtrotted the heavy cargo to nearby scales using hand trucks; then Perkins and MacLean inspected and weighed each box. When they found boxes "smashed open," the two bankers made the repairs themselves using hammers and nails from the Revenge. Perkins was not about to trust anyone else. Each gold bar was worth $14,000, and every time a sailor or stevedore moved a box, he was moving $56,000 worth of gold, or, in today's figures, more than $2 million.[10]

Despite the precautions taken with the special cargo, several mishaps interrupted the work. During the unloading process, one box of gold broke open sending a gold bar down a hatch to the deck below. According to journalist Leland Stowe, a sailor peered down, hollering "Is the bar all right?" An angry sailor shouted up, "What about our bloody heads?" Another mishap involved bags of gold sovereigns falling down a hatch. Commander Jenkins dispatched midshipmen to retrieve them. When the coin bags were reinspected, everything was accounted for.[11]

As the last of the boxes from the Revenge was finally processed, Perkins double-checked the manifest only to discover that three boxes were missing. The battleship was searched "from stem to stern" to no avail. The missing boxes were worth a combined $168,000. As Jenkins recalled, he and the bankers paused in the wardroom completely baffled. Perkins asked Jenkins if he could present the checklist of each box's storage location. "My dear boy," Jenkins told him, "we were in a bit of a rush at the Liverpool end. At any moment, one of those ruddy Junker 88's could have dropped a *bon voyage* present down one of our stacks."[12]

The two men stood staring at each other. The mess steward then piped in: "Maybe I've got what you're looking for, sir. There's something down here under my feet I've been tripping over since we left the Clyde." The three boxes of bullion had been stored beneath several cases of Scotch.[13]

—————————

The unloading operations along the docks at Halifax may have proceeded with scarcely a hitch despite the complex logistics, but passengers on board some of the ships in the convoy were aware that their journey had been fraught with danger. Some of them relayed stories— some apocryphal, others certainly true—about anxious moments spent traversing the North Atlantic.

One harrowing report was relayed by Jozef Polkowski, the museum official in charge of the Polish artifacts on board the *Batory*. Polkowski recalled that on the first day of the trip, an airplane launched by the *Revenge* had spotted a U-boat. One of the convoy's destroyers protectively circled the merchant ships and then dropped a "number of depth charges" about fifty yards from the *Batory*. After about fifteen minutes, life for the convoy went back to normal; the U-boat had apparently been scared off.[14]

Another story of near disaster was recounted by a precocious ten-year-old boy, J. P. Nichols, who kept a journal during the voyage to Canada on board the *Monarch of Bermuda*, a luxury liner converted to wartime use in late 1939. According to Nichols, the convoy leaders had reports of three U-boats in the vicinity. HMS *Bonaventure* raced off in the direction of the submarines. "Depth charges were dropped [and] oil came to the surface." Nichols believed that one U-boat was sunk while "no one could be sure about" the other two.[15]

Two other child evacuees offer additional insights into U-boat activity during this trip. In 1991 Anne Winter recounted her experiences on board the *Monarch of Bermuda*:

> Only one incident of any alarm occurred during the voyage and this happened one evening at dinner. This particular night the dining saloon was crowded

as usual with chattering people. The waiters were moving backwards and forwards smoothly through the swing doors leading to the kitchens, balancing loaded trays on their upturned hands. Suddenly an enormous explosion shook the ship violently one way and then the other, as if rocked by a giant fist. Waiters coming through the doors staggered and sent their trays crashing to the floor. Many diners were jerked off their backless benches, others were quick enough to grab the table in front to steady themselves, and a momentary hush descended on the group as the enormity of what that explosion could mean sank in. Quickly, though, a reassuring voice came over the intercom system. "This is your captain speaking. There is no cause for concern. The convoy has run into a school of porpoises which has been impeding our progress. A depth charge was just now dropped to disperse them. Please resume your normal activities."

I don't know if that is a likely reason for dropping a depth charge. Until reading [Leland Stowe's article in] the *Reader's Digest*,[16] we had entertained the notion that there was a more sinister reason—a U-boat, possibly, infiltrating the defenses of the convoy and being scared away or destroyed by that charge. The article, however, researched carefully with the powers that be, does not hint of such an event, so I guess porpoises it was! After the scare with the porpoises some of the adults thought a concert would be a good diversionary activity to absorb the long days. Other than regular lifeboat drills there was not much to do.[17]

The unusual dinner interruption that Winter described also appeared in the memoir of Patricia Cave, another child evacuee. According to Cave, however, she and the other passengers had been "told after the war that the 'U' boat had been sunk by the depth charge."[18]

The recollections of child evacuees on other ships provide additional glimpses into the dangers of traversing the Atlantic in the summer of 1940. The Cunard passenger ship *Antonia* made half a dozen gold runs in 1939 and 1940. In early June 1940, the *Antonia* was ferrying both gold and civilians (mostly children) from Britain to Canada. John Cooke, a child evacuee, later remembered how hard it was to find places to play on the cramped ship and to escape from his "poor mother's anxious gaze." He also recalled that even the spacious hallway into which the cabin opened "was not much better, for it was blocked with massive wooden crates, rumored to contain gold bullion destined for Fort Knox."[19] The rumor was partially true. The *Antonia* carried a consignment of £6 million in gold. The gold's destination, at least initially, was unlikely to be the United States Bullion Depository at Fort Knox, Kentucky. And it is unlikely that the ship's captain and Bank of England and Treasury officials would have allowed crates of gold to be stored in such public spaces unless guards were posted around the clock.

Nevertheless, Cooke was one of several passengers to describe a U-boat attack on the *Antonia*: "Suddenly alarms sounded, and we were rushed on deck to our lifeboat station—starboard side aft. The life-jackets, which we had been firmly instructed never to be without, were now donned in earnest. As we—my mother, two sisters and I—huddled together cold and bewildered, we learned that we were under attack from a German U-boat."[20]

In his memoir, Cooke added that he was "too young to experience the fear and foreboding that must have gripped the grown-ups. I recall only the intense excitement of the moment, preserved as an indelible mental image of the wake of a torpedo passing just a few feet under our stern—and of the heavy, ponderous explosions of depth charges dropped by our escorting Royal Navy Destroyers. Fear, buried in the subconscious, would only manifest itself later."[21]

Two other passengers on board the *Antonia* were Guy Burgess, a British intelligence officer and agent working for the Soviet Union, and thirty-one-year-old Isaiah Berlin, the distinguished British scholar of social and political theory. The presence of the child evacuees certainly did not go unnoticed. In a letter to his parents, Berlin wrote that it seemed as if there were "millions" of children on the ship, but he specified that there were among them seventy-five Oxford children:

> The noise they make is terrific. The ship is endlessly full of restless children behind, on, in, above, below every piece of furniture and rigging. Peace only comes after 7 p.m. and then it breaks out again somewhere far away below, in the 3d class. We 1st class passengers are peacefully insulated from the lower life below decks. But for the mothers—& the motherless children—it must be hell.[22]

In fact, representatives of the CORB referred to the *Antonia* as one of the "problem ships" because of difficulties associated with many of its child passengers.[23]

In letters to his parents, Berlin's only references to danger during the voyage was to say that "We zig-zag elaborately under Admiralty orders. Some depth charges may or may not have been dropped in the course of our journey, nobody is quite sure." According to Berlin biographer Michael Ignatieff, however, Berlin left out important details to reassure his parents that the journey was "uneventful." Actually, writes Ignatieff, the trip was "slow and nerve-racking. The ship zigzagged through the convoy lanes, with the escort destroyers dropping depth-charges to keep German submarines at bay."[24]

Frances Gray, ten years old at the time, was one of the children on the *Antonia* invited by Yale University to be looked after by American families for the duration of the war. Decades later, she recalled how the *Antonia* and a Polish ship were fired upon twice by a U-boat. "Mercifully," she said, the torpedoes "missed us."[25]

The *Antonia* eventually arrived, unharmed, at Québec on July 19, 1940. According to Cooke, "The arrival of our ship . . . was greeted with profound relief by those on board, and with jubilation by enthusiastic crowds thronging the quayside to welcome us, particularly a contingent of the King's Own Yorkshire Light Infantry waiting to embark for the homeward journey."[26]

Having successfully completed the journey across the Atlantic, the civilian passengers on board the *Antonia* and other Allied ships faced an uncertain future in their new country. They could at least be reassured that they—unlike the compatriots to whom they had recently and tearfully said good-bye—were safe from the Luftwaffe and German invasion forces. "Why, it's a city of light!" Mary Kent, the wife of Bank of England representative Harold Kent, recalled of her first night in Montréal after sailing to Canada on board the *Duchess of Atholl*, a liner requisitioned by the Royal Navy in late 1939. Montréal continued to burn its city lights during the war—unlike London, which had instituted blackouts since September 1939.[27]

For all the anxious moments on the high seas, the Canadian and British bankers in Halifax hoped that unloading the rest of the treasure ships would proceed with the same clockwork efficiency as had the *Revenge*.

========

With the last of the gold from the *Revenge* evacuated, the battleship left its berth to make room for HMS *Bonaventure*. The entire unloading process was now repeated. At noon, Perkins calculated that liberating the gold from the *Bonaventure* would be completed before dark. Excellent progress was made until the boatswain's whistle sounded at 4 p.m. The entire crew suddenly stopped for "a dish of tea."

Perkins was furious, but the *Bonaventure*'s captain, H. J. Egerton, put a hand on his shoulder and said, "We've brought it this far. Don't worry. We'll bring it the rest [of the way]."

After tea, the reinvigorated crew finished the job before sunset, just as Egerton had predicted. The train carrying the *Bonaventure*'s treasure then left Halifax for Montréal.[28]

Perkins and MacLean were far from finished in Halifax. The *Monarch of Bermuda*, *Batory*, and *Sobieski* still needed their attention. Fortunately, circumstances granted the two exhausted Bank of Canada representatives a much-needed break. It took time for the ship's children and other civilian passengers to disembark, and more important, unloading could not take place until dawn the next day. Carrying out the job at night would have required the use of extensive lighting, which would have aroused too much attention.

In the meantime, Perkins and MacLean were invited to dinner on the *Monarch of Bermuda*. They were treated to a "magnificent culinary show" consisting of lobster cocktail, hot rolls, pea soup, roast beef, and Yorkshire pudding. The ship's printing press even rolled out special menus with their names. The captain pointed out that such a feast was definitely not typical. "We've been saving our best for a great occasion," he said. "And this certainly is it."[29]

The next day, July 14, Perkins directed the unloading of the *Monarch of Bermuda* while MacLean took charge of the *Batory* and *Sobieski*. As before, the occasional mishap marred an otherwise smooth process. In one instance, a box of gold bars fell to the ground, spilling the protective sawdust inside the box. A ship's steward came up with the idea of replacing the lost sawdust with straw wine bottle jackets. As it turned out, one gold bar fit neatly into one wine jacket.[30]

By the end of the day, all the special cargo had been transferred to waiting trains. Perkins accompanied the securities to Montréal; MacLean escorted the gold to Ottawa via Montréal. The most valuable treasure in world history was under way once again, this time through the sedate and unsuspecting townships and countryside of Nova Scotia, New Brunswick, and Québec.

As the trains headed west, all other rail traffic—including troop trains—was sidetracked when necessary. The Canadian National Railway blandly listed the cargo on the trains as "fish," probably because railway employees and the Canadian public were used to seeing speedy trains carrying fresh and frozen fish from the Atlantic ports to the rest of the nation.[31] A few also referred to the treasure-filled trains as "Cannonball Specials."[32]

The trains sped toward Montréal, at times reaching speeds of almost sixty miles per hour. At 3 a.m., in the middle of Québec, the train carrying Sidney Perkins and much of the convoy's cargo came to an abrupt halt. As Perkins recalled, "a bitter wind cut through me. Lanterns bobbed several coaches ahead, and dim figures emerged. I sprinted ahead—encountering the conductor. . . . Was it an armed hold-up?"

Then he heard someone cry out, "It's a broken hangar!"[33] A steel rod, part of a car's wheel assembly, was cutting into the wooden rail ties. Flashlights revealed a deep gouge running along the ties behind the train. Fortunately, the workshop of the Canadian National Railway stood only a half mile ahead. The divisional master mechanic told Perkins that, at the speed the train was traveling, "It's a wonder you weren't derailed."

Despite the danger posed by the damaged wheel assembly, the repair job was straightforward. "You're lucky," the mechanic told Perkins. The repairs could be made "without unloading all that fish."[34] The repair crew had no idea that the "fish" were actually a sizable chunk of Britain's wealth.

The crew took about an hour to complete the repairs. At 9 a.m. on July 15, the "fish" finally arrived at Bonaventure Station in Montréal. The securities had reached the end of their line while the gold still had to make the journey westward to Ottawa.

The securities were transferred from the Montréal train station to the Sun Life Assurance Building. The monstrous, twenty-four-story edifice, completed in 1931, took up an entire block and was the largest office building in the British Commonwealth.[35] Accompanying the securities were armed guards from the Canadian National Express, who were dressed in civilian attire so as not to attract attention. Construction workers using wheelbarrows transferred the boxes of securities to the belly of the Sun Life Building. As Leland Stowe reported, "Royal Canadian Mounted Police hovered hawk-like as the boxes were lowered to the 'Buttress Room' in the third basement."[36]

FIG. 11.4. Secure facilities in the basement of the Sun Life Assurance Building in Montréal housed the vast store of British-owned securities. The United Kingdom Security Deposit was created to process the nearly twenty thousand crates of securities that arrived in 1940. *Courtesy of Hayward Studios/ Library and Archives Canada/PA-069265*

The boxes were delivered to one of the most remarkable vaults ever constructed, a hasty makeover of storage rooms that had never been intended for anything like this historic treasure and had the deceptively ordinary name, "United Kingdom Security Deposit." Harold Kent, a Bank of England employee who helped manage the project, recalled that an infant could have broken through the original wooden door, which initially was not even equipped with locks.[37]

The vault's transformation, including the installation of dozens of "super-sensitive" sound-detection devices and alarms, took more than a month. High-pressure lines ran into the building as cement was pumped in. It was impossible to conceal the work from the five thousand or so Sun Life employees who went in and out daily, but a Sun Life executive recalled that no one ever questioned him about the work: "They assumed the foundations were being strengthened." The resulting vault was nearly impenetrable. It was sixty feet wide by sixty feet long and ten feet high against solid rock on two sides. The ceiling and walls were three feet thick. The steel required to reinforce the walls had been scrounged at the last minute from disused railroad rails—870 of them.[38]

When assumptions about "foundation work" in the Sun Life Building no longer sufficed, a new rumor was floated: the activity in the basement related to a very large, but plausible, war loan campaign. According to Draper, even when people found out the truth, they doubted it.[39] At least until late summer, none of the thousands of workers above street level in the enormous office building appears to have discovered the UKSD's existence.

The vault's massive new door was controlled by two combination codes, and only a handful of people were entrusted with one of them. As Kent later recalled, "From first to last I never knew what the other combination was."[40] Security procedures were quickly established for the UKSD staff. According to Stowe, "Every employee had to present a pass (changed each month) first at the elevator entrance and then to Royal Canadian Mounted Police guards below, signing in and out daily."[41] The area beneath the guards' tables concealed trip-hammer alarms connected directly with RCMP and Montréal police headquarters, as well as with the Dominion Electric Protection Company. In addition, twenty-four Mounties guarded the securities around the clock, eating and sleeping in the building.[42]

For all the security apparatus, Sun Life executive H. McAuslane recalled that the workers moving the boxes earned twenty-two dollars a week: "Those fellows . . . were pushing around millions of dollars in wealth—tens of millions each in a few hours—and they had no idea what they were handling . . . but even if someone had wanted to steal a case, it would have been a hopeless job. The only way you could get a case out of that third basement was by the one elevator—and it was always controlled both at the bottom and the top."[43]

The vast number of securities delivered to the UKSD had to be recorded, verified, and classified. They included 200,000 American securities, as well as others from Argentina, Belgium, Canada, France, Holland, Dutch East Indies, Norway, Sweden, and Switzerland.[44]

With the securities safely stowed away, Sidney Perkins moved on to oversee another unusual operation. This job, however, required a different set of skills. It was also one that Perkins found more personal than the job of ensuring the safety of the cargo from the *Revenge* convoy. The representatives of the Bank of England—Alexander Craig and his aids Harold Kent, Harold Forrest, Leslie Phelps, and Charles Hamilton—and their families had left Britain in such a hurry, and security had been so tight, that no one in Canada had found places for them to live. The bankers had arrived with the treasure; their wives and children arrived on the *Duchess of Atholl*. They now all needed a place to call home. Perkins eventually found satisfactory accommodations in various locations around the "war-packed" city.[45]

With the exception of the flood scare of two weeks earlier, discussed in chapter 10, operations at the UKSD proceeded uneventfully. Nearly 130 experts, clerks, and filing staff—about one hundred from Canada and the rest from London—worked in the space immediately outside the vault, twice the size of the vault itself.[46] Alexander Craig's staff worked ten-hour days, six days a week. Everything delivered from Britain had to be properly accounted for before the securities could be marketed. The securities eventually filled more than 900 four-drawer filing cabinets. The job was so complex that it took the staff—mostly women—until the end of September 1940 to finish classifying and checking everything.[47]

Using a card index system, the UKSD staff dispatched over six thousand "Query Slips" to London in order to resolve the inevitable discrepancies that emerged in the processing of so much paperwork. By the end of September, nearly two thousand boxes of securities had found their way to their new home in Montréal.[48] Much to the relief of all those involved, every certificate was accounted for. As UKSD manager Craig put it, "In view of the pressures under which they were assembled and shipped," the safe arrival of the securities "was quite extraordinary."[49] The total value of the UKSD eventually reached nearly $8 billion (about £2 billion). The facility also held gold, roughly a third of the UKSD's total value.[50] At long last, the bankers could get down to the real business of selling off the securities to purchase the matériel Britain so desperately needed to fight the Axis Powers.

━━━━━━

The huge stockpile of gold arriving with the *Revenge* convoy experienced a different fate from the securities. Because of the metal's weight, the railcars carrying the gold were restricted to between 150 and 200 boxes. Each train pulled ten to fourteen baggage cars, a diner, and two sleeping cars for the railway personnel and Canadian National Express guards. Two guards, working four-hour shifts, were locked inside each of the gold cars. At least three hundred rail and security workers were employed in this phase of the operation, including every male employee of the Canadian National Express head office in Montréal.[51] The Canadian National Express Company charged $1 million to deliver the gold safely to the railroad station in Ottawa.[52]

Once in Ottawa and under cover of darkness, the gold was delivered by truck from the railroad station to the Bank of Canada on Wellington Street. By the summer of 1940, the Canadian capital was no stranger to large shipments of gold from overseas. As early as mid-1939, war fears had led many European central banks to ship large quantities of gold to Ottawa for safekeeping. So much gold was arriving at the time that, according to an accountant working at the Bank of Canada facility, crawl spaces were left between the stacks so that Bank auditors could verify that the stacks were all gold.[53] Even more space was needed for the gold shipments of mid-1940.

By the summer of 1940, the Bank's vault had been enlarged to sixty feet by one hundred feet, with a ceiling twenty feet high.[54] Tens of thousands of 27.5-pound bars were neatly stacked in wire cages reaching to the ceiling. The vault also held more than fifty thousand sacks of gold coins from many countries. There were millions of French napoleons as well as countless other coins stamped with the profiles of Louis XIV, Louis XV, and Louis XVI. British gold sovereigns mostly dated from the era of Queen Victoria and King George V, but also included George II's rare "spade guineas" and souvenirs from the Elizabethan era.[55]

The massive quantity of gold shipped by the end of July was formidable. From the start of the war through June 1940, British gold held at the Bank of Canada fluctuated slightly but maintained an average monthly balance of about $330 million. After the gold shipments of June and July 1940, however, the British had amassed a whopping $886 million in their Bank of Canada gold accounts. In the weeks ahead, that number would grow even larger.

Gold was coming in so quickly that the Bank of Canada took days, and sometimes weeks, to record precisely how much had arrived. A Bank ledger for June 24, for example, indicated that the Bank of England had more than $440 million in earmarked gold in Canada. A note at the bottom of the ledger, however, stated that this amount did "not include 740 boxes of special shipment of June 10, 1940 or 1480 boxes of special shipment of June 23, 1940. . . . At an approximate value of $14,000 per bar the value of these shipments would be $124,320,000."[56]

The July gold shipments—including the gold from the *Revenge* convoy—experienced a similar delay in proper registration. The ledger for August 9, for example, lists slightly more than $1 billion in British gold. The note at the bottom of the ledger stated that the amount did not include the following:

518 boxes bullion received July 8/40
11,275 boxes bullion received July 14–16/40
33 boxes coin August 1/40
295 boxes bullion received August 9/40—Australia[57]

Representatives of the Bank of England were apparently not overly concerned about immediately recording the incoming gold. Cameron Cobbold of the Bank of England told his colleagues in Ottawa that there was "no urgency and weighing may be carried out at convenience of Bank of Canada."[58] The magnitude of the task and the lack of pressure from London explain the Bank of Canada's roughly two-week delay in registering all the gold. The episode also reflects the extensive trust the two banks had in each other.

Since much of this gold had been sent to Canada to buy war matériel, the quantity of British gold sent from Canada to the Federal Reserve Bank in New York increased as well. According to an October 1, 1940, Bank of Canada ledger, three gold shipments to New York were listed as follows:

September 29: $12,986,595.41
September 30: $ 8,327,998.00
October 1: $42,090,667.08[59]

Quoting the U.S. Commerce Department, the Associated Press reported that British gold imports had set a twelve-month record of roughly $4.75 billion in 1940. This figure represents British gold sent to the United States directly from the British Empire as well as gold sent through Canada.[60]

After the successful delivery of treasure on board the ships of the *Revenge* convoy, more than seventy-five additional consignments found their way to North America. By the end of 1940, the Bank of England had shipped a total of 82,270 gold bars and 21,680,000 gold sovereigns to Canada.[61] A few additional shipments were dispatched in 1941.[62] By then, the process of shipping British wealth to North America had reached a certain degree of normalcy, as reflected in a letter from Basil Catterns of the Bank of England to Sir Richard Hopkins at the Treasury: "I think that 50–90 convoys a year, assuming escort for full distance, should enable us to keep pace, even if it means only one shipment per convoy, at an average of, say, £2/3 million per shipment."[63]

Even though most of Britain's available liquid assets were securely stowed away in vaults in the United States and Canada, Britain's financial problems were far from over. The British government expected the situation to get worse in the coming months. The minutes from an August 22, 1940, Cabinet meeting reveal that at Britain's rate of gold expenditures, in the twelve-month period ending in June 1941, the nation would burn through some £800 million in gold and foreign exchange, nearly twice the rate of the previous year. Chancellor of the Exchequer Kingsley Wood was particularly glum: "If we continued to [spend] gold at the rate we had experienced in the last six weeks, we should have none left by the end of December [1940]."[64]

The situation was getting dire even with much of the marketable treasury under lock and key in North America. Now some in the Cabinet suggested selling a few of the West Indian islands to the United States.[65] There was even talk of "scraping the pot"—raising money by requisitioning wedding rings and other gold ornaments from the British public, even though Wood thought it would generate no more than £20 million. Churchill put a stop to the proposal but remarked that it could always be adopted "at a later stage, if we wished to make some striking gesture for the purpose of shaming the Americans" into doing more to help Britain.[66]

Nevertheless, American recalcitrance was forcing Britain to contemplate proposals that, under normal circumstances, would otherwise have been considered laughable. Herbert Morrison, Britain's minister of supply, for example, persuaded Churchill that his department should actually increase the rate of purchases in the United States even though Britain's war chest was being drained: "[W]e ought to be prepared to take big financial risks during the next six months, since any marked falling off in our programs, even for a limited period, might materially affect the outcome of the war." In short, he added, "it was better to take a risk on the financial side, rather than to risk losing the

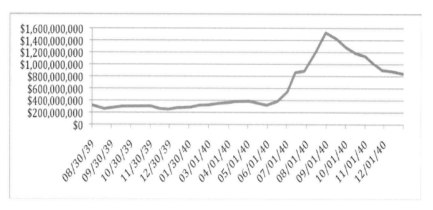

FIG. 11.5. Until early June 1940, the amount of British gold in Canada remained relatively steady, signifying Britain's modest gold shipments to Canada and its concurrent gold expenditures. The graph line starts its steep rise in early June 1940, reflecting the swift German victory over France and the belief in London that Britain was the Nazi's next target. *The data, compiled by the author, are derived from the following Bank of Canada sources: "Gold held in Safekeeping for the Bank of England," File A18-17-9 B of E.—"Gold in Safekeeping at B. of C. Statements 1939–1944; Gold Held in Safekeeping Bank of England, 1939–1946," File 580-44-14A, Vol. 3908-4612.*

war." The minister of aircraft production, Lord Beaverbrook (Maxwell Aitken), made a similar point, although he highlighted the domestic political effects of an America struggling with the Great Depression: "[W]e ought to do everything in our power to fill American factories with British orders. No American Government would dare to tell those factories to cease production, with all the consequences in the shape of unemployment and industrial derangement."[67]

In September 1940, Britain even barred British banknotes used abroad from reentering the country. As *Time* magazine reported, "In effect, she declared worthless for the duration all British paper money in non-sterling countries. U.S. holders of pound notes were given six days to exchange them, but France and other occupied nations were allowed only 24 hours." The purpose behind the unusual move was to prevent Germany from exploiting its own stores of British money by laundering it in the United States, South America, and other neutral countries.[68]

By the end of 1940, it was clear to those central to Britain's wartime financing that the shipments of gold and securities to North America had accomplished their goal; they helped Britain pay for the war and kept its wealth out of German hands. The special shipments did not, however, change the sobering facts about Britain's overall economic health. As Raymond E. Lee put it, "What a wonderful thing it will be if these blokes do win the war. They will be bankrupt but entitled to almost unlimited respect."[69]

Public knowledge of the UKSD slowly emerged in mid-July 1940, even before British and Canadian authorities were prepared to announce its existence. George V. Ormsby of the *Wall Street Journal*, for example, reported on July 19, 1940, that Bank of England representatives would be in charge of the "tremendous volume of securities" shipped to North America in the past few weeks. Though he did not pinpoint the exact location, Ormsby correctly reported the name of the facility, as well as specifying that the securities would be held in Canada.[70]

By July 24, UKSD officials and the British government apparently felt confident enough to formally announce the Deposit's existence. The Associated Press and the *New York Times* reported that arrangements were being completed for the UKSD.[71] The next day, the Associated Press, the *Wall Street Journal*, the *New York Times*, and the *Globe and Mail* (in Canada) published the following notice:

> Arrangements for the establishment of the United Kingdom security deposit in Canada are now practically complete, it was learned today from official sources. The deposit is being established in Montreal and will hold in custody American and Canadian securities which have been sent to Canada under instructions of the British Treasury.
>
> A. S. Craig, an official of the Bank of England, arrived recently in Montreal to assume charge of the work of the British Treasury. He is assisted in his preliminary arrangements for office space, engagement of staff and other matters by the Bank of Canada.[72]

The UKSD staff continued the gradual sell-off of the securities to help pay for Britain's war needs. By the start of 1941, British sales of securities had increased from about $2 million a week to $10 million a week.[73] The sales pace as well as the pressures of the job would ease considerably several months later, when the United States instituted the Lend-Lease program, which finally gave Britain the financial lifeline it needed. As Edward R. Stettinius, an American official central to the Lend-Lease program, put it, Britain and other recipients of Lend-Lease aid could "settle accounts after the danger has passed."[74] In all, the United States would grant Britain $21 billion in Lend-Lease aid, receiving $7 billion of it back.[75]

———

Aside from the *Niagara*, which struck mines laid by a German ship near New Zealand, no other ship involved in Britain's financial flight was lost.[76] For most other ships, subsequent assignments were far less glamorous. The *Manchester Commerce*, for example, delivered £3 million in gold in July 1940 but four years later spent much of its time transporting mules from South Africa to India.[77] The British merchant ship *Aracataca* delivered a similar quantity of gold in trips to North America in May, June, and July 1940, but in late November of that year, the ship was torpedoed and sunk by U-101 while en route from Jamaica to Halifax. Instead of a losing a consignment of gold, the ship went down with most of its crew and sixteen hundred tons of bananas.[78]

Some ships went on to participate in many of the famous battles of the war or deliver other kinds of special cargo. After HMS *Suffolk* delivered £1 million in gold from South Africa to Canada in April 1940, for example, it participated in the May 1941 hunt for the *Bismarck*. HMS *Ramillies* delivered £3 million in gold from Greenock to Halifax in January 1941 and bombarded German positions during D-day in June 1944.[79] Two of the ship's 15-inch guns are on the grounds of the Imperial War Museum in London.

The *Batory*, the liner that delivered both priceless Polish artifacts and £40 million in British gold to Canada in July 1940, left Liverpool in August 1940 and safely evacuated more than four hundred British children to safety in Australia. It became known as the "Singing Ship" after one of the women escorting the child-evacuees organized singing groups among the children. The singing continued for the remaining weeks of the long voyage to Australia.[80]

HMS *Southampton*, one of the warships that escorted the King and Queen (and £15 million in gold) to North America in the spring of 1939, met its fate in the Mediterranean in January 1941. It was attacked by German Ju-87 dive-bombers and finally had to be scuttled by torpedoes from HMS *Orion* and HMS *Gloucester*.[81] HMS *Bonaventure*, which transported £25 million in gold from Greenock to Halifax as part of the *Revenge* convoy, was lost on March 31, 1941, after being torpedoed by the Italian submarine *Ambra* near Crete.[82]

Some of the treasure ships were later lost as a result of accidents. The *Parthenia*, for example, delivered £2 million in gold to Canada in July 1940 and sank on November 29, 1940, after colliding with the *Robert F. Hand* near Scotland.[83] Similarly, the *Bangalore* delivered £1 million in gold from Bombay to Canada in February 1940 and again in June 1940 but on July 21, 1941, collided with the *Richmond Castle*. To prevent the vessel from becoming a hazard to navigation, it was sunk by British gunfire.[84] In 1940 the escort trawler HMCS *Ypres* sank after colliding with HMS *Revenge* at the entrance to the Halifax harbor. (The *Revenge* survived but was forced to listen to mock "abandon ship drills" from other vessels each time it returned to Halifax.)[85]

By the end of the war, some 40 percent of the ships that had previously ferried British wealth to North America had been lost. This loss rate reveals the dangers endured on board merchant ships and warships and the risky nature of Britain's financial evacuation. One is tempted to consider it a miracle that only one gold-laden ship was sunk during the entire operation. If the gold and securities shipments, particularly of the July 1940 *Revenge* convoy, had been lost, the course of the war could have been very different from what we know.

12

Speculation

The enormous risks taken in the global transfers of British wealth demonstrate both the stakes involved and the contingent nature of Britain's survival. The details recounted here invite speculation about how differently history might have unfolded had the Germans intercepted or destroyed the special shipments—especially the July 1940 consignments carried by the *Revenge, Bonaventure, Monarch of Bermuda, Sobieski,* and *Batory.* What would the consequences have been if the Nazis had sunk the ships or—even worse—captured the contents on board the *Revenge* convoy? Challenges marked every phase of the operation, creating opportunities for disaster around every corner. If delays had plagued the operation, might the ships have faced even greater risks? If Britain had lost a significant portion of its wealth at sea, could it have tapped other financial resources to sustain the war effort? And, if significant quantities of British wealth had been lost, how would the United States, Germany, and the Soviet Union have reacted to a bankrupted Britain?

These questions grow out of a branch of historical investigation known as counterfactual analysis. Instead of focusing uniquely on the established facts of events, counterfactual analysis poses what-if questions to tease out plausible, alternative ways in which history could have developed. As Richard Ned Lebow of King's College London has shown, counterfactual analysis highlights bifurcation points where "the context of history could easily have taken a radically different course."[1] This technique is indispensable for many important historical questions, such as, did the Allies ever come close to losing the war? The counterfactual mode of thinking challenges the mainstream approach of the social sciences, which seeks to discover regularities and not the potential conditions or dynamics that can disrupt those regularities.[2] The approach also helps us avoid the bias of hindsight; analysts may be more likely to keep an open mind about what might have been.

While counterfactual analysis has been employed to probe or challenge existing historical accounts, it has also been used to anticipate future developments. In 2008, for example, the U.S. Army War College published a counterfactual study to provide insights into *future* national security, military, and intelligence challenges.[3] Here is a simple application of the idea: if Iran were to acquire nuclear weapons, would it provide this technology to Hezbollah? As author Noel Hendrickson explained, such what-if questions "are essential to intelligence analysis because they are implicit in all strategic assessments."[4]

Counterfactual reasoning often lurks behind theories based on conventional factual analysis. Particularly relevant to the context of World War II is a well-established argument among political science advocates of realism in general and deterrence theory in particular. The realist assertion that British and French prewar appeasement policies whetted Hitler's appetite for more power rests indirectly on counterfactual reasoning. As Lebow describes, the standard argument (based on established facts) is as follows: "Hitler *could* have been restrained *if* France and Britain had demonstrated willingness to go to war in defense of the European territorial status quo."[5] The widely accepted realist lesson of World War II from "factual" analysis—that Allied deterrence policies could have prevented mass slaughter—actually relies on counterfactual analysis.

Turning this approach to Britain's financial evacuation leads to many intriguing questions. One of the most important is the following: would the British government have been willing and able to continue the fight given the loss of a significant amount of wealth to the sea or to the Germans? The assessment of at least one leading figure at the Bank of England is that the loss of securities alone might have forced a British surrender. Alexander Craig, who accompanied one of the huge July 1940 shipments to Canada and managed the UKSD in Montréal, told his counterparts at the Bank of Canada that his team had been rushed at the start of the operation to transfer most of the securities and he could not give a definitive amount for the value of the securities. "All we can say before checking it," Craig asserted, "is that it comprises enough wealth to cost us the war—if it were lost or captured."[6]

Had that, or something comparable, happened, Britain might have chosen to avoid the potential devastation of a German invasion by meeting German terms of surrender. This was an unlikely scenario with Churchill as prime minister, but it was more plausible with another in charge. During the worst months of 1940, for example, Lord Halifax and former prime minister Lloyd George, among others, believed that a negotiated peace with Hitler was preferable to the avoidable catastrophe of relentless German bombing raids.[7]

Churchill warned Roosevelt and Canadian prime minister Mackenzie King several times about an eventual German victory over Britain.[8] As Churchill saw it, with control of Britain, Hitler would have had an easier time consolidating Nazi control over all of Europe. The western front might have been subdued by mid-1941, allowing the Wehrmacht to launch its attack on the Soviet Union with few major distractions. With a pacified western front, Germany could have unleashed a more sizable military force against the Soviet Union. Had the United States, Canada, and other Allies wanted to fight their way back and defeat Germany, they would not have been able to use Britain as an island base to liberate Europe.[9] In addition, if history had unfolded this way, the historical assessment of Hitler's military strategy would have been much more favorable. Future historians would have noted Hitler's wisdom of avoiding a two-front war in Europe.

With Hitler concentrating his forces on the east, would the Soviet Union have been able to repel the German war machine? Since it turned out that the combined efforts of the Soviet Union, Britain, the United States, and the other Allies were not able to defeat Hitler until 1945, it seems unlikely that the Soviet Union, acting alone, could have withstood the Nazis. In light of these considerations, the political and economic face of Europe could be drastically different today.

A German victory over Britain would have been felt in the Americas as well. Fascist groups in Latin America, particularly Argentina and Brazil, would have been emboldened, and the United States would have faced challenges closer to home. In late May 1940, Roosevelt envisioned such a scenario unfolding. As the American president reasoned, Hitler might not at the beginning think he is

> going to conquer the whole world but, when the time comes and he has conquered Europe and Africa and got Asia all settled up with Japan and has some kind of practical agreement with Russia, it may be human nature for

victors of that kind to say, "I have taken two thirds of the world and I am all armed and ready to go—why shouldn't I go the whole hog and control, in a military way, the last third of the world, the Americas?"[10]

The British ambassador to the United States, Lord Lothian, was thinking along the same lines. He envisioned Germany and Italy establishing themselves in Brazil with the help of German and Italian agents operating in those countries. They would then be within bombing distance of the Panama Canal. And if the U.S. Navy were shifted to the Atlantic, Japan could take Hawaii and Alaska.[11]

It is hard to know how Hitler would have responded to a bankrupt Britain. Nevertheless, Hitler's strategic approach to the Soviet Union offers some insights into potential attitudes toward Britain. Some historians have argued that Hitler had already made up his mind to attack the Soviet Union as early as the first week of July 1940, when the Führer disclosed his decision to his chief adjutant and his army's commander in chief.[12] If the goal of invading the Soviet Union was in fact determined at this time, the Führer would not have devoted the necessary military resources to a 1941 invasion of Britain—bankrupt or not. It is also possible that Hitler would have concluded that the March 1941 passage of Lend-Lease had sufficiently stabilized Britain's financial situation, thus reducing the incentives for an invasion.

The loss of a sizable quantity of Britain's wealth at sea in 1940 would have had major repercussions for U.S. policy. Most important, the United States might have abandoned its isolationism in favor of a robust defense of Britain and the other Allies. Such a development, however, should be viewed with a certain degree of skepticism. Historians generally agree that Britain stood on a precipice in the summer of 1940, but the American stance remained firmly against significant intervention in the war. Germany's air campaign in the late summer and fall of 1940 relentlessly pounded both civilian and military targets in Britain.[13] On September 6, 1940, Cordell Hull reported to the Cabinet that it "was actually claimed in some quarters that England would be suing for peace before last week came to an end."[14] Starting the next day, an average of two hundred German bombers attacked London every night for fifty-seven nights.[15] All the while, U.S. isolationism remained entrenched.

FIG. 12.1. London under attack. Despite the unrelenting German barrage against London and other targets, the United States remained unwilling to join the Allies in the fight against the Axis powers. This image was taken on September 7, 1940. *Courtesy of the U.S. National Archives*

On September 23, 1940, Lord Lothian sent a telegram to the Foreign Office about the political mood in Washington. The telegram noted that indiscriminant bombing of London had "created no open movement to intervention on Britain's behalf; repeal of Neutrality or Johnson Acts is not notably discussed, and not much is to be expected before the election, but sympathy is very strong and there are many indications that in due course it will develop into concrete effect."[16] Lothian's phrase "concrete effect" was probably deliberately vague, and it gave no indication of a best-case scenario: a U.S. declaration of war against Germany.

It is thus difficult to conclude that U.S. attitudes would automatically have shifted in the event of the imminent collapse of the British economy. The often strained relations between the United States and Britain—dating back to the start of the war—persisted through Britain's darkest months. The tension was felt at the highest political levels and within the British financial community. Churchill, in January 1941, worried that "the American's love of doing good business may lead them to denude us of all our realizable resources before they show any inclination to be the Good Samaritan."[17] Ten days later, Chancellor of the Exchequer Kingsley Wood lamented that it would be difficult for the British to resist "the American tendency . . . to strip us of everything we possess in payment for what we are about to receive."[18] At the Bank of England and the British Treasury, there was concern that the United States was trying to squeeze Britain financially in order to strengthen its postwar advantage.

Part of Britain's problem was convincing American politicians that its financial situation was so precarious. When Secretary of the Navy Frank

Knox met British ambassador Lothian on August 1, 1940, he described him as "almost tearful in his pleas for help and help quickly."[19] His pleas unanswered, Lothian eventually took his case to the press. On November 22, Lothian bluntly told a group of reporters in New York that "Britain's broke; it's your money we want."[20] As late as January 1941, British Treasury official D. H. Robertson indicated, "It is hard for the American layman to understand how we can have had 4,860 million dollars of resources (whether liquid or not) at the beginning of the war and be without liquid resources now."[21]

The American press acknowledged Britain's desperate financial situation in early 1941. As *Time* magazine reported, for example, "Late last fall it was clear that the British were getting close to the bottom of the barrel. Now spending at the rate of almost $400,000,000 a week, the British will not have enough cash at this year's end to make their 1942 purchasing commitments."[22]

The British eventually presented a memorandum to Congress explaining the nearly exhausted state of their financial resources.[23] U.S. Treasury secretary Henry Morgenthau told the Senate Committee on Foreign Relations that "the problem before us is not whether the British have resources; of course they have, all over the world. The problem is whether the British have got the dollars they need, or can get the dollars they need to spend in this country [the United States]. That, gentlemen, is the problem as I see it."[24]

Thus, even with Britain on the financial brink and with German airplanes bombing the country mercilessly, Britain's diplomatic corps, and Churchill himself, were at great pains to convince the United States that their country needed help on a monumental scale. The U.S. Lend-Lease program was instituted in early 1941, but isolationism in the country would completely collapse only when the threat of war became actual war on December 7, 1941.

It is certainly plausible that if Britain had lost a large portion of its wealth on the high seas, passage of Lend-Lease would have been accelerated. The loss or capture of a sizable quantity of British wealth might have also led to an early declaration of war by the United States. The Roosevelt administration was already sympathetic to Britain's plight. If Britain had actually gone broke, Congress and the American public would have been forced much earlier to confront the possibility of a Nazi victory. In this scenario, enough isolationists might have switched their views in favor of direct confrontation with Germany. While this might not have been as deep a change of heart as the one that occurred immediately after Pearl Harbor, certainly some members of Congress would have been jolted into action in 1940 by the prospects of a world in which western Europe (and, perhaps, central and eastern Europe) were controlled by the Nazis.[25] In such a scenario, history could have played out more or less as it actually did.

═══════════

The loss of a sizeable portion of British wealth at sea, particularly in mid-1940, might have rendered some of the more catastrophic scenarios irrelevant had Britain gained access to an otherwise untapped source of wealth: French gold. Like other European countries of the late 1930s, France sent large quantities of its gold to Canada for safekeeping. In 1940, for example, France shipped to the Bank of Canada 134,798 bars of gold.[26] Once France accepted peace terms with Hitler in the summer of 1940, much of this gold, housed in Ottawa, was up for grabs. Would Canada, a key member of the Allied cause, view the gold as a useful tool for financing the war effort and make it available to Britain? British leaders initially assumed so.

On August 21, 1940, British chancellor of the exchequer Kingsley Wood summarized for the War Cabinet the available gold and foreign exchange resources. In the "Most Secret" document, Wood anticipated a deficit of as much as £800 million by June 1941. To help alleviate the strain on the Treasury, Wood suggested, among other things, that Britain could secure a "certain" amount of French gold.[27] Britain offered sterling to the new Vichy government in France in exchange for the gold, but the French wanted U.S. dollars. To some extent, the offer was beside the point; the French assumed that Britain was done for anyway.[28]

Several days later, on August 25, Churchill cabled Ottawa hoping to persuade the Canadians that French gold should be freed for British use. Prime Minister Mackenzie King told the British that a subcommittee would give the issue a "most careful examination." The disheartening response was a portent of future negotiations. Graham Towers, the governor of the Bank of Canada, felt the British idea deserved serious attention: "While I am not aware how long the gold resources of the United Kingdom will last, I should think that they might manage to get along at least until next spring. . . . Bearing in mind the severe strain under which they are laboring, I can understand that they are desperately anxious to be sure (from a financial point of view) that they can carry on the fight through 1941 . . . rather than be forced to rely on a pious hope that something will turn up."[29] The "pious hope" to which Towers referred probably meant a U.S. war declaration.

In early September 1940, Towers took a more forceful position on Britain's behalf; he wanted his prime minister to grant Britain access to France's gold. "I feel strongly that there is nothing in the slightest degree immoral in making use of such assets. . . . If at the time of the debacle in France there had been four thousand fighting planes owned by the French in Canada, would anyone suggest that these planes should have been packed away for the duration of the war?"[30]

Oskar Skelton, Prime Minister King's right-hand man in foreign affairs, saw the situation very differently. Skelton told Towers that planes were not the same thing as gold because gold carried a "sacred" value. A depositor of gold would feel "gypped if he isn't given back gold or some instrument as certain to be exchanged for equal value" when the war ended.[31] No doubt supporters of granting Britain access to French gold saw this as a specious argument.

In early November 1940, Gerald Pinsent, a financial counselor at the British Embassy, wrote to Frederick Phillips at the British Treasury to suggest that they requisition French gold without telling the French (or the Americans). "The above may look a little like sharp practices," Phillips wrote, "but I am not sure that we ought to boggle even that. The necessity of using this gold for the prosecution of the war, and among other things for the ultimate liberation of France, is so paramount that legal niceties must if necessary be forgotten."[32] Despite the logic employed by British officials and despite recommendations that "legal niceties" not stand in the way, by mid-November 1940, Prime Minister King had made his decision: French gold would remain off limits to the British.[33]

According to historian Duncan McDowall, King's decision rested on both Canada's desire for foreign policy independence as well as domestic political considerations. The Canadian government felt it had "to distance itself from Britain's international agenda" and "cease acting out of colonial obedience."[34] In addition, King's political standing depended on votes from Québec, the province most likely to react negatively to the liquidation of French assets in favor of Britain. Thus, the gold remained in Canadian custody until the fall of the Vichy government and the liberation of France in 1944. The gold was then returned to the Banque de France.[35]

While British gold helped buy the civilian and military goods necessary to keep Britain afloat and hold the line against Nazi dominance, the French gold sat out the war. It is possible that the Canadian government might have changed its mind—and accepted British reasoning—if, for example, the *Revenge* convoy had been lost. The argument that Canada should act independently of British foreign policy might have fizzled with the prospect of a Nazified Britain.

Another fascinating what-if question involves the timing of Britain's most valuable shipments. If Britain had delayed the mid-1940 shipments, would the risks of the operation have increased? In the summer of 1940, the British government and the public at large were convinced by a perceived flood of evidence that a German invasion was imminent. This conviction prompted the Churchill government to undertake the biggest risk the British Empire ever took with its wealth. If the British perception of a German invasion had developed more slowly, however, the government might have sent its most valuable shipments a month or two later. It is also possible that delays could have resulted from organizational complications or from snafus on the banking side of the operation, on the naval side, or both. Regardless of the reasons, a delay in the shipments by a month or two, or even several weeks, could have meant the difference for many of the most valuable consignments shipped to North America. This was because Germany's North Atlantic naval presence grew substantially between 1940 and 1941.

As we have seen, at the start of the war Germany had only fifty-seven operational U-boats, but many of these were not built for action in the North Atlantic. U-boat numbers remained almost static for much of the next twelve months. By July 1940, when the most valuable shipments were undertaken, German U-boat strength stood at just fifty-one.[36] German submarines still had a difficult time patrolling the vast Atlantic Ocean, whether individually or in wolf packs.

By the fall of 1940, however, Erich Raeder and Karl Dönitz had succeeded in putting more U-boats on patrol in the North Atlantic, and wolf-pack operations became more feasible. (Eventually, over one hundred Italian submarines would join the Axis cause in the Atlantic, but the Germans concluded that they were better off without the Italians.[37]) Between November 1940 and March 1941, the strength of the U-boat fleet climbed from 74 to 109 (although the average number of operational U-boats during this time peaked at 27).[38]

The late summer and early fall months of 1940 were so profitable for the U-boat fleet that it was dubbed "the Happy Time." Many a German submarine ace made his name during these months when, in all, German submarines sank 282 ships—almost 1.5 million tons of shipping.[39]

Time was also on the German side regarding the use of French naval bases. According to historian Brayton Harris, from July through September 1940, France-based U-boat kills averaged about five ships a month. By October, U-boats were sinking more than two ships *a day*. On October 19 alone, a wolf pack consisting of eight U-boats sank seventeen Allied ships in a thirty-five-ship convoy. Five of the U-boats in the pack stayed in the hunt and were rewarded the very next day with the sighting of another convoy. These U-boats sank fourteen of the forty-five ships in that convoy. Later that night, another convoy came into view leading to seven more victims. In a three-day period, the Germans sank thirty-eight ships without the loss of a single U-boat.[40] The situation for Allied shipping was just as grim in the months ahead. From November 1940 through March 1941, U-boats took out 180 ships. Germany's surface ships sank an additional ninety ships.[41] The year 1941 proved to be the worst of the war for the Royal Navy.[42] Thus, the German invasion scare of May and June 1940 inadvertently had the beneficial effect of encouraging the British to ship the bulk of its wealth before Germany's Happy Time.

The sad fate of specific treasure ships also suggests how badly things could have gone for the Allied ships if the most valuable shipments of the summer of 1940 had occurred just months later. The story here is also a reminder of the daily peril experienced by Allied ships during the war. The Dutch passenger ship *Volendam*, for example, carried roughly £55,000 in gold from Britain to New York in June 1940. Two months later, however, the ship was torpedoed by U-60 near Northern Ireland. The *Volendam* carried no gold on this trip, but among its passengers were some three hundred children—all of whom survived. According to a twenty-year-old British seaman on board, the children took the experience in stride. "I saw British pluck at the age of five," he said. "One would have thought that boys and girls, roused from their beds, rushed up on deck and passed into lifeboats would have been afraid. What did these 'kids' do? They sang 'Roll out the barrel' and kept on singing it until they were safely on board rescue ships." In less than two hours, the children and other passengers were safely transferred to rescue vessels.[43]

In June 1940 the British cargo ship *Sulairia* successfully delivered over £1 million in gold to Montréal. While en route to the same destination on September 25, 1940—but this time carrying general cargo—the ship was torpedoed and sunk by U-43 near Ireland.[44] Sailing from South Africa, the British merchant ship *Port Gisborne* delivered £500,000 worth of gold to Canada in 1940, but sank on October 11, 1940, after being torpedoed by U-48.[45] The British cargo ship *Manchester Brigade* suffered a similar fate. The ship had made at least two gold runs between May and July 1940. In late September 1940, however, near the start of its journey from Britain to Montréal, the vessel was torpedoed and sunk by U-137.[46]

The *Empress of Britain*, the liner that returned the King and Queen to Britain after their North American tour in the spring of 1939, carried roughly £3 million in gold to North America at the outbreak of the war. In late October 1940, it sank after first being bombed by a German Focke-Wulf aircraft and then torpedoed by U-32.[47]

Despite the losses later in 1940, an extended delay in sending the largest shipments of gold and securities would not necessarily have doomed Britain's chances. Karl Dönitz' hopes for a fleet of three hundred U-boats never materialized. By the time the U-boat fleet came close to that target, Britain's ability to build merchant ships and convoy escort ships had increased, and the United States was a full partner in the war. In fact, at the very start of the war, the top leadership in the Kriegsmarine had serious doubts about Germany's ability to deal a fatal blow to the Allies' North Atlantic supply lines. Erich Raeder was particularly pessimistic about his country's chances:

> Today, the war against England and France broke out, the war which, according to the Fuehrer's previous assertion, we had no need to expect before about 1944. . . . As far as the Navy is concerned, obviously it is in no way adequately equipped for the great struggle with Great Britain. . . . The

submarine arm is still much too weak . . . to have any decisive effect on the war. The surface forces, moreover, are so inferior in number and strength to those of the British Fleet that, even at full strength, they can do no more than show that they know how to die gallantly.[48]

For his part, Karl Dönitz wrote on the first day of the war: "With 22 [oceangoing U-boats] and a prospective increase of one to two boats a month, I am incapable of undertaking efficacious measures against England."[49] Dönitz must also have doubted his country's prospects knowing that from September 1939 to June 1940, German shipyards couldn't build more than two U-boats a month, and only thirteen of the twenty new subs were capable of operations in the Atlantic.[50]

A postponement in the largest shipments of June and July by several months would have also allowed Britain to build much better antisubmarine capabilities—which it did. In addition, British warships that were out of commission as a result of fighting in the Norway campaign were eventually repaired. New ships, including corvettes and antisubmarine trawlers, were added as well. The British also gained (after drawn-out negotiations with the Americans) the use of fifty World War I–era U.S. destroyers. These and other developments helped push U-boat operations farther to the west of the British Isles. In the wide expanses of the Atlantic, U-boats had a harder time finding ships sailing independently or in convoy.

Conditions for Britain improved in other ways as well. First, in August 1940, the Germans were no longer able to decipher British naval communications.[51] Second, the weather also contributed to the British cause in late 1940. On a typical day, U-boats managed to spot four convoys but poor weather prevented wolf-pack operations.[52]

———————

Did the history of World War II pivot on the safe passage of the ships transferring the wealth of the British Empire to North America? An affirmative answer requires considerable qualification. First, the outcome of World War II hinged on many long-term trends, the decisions and actions of specific individuals, and unexpected developments as the war unfolded. Isolating the success of Britain's financial flight as the ultimate determinant of the war would thus exaggerate its importance. Second, if we consider the consequences of Britain's decision *not* to authorize its most valuable shipments in the summer of 1940, the paths of alternate history are not clear or obvious. If, for example, Britain had not sent the *Revenge* convoy in July 1940—and its vast quantity of gold and securities had stayed in Britain—history would not have changed drastically. The main impetus for the June and July 1940 shipments was to keep the wealth of the British Empire out of German hands. Since Germany never invaded Britain, the un-evacuated gold and securities would have remained safe after all.

Nevertheless, the possible failure of the operation is just as relevant to history as the operation's actual success. Depending on the level of detail of German information about the special shipments, Britain's financial situation could have deteriorated so badly that it might have been unable to finance the war. In the context of American isolationism and Germany's seemingly unstoppable march through Europe, the bleak situation of mid-1940 could have been much worse. The potential consequences for the rest of Western Europe, the Soviet Union, and even the Americas could have been devastating.

13

Credit

By 1944, after five years of horrific warfare, the German military was beginning to buckle. That year much of Britain's remaining marketable assets were housed in North America while the Allies—led by the United States and Britain in the west and the Soviet Union in the east—began to finish off the Germans. Hitler's last major offensive to salvage something out of the war had failed by mid-January 1945 as the Allies won what became known as the Battle of the Bulge. In the weeks ahead, Allied forces then closed in on Germany from both sides, liberating city after city from German control. By mid-April, the Allies were in Berlin, and by the end of the month, both Mussolini and Hitler were dead. Following Hitler's suicide, Karl Dönitz became the new and last leader of the Third Reich. Within days, he accepted the futility of continuing the war, and on May 7, he agreed to an unconditional surrender. British prime minister Winston Churchill and U.S. president Harry Truman declared May 8, 1945, Victory in Europe Day, or V-E Day.

The British could now prepare for the repatriation of the remaining assets they had so painstakingly transferred to North America. Britain's gold took separate paths as the war came to a close. The available records do not indicate how much of the gold sent to North America was returned toward the end or right after the war. A good deal of it had been spent to pay for the war, while some remained in North America. Portions of the gold made it back to Britain, although the records of these transfers are incomplete. According to historian Nigel Pickford, HMS *Indomitable* carried twenty tons of gold back to Britain in April 1944 and HMS *Manners* returned with thirteen bags of gold coins in December of the same year.[1] From then on, to the relief of all involved, the returning gold faced no serious risks.[2]

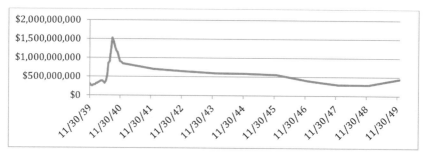

FIG. 13.1. Bank of England gold held in safekeeping in Canada, from near the start of the war to 1949. The values are in U.S. dollars with the price of gold at $35 an ounce. *The data, compiled by the author, are derived from the following Bank of Canada sources: "Gold Held in Safekeeping for the Bank of England," File A18-17-9 B of E.—Gold in Safekeeping at B. of C. Statements 1939–1944; Gold Held in Safekeeping Bank of England, 1939–1946, File 580-44-14A, Vol. 3908-4612; and File A18-17-9 B of E.—Gold in Safekeeping at B. of C. Statements 1945–1951.*

Of far greater concern to the Treasury and the Bank of England was the safe return of the financial securities.[3] Unlike most of the gold, the privately owned stocks and bonds had been requisitioned by the government near the start of the war. The return of the securities would cap the successful operation and allow Britain's financial system to return to normal—albeit in a severely weakened condition.

On September 24, 1944, D. E. Johns of the Bank of England told Ernest Rowe-Dutton of the British Treasury that the value of the securities was "still by any ordinary standards, astronomical and the loss of even one box beyond contemplation." Johns estimated that the securities—some 5 million documents weighing close to seventy-five tons— would fill up roughly 4,500 to 5,000 cubic feet of cargo space and suggested that "a King's ship"—one from the Royal Navy—should be used to ferry the securities to Britain. Johns was implying that all of the securities should return on a single ship.[4]

The Bank of England, the Admiralty, and the Treasury began final preparations for the return of the securities from the UKSD in Montréal. On June 16, 1945, Rowe-Dutton informed F. W. Mattershead at the Admiralty that he should prepare to ship more than a thousand boxes of securities. The next day, Johns wrote to Rowe-Dutton with more precise calculations:

Estimated number of boxes: 1,150
Dimensions of each box: 29" X 14.5" X 14.5"
Est. weight of each box: approx 150 lbs.
Est. total weight: 75 tons
Est. volume: 3,950 cu. ft.[5]

Meanwhile, Alexander Craig and officials at the British Treasury established July 9 as the date to notify the public of the operation's closure. Major newspapers ran the following announcement on that date:

United Kingdom Security Deposit

Notice is hereby given that the United Kingdom Security Deposit, 62 Sun Life Building, Montréal, will close for the deposit of securities on the evening of Wednesday, 15th August, 1945. A. S. Craig, Manager.[6]

To carry the securities back to Britain, the Admiralty chose HMS *Leander*, a light cruiser under the command of Capt. Robert Jocelyn Oliver Otway-Ruthven. Built in 1933 for New Zealand, the ship had an impressive top speed of 32 knots. The *Leander* had last seen action in July 1943 as part of an American task force under the command of Rear Adm. Walden L. Ainsworth. (Coincidentally, another ship in that task force was USS *Honolulu*, the vessel that carried $25 million in gold from England to New York in response to one of the first major war scares back in 1938.) While engaged in the Pacific, the *Leander* was damaged and required minor repairs. The ship eventually sailed to the Boston Navy Yard in Charlestown for a major refit. The *Leander* remained there until late August 1945, when it was finally deemed ready for service.[7]

In Montréal, Craig and the other employees of the UKSD began packing up the financial documents that had not been sold during the war. When everything was ready, Craig destroyed the secret codebooks.[8] On August 31, a fleet of trucks delivered the boxes of securities to the train station for transit on board a Canadian Pacific Express train to the docks. Harbor police stopped all traffic along the waterfront near the *Leander* at the East End dock. Passes were required for anyone trying to get into the sealed-off area. Newspapers devoted little space to the *Leander*'s purpose but did mention that its consignment consisted of over a thousand boxes of British securities from the vault in the Sun Life Building. Naval authorities would only say that all of the unusual activity was of a "confidential nature."[9]

On September 2, 1945—the day of Japan's formal surrender on board USS *Missouri* in Tokyo Bay—the *Leander* and its cargo set sail for Britain. Accompanying the securities were Harold Forrest and Harold Kent of the Bank of England. The two men—having lived in Canada since that frantic month of July 1940—were, like the securities, finally heading home.[10] Harry Higson, a British maintenance worker on board the *Leander*, provided a rare description of the momentous trip in an interview in 2005: "When they'd finished repairing the *Leander* we were all coming back home on that ship and we sailed up the St. Lawrence to Montréal. . . . [We picked] up diplomats, some crown jewels, and bullion." With numerous Mounted Police about, Higson recalled, it was "quite an occasion."[11] Higson, unfortunately, made no reference to the securities. Either he hadn't read the local newspapers or his memory had faltered.

Higson's reference to the *Leander* carrying "some crown jewels" is as tantalizing as it is controversial. According to some accounts, Britain's crown jewels were housed in the vaults of the Bank of Canada in Ottawa or in the Sun Life Building in Montréal. Even today, some of Canada's tourist outlets in Montréal, and on the Internet, make the same assertion. There appears to be little truth to the claim, however. According to Harold Kent, who helped manage the UKSD, it was "absolute nonsense" that the British crown jewels were held in the vaults of the Sun Life Building. Kent believed "that the Crown jewels never got further from London than Chiselhurst, which is about 20 miles from London. There are very deep caves in that region. . . . I suspect the Crown jewels were kept there. . . . At any rate I believe I have good reason for being convinced that they never did leave England."[12] David Mansur, deputy governor of the Bank of Canada at the time, said that he had no knowledge of the location of Britain's crown jewels.[13] Asked in the 1950s about the rumor about the crown jewels, several other banking officials also rejected the claim, including C. E. Campbell, who was in direct charge of the Bank of Canada's vault, and John P. Melvin, the Bank of Canada's deputy chief of the Currency Division.[14]

The *Leander* made an uneventful journey across the Atlantic, arriving at Rosyth in eastern Scotland. According to Bank of England historian Elizabeth Hennessy, over the weekend of September 15 and 16, fifty representatives of twenty of Britain's larger banks and two hundred Bank of England staff checked about 75 percent of the securities.

These securities were then delivered to the "owner" banks. Through the following week, thirty-three other banks took delivery of the rest of the securities. "The whole of this gigantic task," wrote Hennessy, "from packing to redelivery, was accomplished within a seven week period, eliciting a letter from the Chancellor to the Governor thanking the Bank for its 'hard work and ingenuity.'"[15]

<hr/>

Thanks to advances in technology, the physical transfer of such fantastic portions of a great power's wealth is unlikely to be needed, or successful, again. Modern national economies, and indeed the global economy in general, rely extensively on electronic transfers of money. In addition, if a great power were to physically transport a comparable share of its national wealth today, modern technology would pose a daunting array of new challenges for the operation's secrecy. The planners of Britain's gold and securities shipments during World War II did not have to contend with satellite technology, twenty-four-hour cable television, phones with cameras, handheld video cameras, devilishly clever computer hackers, drones, and pro-transparency organizations like WikiLeaks.[16]

When it counted most, and during Britain's bleakest phase of World War II, thousands of individuals, of all ranks and from all walks of life, helped safeguard the transit of Britain's liquid assets. Their efforts are reminiscent of the sentiments of the sixteenth-century English sea captain Sir Francis Drake, paraphrased by HMS *Emerald*'s captain Augustus Agar: "Everyone must pull together on the rope, the Mariners to haul and draw with the Gentlemen and the Gentlemen with the Mariners."[17]

War stories both real and fictional often revolve around heroic figures—individuals known for their decisive political choices, military exploits, noble sacrifices, cunning espionage, or physical and mental endurance under seemingly unbearable strain. Much of the success of Britain's financial flight depended on a different sort of figure. Many of those who helped Britain survive the first harrowing months of the war and who helped protect the wealth of the British Empire were simply men and women sitting behind desks. We do not call such people heroes for authorizing a particular ship to carry a given amount of cargo to Halifax, Vancouver, or New York. However, it is thanks to their efforts that Britain managed to hang on financially and allow the country to prosecute the war until U.S. Lend-Lease aid materialized in 1941. The civil servants and bankers, as well as those who sailed to and from North America, the truck drivers, the security guards, the rail employees, and the file clerks all played vital roles in the success of the operation. Without ever asking for credit, they all helped save Britain and the broader Allied cause.

Appendix 1
Code Names and Nicknames

Many of the published references to Britain's World War II financial transfers refer to the scheme as Operation Fish. This nickname derives not from actual use during the war but from Alfred Draper's 1979 book of the same name. Despite the occasional references to "fish" or "fish trains," no code name was used at the secret meetings held in Allied political, banking, and military circles.[1] Instead, the British and Canadians used "fish" more as an occasional nickname. Moreover, "fish" was only one of several expressions used to refer to British wealth.[2] "Fish" was actually more likely to have been used as a code word for subjects unrelated to gold or securities. "Fish" was a term used in connection with the decryption of German messages sent on a non-Morse cipher machine called a Geheimschreiber (secret writer). British and American cryptologists also used "fish" as a description for Sturgeon and Tunny cipher machines. Among Germans, "fish" (and "eels") was also the nickname for torpedoes.[3]

Another unofficial nickname specifically related to the treasure shipments was "Bundles from Britain,"[4] although this expression does not appear to have been used often and it typically referred to things other than gold. For example, some of the Canadian staff of the UKSD used the expression to refer only to the securities.[5] *Time* magazine also used the expression "Bundles from Britain" with a short statement in its February 24, 1941, edition: much of "Wall Street buying power has been absorbed by the liquidation of Britain's US securities. For these unloadings Wall Street had a new name last week: Bundles from Britain."[6] The expression is actually a play on words from Bundles For Britain, an American civilian organization founded in early 1940 to provide nonmilitary aid to the British.

In short, those involved in the transfer of British wealth to North America in World War II did not use code names in any systematic way. In the operation's many encrypted messages, bland, bureaucratic wording such as "special shipment" was used far more often than "fish."

Appendix 2

Tracking Ships and Shipments

Precise information about many ships that carried British wealth to North America and the value of their consignments is probably lost to history because of a combination of security precautions and inadequate record keeping in Britain and Canada. The two most valuable sources are the British Admiralty and the research of Nigel Pickford. The Admiralty's list of gold shipments was originally sent in 1955 to Leland Stowe, who had asked the Admiralty for any information it could provide regarding the British gold shipments to North America. Until then, no one outside a select few knew exactly how extensive the operation had been, and no such list was likely to have existed outside Admiralty offices. Upon receiving the Admiralty's ten-page document, Stowe wrote across the top of the first page that the information was "Like a gift from the gods." The Admiralty's letter to Stowe, dated July 23, 1955, is among the Leland Stowe Papers at the Wisconsin Historical Society in Madison. The Admiralty's list does not appear in Stowe's *Reader's Digest* article of that year,[1] but it does appear, unattributed, in the appendixes of Alfred Draper's *Operation Fish*.[2]

The Pickford list, derived from documents at the National Archives in London and elsewhere, can be found in *Lost Treasure Ships of the 20th Century* or online at http://www.defence.gov.au/sydneyii/EXH/EXH.138.0111.pdf.[3]

Unfortunately, neither the Admiralty's 1955 list nor the Pickford list is complete. Several factors explain gaps or discrepancies, although most generally fall under the umbrella of organizational complexity. Sometimes, a gold-laden ship would sail for one city but end up in another. For example, according to documents at the Bank of Canada, two shipments in March 1940 went from England to Montréal, but the gold was then "diverted" to New York.[4] Another complication is that it is unclear whether the Admiralty consistently referred to the ship's destination city or the gold's destination city. In addition, sometimes the ports of departure are provided on one list but not the other; sometimes the exact amount of gold differs; sometimes the departure dates are specific while others are not.

Some shipments do not appear on the Admiralty list because Stowe did not request information about gold shipments before 1939. Stowe's oversight is understandable because—as the first researcher to try to solve the puzzle of Britain's financial flight—he did not realize how prewar political tensions had driven Britain's initial special shipments. Thus, Stowe (and by extension, Draper) missed, for example, the shipments made by the American cruisers *Nashville* and *Honolulu* in October 1938. Each of these ships delivered $25 million in gold from southern England to New York.[5] Pickford's list does not include these shipments either. Also, the Admiralty and Pickford lists refer only to official (Bank of England) gold transfers and do not include private gold transfers involving commercial banks.

Information that supplements the Admiralty and Pickford lists comes from declassified documents from the Bank of Canada and the Library and Archives Canada, as well as information from the Bank of England and the National Archives in London. Additional information is derived from some of the sources listed in this book's bibliography, such as Karl Dönitz's *Memoirs: Ten Years and Twenty Days* and articles from the *New York Times*.

The following websites also proved helpful for some, but not all, of the ships:

U-boat.net: http://www.u-boat.net and, in particular, http://www.uboat .net/allies/merchants/

The Ships List: http://www.theshipslist.com/ships/lines/cunard.shtml

Naval History: http://www.naval-history.net/WW2BritishLossesby Name3.htm

U-boat Archive: http://www.uboatarchive.net/index.html

Norway Heritage: Hands Across the Sea: http://www.norwayheritage.com/

Battleships-cruisers.co.uk: http://www.battleships-cruisers.co.uk/ merchant_navy_losses.htm

Warsailors.com: http://www.warsailors.com/freefleet/shipindex.html

Cofepow: http://www.cofepow.org.uk/pages/ships_list.html

Roll of Honour (Ministry of Defence): http://www.roll-of-honou
MerchantNavy/index.html

American Merchant Ships Sunk in WWII: http://www.armed-gu
.com/sunk.html[6]

HyperWar: A Hyptertext History of the Second World War: http:/
.ibiblio.org/hyperwar/index.html

Warships of World War II: http://www.warshipsww2.eu/shipsph
.php?language=E&id=20058

Notes

Preface

1. Alfred Draper, *Operation Fish: The Race to Save Europe's Wealth, 1939–1945* (Don Mills, Ontario, Canada: General Publishing Co. Limited, 1979), 148.

2. Augustus Agar, *Footprints in the Sea* (London: Evans Bros., 1959). An exception was midshipmen's journals kept by young officers in training.

3. Winston Churchill, *The Second World War*, vol. 2, *Their Finest Hour* (Boston: Houghton Mifflin, 1949), 398.

4. Robert Self, ed., *The Neville Chamberlain Diary Letters*, vol. 4, *The Downing Street Years, 1934–1940* (Aldershot, England: Ashgate, 2005); Chamberlain Archives, Birmingham, NC 7/11/32 1-304.

5. Colville was aware of Britain's precarious financial conditions but was apparently not informed about the shipments of gold and securities. Colville served as secretary to Chamberlain from 1939 to 1940 and to Churchill from 1940 to 1941 and—after a stint in as a pilot in the Royal Air Force Volunteer Reserve—from 1943 to 1945. Colville also served as assistant secretary to Prime Minister Clement Attlee in 1945. The diaries are housed in the Churchill Archives Center in Cambridge. Much of the work is found in John Colville, *The Fringes of Power: Downing Street Diaries, 1939–1955* (London: Phoenix, 2005), 213.

6. David Dilks, ed., *The Diaries of Sir Alexander Cadogan, O.M.: 1938–1945* (New York: Putnam, 1972).

7. Letter from Sidney Perkins to Leland Stowe, June 6, 1955; and Leland Stowe, "Note to RD Editors," June 15, 1955, Leland Stowe Papers, Wisconsin Historical Society.

8. Draper, *Operation Fish*, 357.

9. Oliver Lascelles, "Memoirs of Commander Oliver Lascelles," Lascelles, Commander O MBE OSC RN 99/75/1 and MBE DSC RN 99/71/1, Imperial War Museum, London. For another account, see Jack Cockrill, "Wartime Service in the Navy," WW2 People's War, BBC, accessed September 20, 2011, http://www.bbc.co.uk/ww2peopleswar/stories/19/a3837819.shtml. A similarly low priority given to gold shipments is found in Ivy Chapman's account, "Married to the Navy," WW2 People's War, BBC, accessed September 20, 2011, http://www.bbc.co.uk/ww2peopleswar/stories/47/a8652747.shtml.

10. The large number of key events during the war also may explain why Ronald Lewin

does not include the failure of Germany to detect Britain's operation in his book *Hitler's Mistakes* (New York: Morrow), 1984.

11. Leland Stowe, "The Secret Voyage of Britain's Treasure," *Reader's Digest*, November 1955, 17–26.

12. Draper, *Operation Fish*.

13. An exception is the chapter "Churchill's Amazing Gamble" in William B. Breuer, *Top Secret Tales of World War II* (New York: Wiley, 2000), 59–63. The chapter, however, relies heavily on Stowe's article in *Reader's Digest*.

14. Thomas Parrish, ed., *The Simon and Schuster Encyclopedia of World War II* (New York: Simon and Schuster, 1978); I. C. B. Dear and M. R. D. Foot, eds., *The Oxford Companion to World War II* (Oxford: Oxford University Press, 1995).

15. Bernard Ireland, *The Battle of the Atlantic* (Annapolis, MD: Naval Institute Press, 2003); Marc Milner, *Battle of the Atlantic* (St. Catherines, ON: Vanwell Pub., 2003); David Fairbank White, *Bitter Ocean: The Battle of the Atlantic, 1939–1945* (New York: Simon and Schuster, 2006). The operation is also neglected by Richard Overy, *Why the Allies Won* (New York: W. W. Norton, 1995).

16. Thomas Parrish, *To Keep the British Isles Afloat: FDR's Men in Churchill's London, 1941* (New York: Smithsonian Books/HarperCollins, 2009).

17. Peter Fleming, *Operation Sea Lion: the Projected Invasion of England in 1940, an Account of the German Preparations and the British Countermeasures* (New York: Simon and Schuster, 1957), 95.

18. David Lampe, *The Last Ditch* (New York: Putnam, 1968); Norman Moss, *Nineteen Weeks: America, Britain, and the Fateful Summer of 1940* (Boston: Houghton Mifflin, 2003); and John Lukacs, *The Duel: The Eighty-Day Struggle between Churchill and Hitler* (New Haven, CT: Yale University Press, 2001). In addition, David Irving includes one sentence on the subject: "The transatlantic incandescence in 1940 was the glow of Europe's Gold, as it was carted to America by cruiser and battleship." Most of the gold was actually first "carted" to Canada, not the United States; the fact that securities were also shipped is not mentioned. David Irving, *Churchill's War: The Struggle for Power* (Maryborough, Australia: Veritas, 1987).

19. David M. Kennedy, ed., *The Library of Congress World War II Companion* (New York: Simon and Schuster, 2007), 86.

20. "Incidentally, as a precaution, the gold and dollar securities were being moved in June to Canada and two-thirds of the gold was there by the end of that month." H. Duncan Hall, *North American Supply* (London: Her Majesty's Stationery Office, 1955), 245–46.

21. Duncan McDowall, "Earmarked Gold in Canada 1935–56," in *Due Diligence: A Report on the Bank of Canada's Handling of Foreign Gold During World War II* (Ottawa: Bank of Canada, November 27, 1997), accessed September 19, 2001, http://www.bankofcanada.ca/wp-content/uploads/2010/07/gold97-4.pdf; and Elizabeth Hennessy, *A Domestic History of the Bank of England, 1930–1960* (Cambridge: Cambridge University Press, 1992).

22. The staff at the Naval War Museum and the Royal Marines Museum in Portsmouth in southern England found no information directly related to the operation.

1. Shoring Up Support

1. "The Press: Royal Press," *Time*, May 29, 1939; and "Canada: Royal Visit," *Time*, May 29, 1939.

2. "Canada: Royal Visit," *Time*, May 29, 1939.

3. Ibid.

4. "Foreign News: Isn't It Wonderful?" *Time*, June 5, 1939.

5. Chuck Davis, "A History of Metropolitan Vancouver," accessed May 7, 2013, http://www.vancouverhistory.ca/archives_1939.htm.

6. Moss, *Nineteen Weeks*, 50.

7. Peter Pigott, *Royal Transport: An Inside Look at the History of Royal Travel* (Toronto: Dundurn Group, 2005), 45; *Ottawa Citizen*, June 9, 1939.

8. "The Presidency: Here Come the British," *Time*, June 19, 1939; and David Reynolds, "FDR's Foreign Policy and the British Royal Visit to the U.S.A., 1939," *The Historian* 45, no. 4 (August 23, 1983): 461–72.

9. Transcript of a conversation between Bolton and the deputy governor of the Bank of Canada, April 14, 1939, File A18-17-2 1936-1945, Gold Earmarked for B. of E. Arrangements Shipped from B. of C. to NY, Bank of Canada Archives.

10. "Behind the Diary: Politics, Themes, and Events from King's Life: The Royal Tour of 1939," Library and Archives Canada, accessed January 14, 2013, http://www.collectionscanada.gc.ca/king/023011-1070.06-e.html.

11. McDowall, "Earmarked Gold," 14–15; and William A. B. Douglas and Brereton Greenhous, *Out of the Shadows: Canada in the Second World War* (Toronto: Oxford University Press, 1977), 14.

12. Disunion referred to not only the French-English split but also the east-west division within Canada that was exacerbated by the Great Depression. J. L. Granatstein, *Canada's War: The Politics of the Mackenzie King Government, 1939–1945* (Toronto: Oxford University Press, 1975), 5.

13. King was prime minister from 1921 to 1930 and again from 1935 to 1948. See Chamberlain's letter to his sister Ida, June 20, 1937, and the letter to his sister Hilda, January 13, 1940, in Self, *Downing Street Years*, 255.

14. Douglas and Greenhous, *Out of the Shadows*, 235–36.

15. Joseph P. Lash, *Roosevelt and Churchill 1939–1941: The Partnership That Saved the West* (New York: Norton, 1976), 63; "Behind the Diary," Library and Archives Canada; Draper, *Operation Fish*, 15–16.

16. David Reynolds, *The Creation of the Anglo-American Alliance, 1937–41: A Study in Competitive Co-operation* (Chapel Hill: University of North Carolina Press, 1981), 43.

17. Letter from M. F. Hepburn, premier of Ontario to King George VI, May 24, 1939, Reel 3744, Library and Archives Canada.

18. Letter from W. L. Mackenzie King to Sir Alexander Hardinge, private secretary to His Majesty the King, August 20, 1939, Reel 3744, Library and Archives Canada.

19. Douglas and Greenhous, *Out of the Shadows*, 20.

20. W. L. M. King Papers, Correspondence, June 12, 1940, Microfilm reel C-4566, image 239203, Library and Archives Canada.

21. "The British Royal Visit: June 7–12, 1939," Franklin D. Roosevelt Presidential Library and Museum, accessed January 14, 2013, http://docs.fdrlibrary.marist.edu/royalv .html.

22. Reynolds, "FDR's Foreign Policy," 464.

23. B. J. C. McKercher, *Transition of Power: Britain's Loss of Global Pre-eminence to the United States 1930–1945* (Cambridge: Cambridge University Press, 1999).

24. Bank of England folder C43/240 contains a set of receipts, one of which states, "Please write off from the account of HM Treasury 815501.115 ozs fine 2026 gold bars for special export, part of £30.000.000." The Bank of Canada registered the delivery on May 18, 1939, at the value of $141.4 million. "Bank of England: Gold in Safekeeping—1939," File A18-17, Bank of Canada Archives. The $151 million figure is noted in the July 7, 1939, "Secret and Personal" letter from C. W. Dixon of the Dominions Office in London to Sigismund Waley of the British Treasury, T 236/721, National Archives. See also Draper, *Operation Fish*, Appendix I, 358.

25. The consignment consisted of over 3.4 million troy ounces of gold. The contemporary dollar value is based on gold worth $1,300 an ounce.

26. McDowall, "Earmarked Gold," 10.

27. Ibid.

28. Osborne to Siepmann, May 11, 1938, Bank of Canada file A18-17 as quoted in McDowall, "Earmarked Gold," 10.

29. Gordon to Bolton, Bank of England, Folder C43/240, May 22, 1939.

30. Haskell added that the "battle-cruiser HMS *Repulse* was to have accompanied this trio, but the Admiralty felt that she should not leave home waters and was subsequently withdrawn." George Purkiss Haskell, "D'You Hear There?" Haskell, G P 94/6/1, Imperial War Museum, London. Emphasis in the original.

31. "Sir Otto Niemeyer: Purpose of American Visit," *Sydney Morning Herald*, January 22, 1937.

32. T 236/721, April 27, 1939, National Archives; and Folder C43/240, Bank of England.

33. Letter from Basil Catterns to Sir Frederick Phillips regarding the May 6, 1940, sailing involving the *Repulse*, *Southampton*, and *Glasgow*, April 5, 1939, T 236/721, National Archives.

34. Based on a 1939 Anglo-French Staff analysis quoted in Terry Hughes and John Costello, *The Battle of the Atlantic* (New York: Dial Press, 1977), 9.

35. Bullitt, in turn, told FDR that, in the opinion of the U.S. military attachés in Paris, "They are not sure that the British and French can hold out until trans-Atlantic production can be brought into the struggle. . . . [I]f the Neutrality Act remains in its present form, France and England will lose." Parrish, *To Keep the British Isles Afloat*, 78.

36. Hughes and Costello, *Battle of the Atlantic*, 9.

37. Ireland, *Battle of the Atlantic*, vi, 219; Ian Friel, *Maritime History of Britain and Ireland* (London: British Museum Press, 2003), 245–50.

38. McDowall, "Earmarked Gold," 12.

39. Siepmann to Towers, March 31, 1938, Bank of Canada file A18-17, as quoted in ibid., 9–10.

40. Letter from Towers to Siepmann, April 4, 1938; letter from Norman to Towers, April 1938; cable from the Bank of England to Towers, April 27, 1938; letter from the secretary to the chief of Currency Division, May 6, 1938; and letter from Osborne of the Bank of Canada to Siepmann, May 10, 1938, all of which are in File A18-17-2 1936–1945, Gold Earmarked for B. of E. Arrangements Shipped from B. of C. to NY, Bank of Canada Archives. See also the letter from the secretary to the chief of Currency Divisions, Bank of Canada, Ottawa, May 3, 1938, File 580-42-14D, Banking Operations, Bank of Canada Archives.

41. Norman to Towers, April 19, 1939, Bank of Canada file A18-17, as quoted in, McDowall, "Earmarked Gold," 10.

42. Letter from the Foreign Department of the Federal Reserve Bank in New York to the Bank of Canada, September 21, 1938, File 580-42-14D "Bank of England 1938 1939," and File 135-6 Gold Under Earmark Abroad 1938, Bank of Canada Archives.

43. Interoffice correspondence from the secretary to chief of the Currency Division, for April 19 and 20, 1939, and May 2, 1939, File 580-42-14D "Bank of England 1938 1939," Bank of Canada Archives; memo from chief of the Currency Division at the Bank of Canada for the Bank's Control Ledger, June 3, 1939, Bank of Canada Archives; and the ledger, June 5, 1939, File 580-42-14D, Banking Operations, Bank of Canada Archives. By the end of 1938, the Bank of England had 10,219 bars of gold (4,087,731 fine ounces) worth slightly more than $143 million. McDowall, "Earmarked Gold," 11.

44. Chamberlain letter to "My dear Ida," May 7, 1939, in Self, *Downing Street Years*, 413.

45. Anthony Martienssen, *Hitler and His Admirals* (New York: Dutton, 1949), 15.

46. No record has been found of the British contemplating airlifting their wealth to North America; security focused on the ocean passage across the North Atlantic. Government discussions about the air option were most likely absent because Britain's air transport capabilities were not up to the task in the first year of the war. Trans-Atlantic aviation had improved in the interwar years but was far from mature at the outbreak of the war. Some commercial services—with circuitous routing—existed in 1938 and 1939, but these were not the years for enhancing a preexisting air transportation fleet for the Atlantic; this was a time for trial and proving flights between Europe and New York. Given the importance of the financial cargo, Britain also could not yet sufficiently rely on its meteorological service—an important impediment given the frequently terrible weather over the North Atlantic. See David Beaty, *The Water Jump* (London: Secker & Warburg, 1976); Carl Christie, "World War II: Ferry Command," *Canada: A Country by Consent*, accessed February 16, 2013, http://www.canadahistoryproject.ca/1939-45/1939-45-09-ferry-command.html; Royal Air Force, "The Second World War 1939–45," chap. 3 in *A Short History of the Royal Air Force*, accessed February 10, 2013, http://www.raf.mod.uk/history/shorthistoryoftheroyal airforce.cfm; and Alan Wykes, *Air Atlantic: A History of Civil and Military Transatlantic Flying* (New York: David White, 1968).

2. For the Sake of the Realm

1. CAB 24/287, reference 0032, July 3, 1939, National Archives.

2. CAB 23/100, reference 0004, July 5, 1939, National Archives.

3. Ibid.

4. Draper, *Operation Fish*, 153, 247.

5. Stowe, "Secret Voyage," 18. On February 11, 1940, the Bank of England sent a cipher telegram to Lord Lothian. The draft of communiqué read as follows: "Arrangements were made on the outbreak of war for registration with the Bank of England of UK Residents-holding of foreign securities in particular United States dollar securities. The owners of these securities have been able to proceed with sales on obtaining a form of permission from the Bank of England which has been necessary for the purpose of keeping up to date the Bank's records of holdings of these securities. The next step, now being taken, is vesting of a certain number of United States dollar securities in His Majesty's Treasury. A vesting order has now been issued and is made public today. Further vesting orders may be issued from time to time." Folder G1/46, Bank of England.

6. Moss, *Nineteen Weeks*, 27, 34.

7. Keith Feiling, *The Life of Neville Chamberlain* (London: Macmillan, 1970), 320.

8. John F. Kennedy, *Why England Slept* (New York: W. Funk, 1940), as noted in Robert J. Caputi, *Neville Chamberlain and Appeasement* (Cranbury, NJ: Associated University Presses, 2000), 32, 230.

9. John Keegan, *The Second World War* (New York: Viking Penguin, 1990), 40.

10. Letter from Wilson Carlile, C.H., D.D. to Chamberlain, February 7, 1939, Chamberlain Archives, Birmingham, 7/11/32 1-304.

11. Joseph S. Nye, *Understanding International Conflicts: An Introduction to Theory and History*, 5th ed. (New York: Pearson/Longman, 2005), 861; U.S. Department of Justice, "WWI Casualty and Death Tables," PBS, accessed January 15, 2013, http://www.pbs.org/greatwar/resources/casdeath_pop.html.

12. William Douglas Home, ed., *The Prime Ministers: Stories and Anecdotes from Number 10* (London: W. H. Allen, 1987), 221.

13. Hadley's comment was made in a letter to the *Sunday Times*. Chamberlain Archives, Birmingham, England, NC 7/11/32 1-304. Nearly fifty years later, Robert Kee concluded that Chamberlain was neither outwitted nor duped by Hitler at Munich; he acted as an honorable man of peace. Keith Robbins drew a similar conclusion and emphasized *underlying* causes (the decline of the British Empire) more than *immediate* causes (Chamberlain's influence on British foreign policy). He described appeasement as "neither stupid nor wicked: it was merely inevitable." Keith Robbins, *Appeasement* (London: Basil Blackwell, 1988), 6; Robert Kee, *Munich: The Eleventh Hour* (London: H. Hamilton, 1988), 107; and Caputi, *Chamberlain and Appeasement*, chap. 9.

14. Regarding King's meeting with Hitler, High Commissioner Gerald Campbell is quoted in Granatstein, *Canada's War*, 4. See also Douglas and Greenhous, *Out of the Shadows*, 12.

15. "A Real Companion and Friend: The Diaries of William Lyon Mackenzie King," Library and Archives Canada, September 29, 1938, accessed January 20, 2013, http://www .collectionscanada.gc.ca/databases/king/index-e.html.

16. Letter of April 11, 1939, Chamberlain Archives, Birmingham, NC 7/11/32 1-304, 2nd box.

17. Richard Langworth, *Churchill by Himself: The Definitive Collection of Quotations* (New York: PublicAffairs, 2011), 4.

18. Letter of September 11, 1938, Kennedy, *World War II Companion*, 63–64.

19. Letter from Davidson to Chamberlain, July 5, 1939, Chamberlain Archives, Birmingham, NC 7/11/32 1-304.

20. Lukacs, *Duel*, 22. A similar description of Churchill is offered by John Colville (whose views would later change somewhat), Chamberlain's private secretary at the time. Colville, *Fringes of Power*, 54, 108.

21. William Manchester and Paul Reid, *The Last Lion: Winston Spencer Churchill*, vol. 3, *Defender of the Realm, 1940–1965* (Boston: Little, Brown, 2012), 50.

22. Donald Macintyre, *The Naval War against Hitler* (New York: Scribner, 1971), 48.

23. Other available ships included coastal patrol vessels and twenty-four sloops. Macintyre, *The Naval War against Hitler*, 57.

24. Stephen Broadberry and Peter Howlett, "The United Kingdom: 'Victory at All Costs,'" in *The Economics of World War II: Six Great Powers in International Comparison*, ed. Mark Harrison (Cambridge: Cambridge University Press, 1998), 58.

25. Robert Self, *Neville Chamberlain: A Biography* (Aldershot, England: Ashgate, 2006), 314. According to Chamberlain's private secretary, John Colville, Chamberlain said he was "sure Hitler was sincere at Munich, but [Chamberlain] changed his mind a few days later." Colville, *Fringes of Power*, 18.

26. Self, *Downing Street Years*, 48–49.

27. Chamberlain's letter to Ball is dated October 28, 1940. Regarding the ultimate merits of appeasement, Robert Self concludes that "of all the optimistic miscalculations of his political career, this unquestionably would be the greatest." Ibid. A consensus view of Britain's appeasement policy is elusive, even today. It was true that France and the Soviet Union were reluctant to defend Czechoslovakia without British help. In addition, members of the British Commonwealth—notably Canada, South Africa, and Australia— were not advocating a firm stand against Hitler. Moreover, the British economy was in poor shape, and the military of 1938 was far from prepared for all-out war against Germany.

28. Chamberlain Archives, Birmingham, NC 7/9/1-109.

29. Department of the Navy, "Nashville," Dictionary of American Naval Fighting Ships, accessed September 17, 2011, http://www.history.navy.mil/danfs/n2/nashville-ii.htm; and "Crews of Warship Honored for Record Gold Transport," *Los Angeles Times*, December 24, 1939.

30. "The Gold Movement," *New York Times*, August 23, 1939.

31. The description draws on Hennessy, *Bank of England*, 5–42.

32. Alma Arnall-Culliford, "54 Lombard Street," WW2 People's War, BBC, accessed September 17, 2011, http://www.bbc.co.uk/ww2peopleswar/stories/62/a3317762.shtml.

33. Hennessy, *Bank of England*, 11.

34. See the series of letters from the secretary in Ottawa to the chief of the Currency Division in Ottawa for August 24, 1939, September 2, 1939, September 7, 1939, and September 11, 1939. For the number of U-boats and their location prior to the start of hostilities, see Martienssen, *Hitler and His Admirals*, 18.

35. "The Transcript of Neville Chamberlain's Declaration of War," BBC Archive, accessed January 16, 2013, http://www.bbc.co.uk/archive/ww2outbreak/7957.shtml?page=txt.

36. Jochen Brennecke, *The Hunters and the Hunted: German U-Boats, 1939–1945* (New York: Norton, 1958), 9, 15.

37. Raymond Dutton, "What No Isambard? (A Sort of Autobiography)," Dutton R 85/49/1, Imperial War Museum, London, 26. See also "Private Papers of R Dutton," Imperial War Museum.

38. Agar, *Footprints in the Sea*, 236.

39. Colville, *Fringes of Power*, 3.

40. In addition, when the bombs started falling, the lions, tigers, polar bears, and full-grown apes were shut in their sleeping dens. Fleming notes that the only escapee was a zebra, which was later captured. When the bombing did commence, both the Monkey Hill and the Zebra House "received a direct hit, but the morale of the monkeys remained unaffected." Fleming, *Operation Sea Lion*, 99. See also "Invasion: Preview and Prevention," *Time*, June 3, 1940, accessed September 17, 2011, http://www.time.com/time/magazine/article/0,9171,789811,00.html.

41. "Great Britain: War Is Very Near," *Time*, September 4, 1939.

42. Martin Gilbert, *The Second World War: A Complete History* (New York: H. Holt, 1989), 1, 5.

43. At the Bank of Canada Archives, information on these ships is found in letters from the secretary in Ottawa to the chief of the Currency Division in Ottawa for August 24, 1939, September 2, 1939, September 7, 1939, and September 11, 1939. See also Nigel Pickford, *Lost Treasure Ships of the 20th Century* (Washington, DC: National Geographic, 1999), 183.

3. Seeking Refuge from the Storm

1. "The Great Change," *Time*, September 11, 1939.

2. September 9, 1939, Chamberlain Archives, Birmingham, NC 2/26.

3. Kennedy, *World War II Companion*, 467; and Brayton Harris, *The Navy Times Book of Submarines: A Political, Social, and Military History* (New York: Berkley Books, 1997), 275.

4. Kennedy, *World War II Companion*, 485.

5. Ibid., 436.

6. November 2, 1939, NC 7/11/32 1-304, Chamberlain Archives, Birmingham.

7. Chamberlain letter to sister Hilda, October 15, 1939, NC 18/1/1125, Chamberlain Archives, Birmingham; Self, *Downing Street Years*, 458–60.

8. Hall, *North American Supply*, 46–47; and Chamberlain Archives, Birmingham, NC 8/34/1-109.

9. Martin Gilbert, *Churchill and America* (New York: Free Press, 2005), 92; Justus D. Doenecke, *The Battle against Intervention, 1939–1941* (Malabar, FL: Krieger, 1997), 39.

10. Letter of February 16, 1921, Baroness Spencer-Churchill Papers, as quoted in Gilbert, *Churchill and America*, 93.

11. National Archives, CAB 24/288 Reference 0026, August 26, 1939.

12. Letter dated August 27, 1940, Folder G1/46, Bank of England.

13. Office of the Historian, "Milestones 1921–1936: The Neutrality Acts, 1930s," U.S. Department of State, accessed September 28, 2011, http://history.state.gov/milestones/1921-1936/Neutrality_acts.

14. "Europe Gold Shipments Yesterday Largest since Tension Began," *Wall Street Journal*, September 14, 1938.

15. Feiling, *Life of Neville Chamberlain*, 322.

16. "Transcript of King George VI's Handwritten Notes for a Memorandum on His Conversations with President Roosevelt on June 10 and 11, 1939," Franklin D. Roosevelt Presidential Library and Museum, accessed February 8, 2010, http://docs.fdrlibrary.marist.edu/memorand.html.

17. Seyom Brown, *The Causes and Prevention of War*, 2nd ed. (New York: St. Martin's Press, 1994), 119.

18. Allen W. Dulles, "Cash and Carry Neutrality," *Foreign Affairs* 18, no. 2 (January 1940): 181.

19. Parrish, *To Keep the British Isles Afloat*, 79. The tension Roosevelt faced between his desire to intervene and resistance from the American public is also evident from polls taken before and at the end of the war. According to a Gallup poll in October 1939, 84 percent of Americans wanted the Allies to win. However, near the end of the war in Europe, in April 1945, another poll found that 80 percent of Americans believed that until Pearl Harbor, the president was right not to have intervened in the war. Thomas A. Bailey and Paul B. Ryan, *Hitler vs. Roosevelt: The Undeclared Naval War* (New York: Free Press, 1979), 29.

20. Edward R. Stettinius, *Lend-Lease: Weapon for Victory* (New York: Macmillan, 1944), 20.

21. A. H. Vandenberg Jr. and J. A. Morris, eds., *The Private Papers of Senator Vandenburg* (Boston: Houghton Mifflin, 1952), 3, as quoted in Alan P. Dobson, *US Wartime Aid to Britain, 1940–1946* (London: Croom Helm, 1986), 15.

22. Kennedy, *World War II Companion*, 77.

23. Walsh's comments were made on June 21, 1940, ibid., 83. See also Draper, *Operation Fish*, 268.

24. Pittman's comments were made in mid-July 1940. Moss, *Nineteen Weeks*, 248. In addition, in late September 1940, American general Raymond Lee met with Britain air commodore James Warburton and Captain Balfour, parliamentary undersecretary for air. During the discussion, Warburton and Balfour expressed concern that Japan's threat to the United States would encourage the Americans to keep their weapons for themselves.

James Leutze, ed., *The London Journal of General Raymond E. Lee: 1940–1941* (Boston: Little, Brown, 1971), 74. This was the same congressman who, incidentally, in 1933 represented the United States at the World Economic Conference in London. One evening, a drunken Pittman used his pistol to shoot out all of the streetlamps on Upper Brook Street. Liaquat Ahamed, "Currency Wars, Then and Now," *Foreign Affairs* 90 (March/April 2011): 93.

25. John Morton Blum, *From the Morgenthau Diaries*, vol. 2, *Years of Urgency: 1938–1941* (Boston: Houghton Mifflin, 1965), 66; and Lynne Olson, *Those Angry Days: Roosevelt, Lindbergh, and America's Fight over World War II, 1939–1941* (New York: Random House, 2013), 101.

26. Joseph E. Persico, *Roosevelt's Secret War: FDR and World War II Espionage* (New York: Random House, 2001), 14–15; Gilbert, *Churchill and America*, 178–79; Richard Overy, *1939: Countdown to War* (New York: Viking, 2010), 33.

27. Moss, *Nineteen Weeks*, 159, 165. See also Olsen, *Those Angry Days*, chap. 15.

28. AmericaFirstCommittee.org, accessed June 20, 2009, http://www.americafirst committee.org/ourhistory.html (site discontinued). Lindbergh joined the AFC in April 1941.

29. Kennedy, *World War II Companion*, 78.

30. Persico, *Roosevelt's Secret War*, 82.

31. Moss, *Nineteen Weeks*, 240; Wellington Jeffers, "Finance at Large," *Globe and Mail*, June 27, 1940.

32. Justus D. Doenecke, "Non-Interventionism of the Left: The Keep America Out of the War Congress, 1938–41," *Journal of Contemporary History* 12, no. 2 (April 1977): 222, 225–26.

33. Ibid., 222; Moss, *Nineteen Weeks*, 66.

34. Doenecke, "Non-Interventionism," 225–26.

35. "Charges Roosevelt with Defense Subterfuge," *Los Angeles Times*, September 17, 1940.

36. Blum, *Years of Urgency*, 108; Richard A. Lauderbaugh, *American Steel Makers and the Coming of the Second World War* (Ann Arbor, MI: UMI Research Press, 1980), 22.

37. September 11, 1939, Chamberlain Archives, NC 7/11/32 1-304, 2nd box.

38. T160/1089, Memo No. 87, January 22, 1940, National Archives.

39. Lord Riverdale letter to Minister of Supply Leslie Burgin. CAB 24/288 Reference 0026, August 26, 1939, National Archives; the Cabinet minutes from a week into the war, CAB 66/1/15, September 8, 1939, National Archives.

40. Stettinius, *Lend-Lease*, 20.

41. Keith Sainsbury, *Churchill and Roosevelt at War: The War They Fought and the Peace They Hoped to Make* (New York: New York University Press, 1994), 11.

42. CAB 23/100, Reference 0004, July 5, 1939, National Archives.

43. Warren F. Kimball, *Churchill and Roosevelt: The Complete Correspondence*, vol. 2, *Alliance Forged, November 1942–February 1944* (Princeton, NJ: Princeton University Press, 1984), 49–51.

44. Reynolds, *Creation of the Anglo-American Alliance*, 23–25. Regarding intelligence and military cooperation, historian Stephen Budiansky wrote that it is "difficult for us today to realize just how insular Britain and America were in 1940, and the extent to which cultural

differences posed a significant obstacle to establishing cooperation." Stephen Budiansky, "The Difficult Beginnings of US-British Codebreaking Cooperation," in *American-British-Canadian Intelligence Relations, 1939–2000*, ed. David Stafford and Rhodri Jeffreys-Jones (Portland, OR: Frank Cass, 2000), 50–53.

45. The advice offered by Sir Frederick Phillips, a senior official at the British Treasury, to his colleague D. H. Robertson offers a specific example: "If you ever get asked advice about [British] financial procedures, never forget . . . [u]nlike the House of Lords, the Senate can and does debate Finance Bills enthusiastically and modifies them to its taste." T160/1054, May 23, 1940, National Archives. Similarly, British author H. Duncan Hall found it important to write that the British political system was not like that of the United States. Hall, *North American Supply*, 42.

46. PREM 15/425, February 24, 1945, National Archives.

47. The discussion here focuses on 1939 and 1940, but trans-Atlantic misunderstanding persisted. For example, on February 3, 1941, Arthur Purvis dined with Canadian prime minister Mackenzie King and told him that "he felt 'very strongly that the English do not understand or appreciate the Americans even yet and that, but for Canada and our interpretation, the two countries would be wide apart.'" Douglas H. Fullerton, *Graham Towers and His Times: A Biography* (Toronto: McClelland and Stewart, 1986), 135. For additional evidence of Britain's need for delicate diplomacy across the Atlantic, see the exchange between Lothian and Chamberlain in NC 7/11/32 1-304, Chamberlain Archives, Birmingham, 2nd box. See also the discussion between John Colville and Herschel Johnson, a State Department official at the U.S. Embassy in London in Colville, *Fringes of Power*, 82.

48. Lash, *Roosevelt and Churchill*, 24.

49. "Great Britain: War Is Very Near," *Time*, September 4, 1939. See also Louis Lyons, "Pinch Coming in the United States Trade Loss," *Boston Globe*, November 10, 1940; Michael O'Brien, *John F. Kennedy: A Biography* (New York: St. Martin's Press, 2005), 110; and David Nasaw, *The Patriarch: The Remarkable Life and Turbulent Times of Joseph P. Kennedy* (New York: Penguin Press, 2012), 373.

50. Balfour replied, "I am of the belief that the Catholic votes are in his jacket." Letter from Mr. Warner to Balfour, March 3, 1940, National Archives, FO 371/24251, 63. Henry Morgenthau also said, on at least one occasion, "Kennedy is too dangerous to have around here [Washington]." Nasaw, *Patriarch*, 274, 430, 492, and 496.

51. Nasaw, *Patriarch*, 272.

52. National Archives, FO 371/24251, August 22, 1940. After the start of the war, the Foreign Office began to monitor Kennedy's defeatist remarks and created a secret "Kennedyiana" file, Nasaw, *Patriarch*, 417. The expression "fifth column" dates to the Spanish Civil War. In October 1936, one of Francisco Franco's generals proclaimed that, "in addition to their four columns in the field, there is one in Madrid." Fleming, *Operation Sea Lion*, 57–58; Lukacs, *Duel*, 188.

53. As quoted in Blum, *Years of Urgency*, 293.

54. Kennedy says that he never made anti-British statements and that he never said "on or off the record" that he did not expect Britain to win the war. Kennedy believed he

was getting a bad rap. See newspaper articles November 12, 1940, noted in FO 371/24251, 70–71, National Archives.

55. Leland Stowe, *No Other Road to Freedom* (New York: Knopf, 1941), 376.

56. Dulles, "Cash and Carry Neutrality," 195.

57. Colville, *Fringes of Power*, 42.

58. Parrish, *Encyclopedia of World War II*, 109; and Office of the Historian, "The Neutrality Acts."

59. Dulles, "Cash and Carry Neutrality," 188.

60. Kennedy, *World War II Companion*, 75.

61. Gilbert, *Churchill and America*, 159.

62. Blum, *Years of Urgency*, 294.

63. Gilbert, *Second World War*, 25. Regarding various proposed methods for directing French and British requests in the United States, see Blum, *Years of Urgency*, 290–94.

64. Gilbert, *Second World War*, 139.

65. Blum, *Years of Urgency*, 301–2, 304.

66. Gilbert, *Second World War*, 81. See also Bailey and Ryan, *Hitler vs. Roosevelt*, 80–81.

67. Norman H. Robison letter to Leopold Stennet Avery, the secretary of state for Indian Affairs, CHAR 20/11, Churchill Archives, Cambridge.

68. September 8, 1939, CAB/66/1/15, National Archives.

4. Gold and the Phony War

1. The Army preferred a more defensive position toward the West, but Hitler's plan prevailed. Walter Ansel, *Hitler Confronts England* (Durham, NC: Duke University Press, 1960), 41–42.

2. Ibid., 99.

3. Martienssen, *Hitler and His Admirals*, 19.

4. Karl Dönitz, *Memoirs: Ten Years and Twenty Days*, trans. R. H. Stevens and David Woodward (Annapolis, MD: Naval Institute Press, 1990), 67; Barrie Pitt, *The Battle of the Atlantic* (Alexandria, VA: Time-Life Books, 1977), 17; Lash, *Roosevelt and Churchill*, 67.

5. Britain had 120 million ounces of gold at the start of 1938. The day before the war, this figure had dropped to 53 million ounces. According to Simon, "At the beginning of the war in 1914 we had something under 40 million ounces of gold, rather less than at present, but the purchasing value of the gold in 1914 was higher." CAB 65/2/12, November 10, 1939, National Archives. A similar conclusion is found in CAB 65/5/40, February 13, 1940, National Archives.

6. This figure is extrapolated from Admiralty records reprinted in Draper, *Operation Fish*, 358–66.

7. "Canada Held Bolstering Gold Reserves in U.S. against Future Needs," *Wall Street Journal*, December 15, 1939.

8. Folder G1/20, Bank of England.

9. According to a telegram from Ambassador Lord Lothian. T231/267, October 27, 1939, National Archives. Back on July 3, 1939, Cabinet officials had raised the issue of

selling some £200 million in foreign securities. CAB 24/287 Reference 0032, July 3, 1939, National Archives. At the Cabinet meeting two days later, discussions continued to focus on how Britain could pay for and acquire the goods necessary in the event of war. As laid out by Simon, there were four possibilities: (1) Britain's export trade, (2) stocks of gold, (3) foreign securities owned by British subjects that the Government could acquire in order to increase Britain's purchasing power in the United States, and (4) loans abroad. Increasing exports was not considered viable because of the risk of offending the United States, which would likely suffer from more unfavorable balance of payments terms. A similar concern applied to the devaluation of the British pound (which would boost British exports at the expense of the U.S. balance of payments account). The sale of foreign securities was also considered, but the Cabinet concluded that it could only rely on the sale of £200 million worth. The Cabinet understood that further borrowing from the United States was also impossible because of the Johnston Act. CAB 23/100, July 5, 1939, National Archives.

10. T231/267, October 27, 1939, National Archives.

11. Documents from the Bank of Canada Archives indicate that two shipments, departing on September 3 and September 5, each carried $14 million in gold. The destination was not provided. The third shipment, leaving Britain on September 10 involved $13.2 million in gold. It was "diverted by us" (the British) to New York—presumably the Federal Reserve Bank of New York. "Bank of England: Gold in Safekeeping—1939," File A18-17, January 15, 1940, Bank of Canada.

12. Geoffrey Haskins, *The Irish Flagship: The Story of HMS* Emerald *1925–1948* (London: Arcturus, 2000), 35.

13. Augustus Agar Papers, 69/1/5 (box 5 from 69/1/10), Imperial War Museum, London.

14. Draper, *Operation Fish*, 40.

15. Haskins, *Irish Flagship*, 36.

16. Agar, *Footprints in the Sea*, 238.

17. Ibid., 239; Draper, *Operation Fish*, 44–46; and ADM 53/11021, October 1939, National Archives.

18. ADM 53/10851, October 1939, National Archives.

19. Agar, *Footprints in the Sea*, 247–48.

20. The ships are HMS *Revenge*, HMS *Resolution*, HMS *Emerald*, HMS *Enterprise*, HMS *Caradoc*, and HMS *Ascania*. Draper, *Operation Fish*, Appendix I, 358–59; and Pickford, *Lost Treasure Ships*, 184.

21. CAB 66/2/22, October 6, 1939, National Archives. Cabinet minutes from the following day indicated that the preference was for Belgian and Dutch gold to be shipped to Britain. CAB 65/3/21, October 7, 1939, National Archives.

22. Draper, *Operation Fish*, 49.

23. Leland Stowe, "Project XFF: England—Jenkins," July 1955, Wisconsin Historical Society.

24. T. W. Pope, 01/39/1, Imperial War Museum, London.

25. Terry Hulbert, "Lady Luck Part 1," WW2 People's War, BBC, accessed January 20, 2013, http://www.bbc.co.uk/history/ww2peopleswar/stories/41/a7046741.shtml.

26. Lewis John Jackson, "Jacko's Story," WW2 People's War, BBC, accessed September 18, 2011, http://www.bbc.co.uk/ww2peopleswar/stories/19/a5970819.shtml.

27. Douglas and Greenhous, *Out of the Shadows*, 64–65.

28. Andrew Williams, *The Battle of the Atlantic: The Allies' Submarine Fight against Hitler's Grey Wolves of the Sea*, large print ed. (London: BBC Worldwide, 2002), 76.

29. Barney Roberge, "Heroes Remember," Veterans Affairs Canada, accessed January 20, 2013, http://www.veterans.gc.ca/eng/collections/hrp/alpha_results/197.

30. Gerald R. Bowen, "Heroes Remember," Veterans Affairs Canada, accessed January 20, 2013, http://www.veterans.gc.ca/eng/collections/hrp/alpha_results/540.

31. "Unmentionable Weather," *Time*, February 12, 1940, accessed September 18, 2011, http://www.time.com/time/magazine/article/0,9171,883962,00.html; Hughes and Costello, *Battle of the Atlantic*, 60.

32. Manchester and Reid, *Defender of the Realm*, 37.

33. Günter Hessler, *The U-Boat War in the Atlantic, 1939–1945* (London: Her Majesty's Stationery Office, 1989), 13.

34. John Campbell, ed., *The Experience of World War II* (New York: Oxford University Press, 1989), 108.

35. Agar, *Footprints in the Sea*, 241–44.

36. Pitt, *Battle of the Atlantic*, 62.

37. Williams, *Battle of the Atlantic*, 122.

38. Home, *Prime Ministers*, 221–22. John Colville makes reference to the three U-boat sinkings, although not the Chamberlain-Churchill dinner. Colville, *Fringes of Power*, 23.

39. T 236/721, November 6, 1939, National Archives. See also B. L. Johnson, Naval officer-in-charge, Vancouver to Commanding Officer pacific coast H.M.C. Dockyard Esquimalt, December 4, 1939, "Finance and Bullion," RG 24, Vol. 11, 801, Library and Archives Canada.

40. T 236/721, December 20, 1939, National Archives.

41. T160/982, September 20, 1939, National Archives.

42. T 236/721, November 6, 1939, National Archives

43. Folder G1/17, Bank of England.

44. Letter from Marble to Rear Adm. Percy W. Nelles, November 7, 1939, RCN, File A18-17-2 1936–1945, Gold Earmarked for B. of E. Arrangements Shipped from B. of C. to NY, Bank of Canada Archives.

45. T 236/721, October 16, 1939, National Archives.

46. According to Joseph P. Lash, the expression "Phony War" was coined by isolationist U.S. senator William E. Borah. In German, some also used the phrase, *der Katlekrieg* (cold war). Lash, *Roosevelt and Churchill*, 75.

47. A comment relayed by Sir Eric Phipps (British ambassador to France from 1937 to 1939), as quoted in Colville, *Fringes of Power*, 11.

48. Stowe, *No Other Road*, 18, 23.

49. Letter from January 10, 1940, Chamberlain Archives, Birmingham, NC 7/11/33/1-186, specifically 117.

50. A. F. W. Plumptre, "Organizing the Canadian Economy for War," in *Canadian War Economics*, ed. J. F. Parkinson (Toronto: University of Toronto Press, 1941), 4.

51. Peter Stursberg, "War on B. C. Front Hum-Drum," *Victoria Times*, October 23, 1939.

52. As Basil Catterns of the Bank of England relayed to representatives of the Bank of Canada, "[The] French contemplate sending you some 30 millions and the Swiss some 20 millions of gold as soon as arrangements can be made. These may turn out to be only first installments. You are already in direct touch with the Belgians, who are also sending large amounts to London for safe custody here." Letter from Catterns to Graham Towers, April 14, 1939, File A18-17-2 1936–1945, Gold Earmarked for B. of E. Arrangements Shipped from B. of C. to NY, Bank of Canada Archives. See also McDowall, "Earmarked Gold," 11, 19.

53. At the end of 1940, British gold holdings at the Bank of Canada peaked at 60,575 bars. French gold amounted to more than 47,000 bars. McDowall, "Earmarked Gold," 13, 18. The French gold bar total is extrapolated from 108,000 bars for the two countries.

54. George S. Watts, "A Note on the 'Shadow' Bank of England in Ottawa, 1940," File GSW-89-20, GWS—Memoranda 1981–1984, Bank of Canada Archives.

55. Memo, November 7, 1939, File A18-17-2 1936-1945, Gold Earmarked for B. of E. Arrangements Shipped from B. of C. to NY, Bank of Canada Archives.

56. Colville, *Fringes of Power*, 27. Chamberlain made the same comment in early April 1940 in a speech delivered to the Central Council of the Conservative and Unionist Association. Walter H. Thompson, *Assignment: Churchill* (New York: Farrar, Straus and Young, 1955), 158.

57. Joanna Mack and Steve Humphries, *London at War: The Making of Modern London, 1939–1945* (London: Sidgwick & Jackson, 1985), 14, 19.

58. "Great Britain: Interesting, If Not True," *Time*, January 1, 1940.

59. Thompson, *Assignment: Churchill*, 158.

60. "Britain Ready, Says Premier," *Globe and Mail*, January 17, 1940; "War Situation," House of Commons Debates, HC Deb 16 January 1940, Vol. 356, cc33-102, accessed September 18, 2011, http://hansard.millbanksystems.com/commons/1940/jan/16/war -situation.

61. Lukacs, *Duel*, 115.

62. Hughes and Costello, *Battle of the Atlantic*, 54; and Colville, *Fringes of Power*, 16.

63. Hughes and Costello, *Battle of the Atlantic*, 54.

64. Germany's weekly rations were much more generous. The government allowed for 1.5 pounds of meat, 8 ounces of fats, 8 ounces of sugar, 2 pints of milk, and 3/4 ounces of tea a month. Hughes and Costello, *Battle of the Atlantic*, 55. In a year, the British government would be subsidizing foodstuffs on the order of £100 million per year. Broadberry and Howlett, "The United Kingdom," in Harrison, *Economics of World War II*, 49. See also Folder OV11/1, Bank of England, Exchange Position, extract from W.P.(30) 15 approved by War Cabinet, September 11, 1939.

65. Self, *Downing Street Years*, 494.

66. "Great Britain: What They Deserve!" *Time*, December 11, 1939.

67. As quoted in Colville, *Fringes of Power*, 39.

68. Hennessy, *Bank of England*, 85.

69. Thompson, *Assignment: Churchill*, 148.

70. Sidney Davies, "A View from the Merchant Navy 1939–1940," in *Destroyer: An Anthology of First-Hand Accounts of the War at Sea, 1939–1945*, ed. Ian Hawkins (London: Conway Maritime Press, 2003), 110.

71. The message was delivered on December 30, 1939. Kennedy, *World War II Companion*, 75.

5. Thin Armor

1. Ireland, *Battle of the Atlantic*, 49.

2. FO 371/24251, March 21, 1940, National Archives, 495.

3. Kennedy, *World War II Companion*, 430. Pound's comment was made in March 1942 but was just as applicable to the start of the war.

4. Martienssen, *Hitler and His Admirals*, 36.

5. Six weeks into the war, Hitler convened a conference of his military chiefs to reaffirm his country's strategy for controlling western Europe. Note, in particular, his Directive Number 6. The meeting was held on October 10, 1939. While the army preferred a more defensive position toward the West, Hitler's plan prevailed. See Ansel, *Hitler Confronts England*, 41–42.

6. Charles S. Thomas, *The German Navy in the Nazi Era* (Annapolis, MD: Naval Institute Press, 1990), 194.

7. Dönitz, *Memoirs*, 38.

8. Hughes and Costello, *Battle of the Atlantic*, 56.

9. Campbell, *Experience of World War II*, 129.

10. Martienssen, *Hitler and His Admirals*, 13. See also Thomas, *German Navy*, 179–79.

11. Ireland, *Battle of the Atlantic*, 20, 42; Patrick Abbazia, *Mr. Roosevelt's Navy: The Private War of the U.S. Atlantic Fleet, 1939–1942* (Annapolis, MD: Naval Institute Press, 1975), 56.

12. Even after the war started, Hitler expected France and Britain to reach a political accommodation after the German army had gained control of Poland. Influenced by Hitler's optimism, Grand Admiral Raeder did not believe his fleet would be needed until 1946. Moss, *Nineteen Weeks*, 176; Kennedy, *World War II Companion*, 236; and Harris, *Book of Submarines*, 270.

13. Martienssen, *Hitler and His Admirals*, 14.

14. Edward P. Von der Porten, *The German Navy in World War II* (New York: Cromwell, 1969), 23; Manchester and Reid, *Defender of the Realm*, 132.

15. Von der Porten, *German Navy*, 32.

16. Ibid., 31.

17. Kennedy, *World War II Companion*, 236; Macintyre, *Naval War*, 60; Jürgen Rohwer, "Codes and Ciphers: Radio Communication and Intelligence," in *To Die Gallantly: The Battle of the Atlantic*, eds. Timothy J. Runyan and Jan M. Copes (Boulder, CO: Westview, 1994), 41. Some sources offer slightly different figures. For example, Ian Friel of the British Museum claims Germany had only forty-six U-boats. Friel, *Maritime History*, 245.

18. Macintyre, *Naval War*, 60.

19. Hessler, *U-Boat War*, 15; Von der Porten, *German Navy*, 174, 248; V. E. Tarrant, *The U-Boat Offensive 1914–1945* (London: Arms & Armour, 1989), 89.

20. Ireland, *Battle of the Atlantic*, 48; and Tarrant, *U-Boat Offensive*, 85.

21. Hessler, *U-Boat War*, 10, 27.

22. "Private and Personal" letter from Churchill to Chamberlain, September 10, 1939, NC 7 /9 / 1-109, Chamberlain Archives, Birmingham.

23. September 11, 1939 letter from Churchill to Chamberlain, Chamberlain Archives, Birmingham, NC 7 /9 / 1-109.

24. Pitt, *Battle of the Atlantic*, 18; Ireland, *Battle of the Atlantic*, 53.

25. Tarrant, *U-Boat Offensive*, 89, 94; Abbazia, *Mr. Roosevelt's Navy*, 109.

26. Dönitz, *Memoirs*, 55, 71; Von der Porten, *German Navy*, 40; Harris, *Book of Submarines*, 278; "HMS *Nelson*, British Battleship, WW2," Naval-History.net, accessed September 18, 2011, http://www.naval-history.net/xGM-Chrono-01BB-Nelson.htm.

27. Harris, *Book of Submarines*, 278.

28. Ireland, *Battle of the Atlantic*, 49; Harris, *Book of Submarines*, 279–81; Timothy P. Mulligan, *Neither Sharks nor Wolves: The Men of Nazi Germany's U-boat Arm, 1939–1945* (Annapolis, MD: Naval Institute Press, 1999), 73. Dönitz's own statistics showed that up to January 6, 1940, nearly 41 percent of torpedo misses were attributable to this problem. He estimated that the torpedo failures cost the U-boat service at least 300,000 tons of Allied shipping. Tarrant, *U-Boat Offensive*, 83.

29. Hughes and Costello, *Battle of the Atlantic*, 67.

30. Submarines in World War II used either gasoline or diesel engines while on the surface and electric batteries under the water. As a result, submarines had to surface periodically to recharge their batteries and allow fresh air in. The Germans developed snorkel technology designed to provide a semi-submerged U-boat with air for the diesel engines. However, the technology was introduced near the end of the war. Mulligan, *Neither Sharks nor Wolves*, 20; "Guppy," GlobalSecurity, accessed June 15, 2012, http://www.globalsecurity.org/military/systems/ship/guppy.htm.

31. Pitt, *Battle of the Atlantic*, 21.

32. The British stated publicly that they expected Germany to operate U-boats in surfaced night attacks. Tarrant, *U-Boat Offensive*, 80, fn 8.

33. Ibid., 93.

34. Cajus Bekker, *Hitler's Naval War*, trans. and ed. Frank Ziegler (Garden City, NY: Doubleday, 1974), 188; Tarrant, *U-Boat Offensive*, 80, fn 7.

35. Brennecke, *Hunters and the Hunted*, 63–64. Nighttime surface attacks on convoys formed part of Dönitz's prewar training program. Mulligan, *Neither Sharks nor Wolves*, 59.

36. For example, H. Duncan Hall, a chronicler of Britain's purchasing history during the war, described how Britain could get what it could afford from the United States but that Britain still had to cross the Atlantic "through the U-boat packs." Hall, *North American Supply*, 40. The description of the Battle of the Atlantic provided by Uboataces.com is accurate but also inadvertently perpetuates this false impression. "For nearly six years, Germany

launched over 1,000 U-Boats into combat, in an attempt to isolate and blockade the British Isles, thereby forcing the British out of the war." "German U-Boats and the Battle of the Atlantic," German U-Boat, accessed September 18, 2011, http://www.uboataces.com.

37. Ireland, *Battle of the Atlantic*, 220–21.

38. Dönitz believed that three or perhaps four steamers had been sunk in the joint attack. Dönitz, *Memoirs*, 62. This view is also held by Von der Porten, *German Navy*, 59. According to Ireland, it took time for Dönitz to discover that the attack had not been coordinated and that three boats had been lost. Ireland, *Battle of the Atlantic*, 46–47. Analyses by David Fairbank White and Jürgen Rohwer of the pack indicates that nine U-boats were to be involved in a coordinated attack on Convoy HG 3 off of Ireland (HG representing Homeward from Gibraltar). Only three U-boats were ultimately involved, but problems of faulty torpedoes and poor coordination "fouled the operation." White, *Bitter Ocean*, 19; Rohwer, "Codes and Ciphers," 41–42.

39. Dönitz, *Memoirs*, 130.

40. Hughes and Costello, *Battle of the Atlantic*, 53.

41. Pitt, *Battle of the Atlantic*, 42; Macintyre, *Naval War*, 13. Others put the number of hunting parties at eight. Hughes and Costello, *Battle of the Atlantic*, 50–51.

42. Hughes and Costello, *Battle of the Atlantic*, 61.

43. After six months of war, mines had claimed 114 merchant ships. Ibid., 49; Pitt, *Battle of the Atlantic*, 23; Von der Porten, *German Navy*, 35; Ireland, *Battle of the Atlantic*, 41.

44. Iain Nethercott, "Early Days," in Hawkins, *Destroyer*, 32.

45. Hughes and Costello, *Battle of the Atlantic*, 50.

46. Ibid., 48, 50. See also the following documents at the National Archives: ADM 1/10315 (German magnetic mine: proposed countermeasures), ADM 1/11024 (Detonation of magnetic mines), ADM 204/264 (Magnetic sweep for non-contact mines: investigation to determine weight and winding of electromagnet capable of operating magnetic mine), ADM 253/713 (Methods of counteracting magnetic mines and torpedoes), CAB 63/141 (Magnetic mines; suggestions for combatting), CAB/65/2/50, December 15, 1939, and FO 371/23949 (Safe channels for shipping—magnetic mines). See also Gilbert, *Second World War*, 35.

47. From the Bank of Canada Archives, see the February 29, 1940, letter from George Bolton at the Bank of England to Dean Marble at the Bank of Canada; the April 16 and 18, 1940, letters from Percy Nelles to Marble; the June 21, 1940, letter from Bolton to Gordon at the Bank of Canada. The June 20, 1940, cable from Bolton to Gordon (both of the Bank of England) lists the *Niagara* as having carried £2 million in gold. A18-17-2, Banking Operations. See also Keith Gordon, *Deep Water Gold* (Whangarei, New Zealand: SeaROV Technologies, 2005); and Draper, *Operation Fish*, 232–33.

48. Keegan, *Second World War*, 105.

49. Williams, *Battle of the Atlantic*, 74–75; Hughes and Costello, *Battle of the Atlantic*, 9, 45; Macintyre, *Naval War*, 57–58.

50. Macintyre, *Naval War*, 105. While the Royal Canadian Navy was instrumental in protecting Allied convoys, it was in no position to tip the balance in the Battle of the Atlantic.

Before the war the total payroll of the Canadian shipbuilding industry was less than $1 million, and its main activity was ship repair, not ship construction. Charles P. Stacey, *Arms, Men and Governments: The War Policies of Canada, 1939–1945* (Ottawa: Queen's Printer, 1970), 107.

51. James B. Reston, "Rise in U-boat Toll Laid in Part to New Nazi Bases," *New York Times*, November 10, 1940.

52. Tarrant, *U-Boat Offensive*, 86.

53. Ibid., 90; Williams, *Battle of the Atlantic*, 116; Reston, "Rise in U-boat Toll."

54. T 236/721, January 25, 1940, National Archives. A January 29, 1940, letter from Cobbold to Waley indicated that current shipment plans should be maintained, suggesting that there was no panic to ship much larger quantities—a situation that would change in several months. T 236/721, January 29, 1940, National Archives.

55. Harris, *Book of Submarines*, 277.

56. Bernard Ireland provides the example of the carriers *Ark Royal* and *Courageous* being engaged in ultimately unsuccessful antisubmarine operations. Ireland, *Battle of the Atlantic*, 41. See also Pitt, *Battle of the Atlantic*, 21; and Hughes and Costello, *Battle of the Atlantic*, 9, 63.

57. Tarrant, *U-Boat Offensive*, 86.

58. Macintyre, *Naval War*, 58.

59. Williams, *Battle of the Atlantic*, 85; Stephen Wentworth Roskill, *A Merchant Fleet at War: Alfred Holt & Co., 1939–1945* (London: Collins, 1962).

60. ASDIC refers to the organization that helped develop the technology: the Anti-Submarine Detection Investigation Committee. Led by British scientists, the committee built on a French breakthrough in quartz and steel transducers. It conducted the first successful trials of an active underwater location system in March 1918, when echoes were received from a sub at a range of five hundred yards. Milner, *Battle of the Atlantic*, 11. The term ASDIC was replaced in 1943 by the new, U.S.-originated sonar (sound navigating and ranging). Tarrant, *U-Boat Offensive*, 80.

61. Tarrant, *U-Boat Offensive*, 80.

62. Hughes and Costello, *Battle of the Atlantic*, 63.

63. Ireland, *Battle of the Atlantic*, 29. The captain of HMS *Glasgow* in early January 1940, said that, although he did not "place any great faith in the ASDIC set as fitted in *Glasgow*, I consider that, when a firm contact is obtained, depth charges should be dropped." ADM 188.122, National Archives, 52.

64. Von der Porten, *German Navy*, 59; Ireland, *Battle of the Atlantic*, 53.

65. Brennecke, *Hunters and the Hunted*, 13.

66. Gilmour's last comment reflected the fact that fast ships could outrun U-boats. T 236/721, February 5, 1940, National Archives.

67. "Rand Gold Output Sets New Record in March," *Wall Street Journal*, April 11, 1940. South Africa accounted for 40 percent of the world's gold output, and the British Empire accounted for half of the world's gold supply at the time—$700 million a year from its mines. B. H. McCormack, "Following the News: The Gold Pours In," *Wall Street Journal*,

November 30, 1940; "The Dominions War Report," *Globe and Mail*, April 20, 1940. In the first nine months of 1940, gold from South Africa alone reached a record of approximately 10,463,000 fine ounces. "South African Gold Output at New High for 9 Months," *Wall Street Journal*, October 11, 1940; "Gold by Warship," *New York Times*, February 6, 1941.

68. See, for example, the letter from Bolton to Marble, February 9, 1940, File A18-17-2 1936-1945, Gold Earmarked for B. of E. Arrangements Shipped from B. of C. to NY, Bank of Canada Archives.

69. Draper, *Operation Fish*, 358–59.

70. It is possible that some larger shipments took place in January. Documents from the archives of the Bank of Canada indicated that in mid- to late January a ship carrying $20 million in gold sailed from Britain to an undisclosed port in North America. File A18-17, January 15, 1940, Gold Earmarked for B. of E. Arrangements Shipped from B. of C. to NY, Bank of Canada Archives. See also the letter from Bolton to Marble, January 25, 1940, and the letter from the Bank of England to Dean Marble at the Bank of Canada, February 27, 1940, File A18-17-2, Gold Earmarked for B. of E. Shipped via Vancouver, Nov. 8/40–June 28/40, Bank of Canada Archives.

71. Agar, *Footprints in the Sea*, 221–22.

72. Ibid.

73. Ibid., 253.

74. Ibid.

75. Ibid., 242.

76. Ibid., 222, 245.

77. Ibid., 250–51; Haskins, *Irish Flagship, 36*.

78. CAB 65/5/40, February 13, 1940, National Archives. By the end of 1939, the British had quietly sold $144.5 million worth of American securities to help pay for war matériel. "Stock Sales Here by Britain Listed," *New York Times*, March 27, 1942. For a November 1939 estimate of securities sales, see T231/267, National Archives.

79. Nasaw, *Patriarch*, 429.

80. Folder G1/17, Bank of England. According to the November 22, 1939, telegram from Lord Lothian, "Individual sales are proceeding steadily at a satisfactory rate little short of 100 millions a year as advised in the Bank of England . . . private sales to date have been about £16 millions." U.S. markets were able to absorb without disruption further sales of British-owned securities over the next six months. Blum, *Years of Urgency*, 296.

81. GHS Pinset, an economic adviser at the British Embassy in Washington, quotes figures from American Treasury secretary Henry Morgenthau Jr. Letter from GHS "Jerry" Pinset to Sigismund Waley, December 18, 1939, Folder G1/46, Bank of England. The situation remained essentially unchanged in February 1940. See February 7, 1940, Bank of England cipher telegram to Lord Lothian, Folder G1/46, Bank of England. For a summary of dollar and securities figures from the start of the war to mid-January 1940, see the description of the January 19, 1940, phone call involving Ernest Rowe-Dutton, Folder G1/46, Bank of England.

82. Clinton R. Harrower, "British Resources," *Wall Street Journal*, November 4, 1939.

See also Edward J. Condlon, "Alien Liquidation Found Slackening," *New York Times*, December 24, 1939; Blum, *Years of Urgency*, 295–96; CAB 65/5/40, February 13, 1940, National Archives.

83. Draper, *Operation Fish*, 164.

84. Many of the titles of the securities were shown inaccurately on the registration documents, and sorting them out proved to be like solving a "super jig-saw puzzle." Hennessy, *Bank of England*, 91.

85. Folder G1/46, Bank of England.

86. CAB 65/5/40, February 13, 1940, National Archives.

87. U.S. treasury secretary Henry Morgenthau opposed Kennedy's idea because it would force Britain to sell even more of its securities, flooding the market and depressing American stock prices. Nasaw, *Patriarch*, 437–38.

88. Letter from Balfour to T. K. Bewley at the British Treasury. FO 371/24251, May 1, 1940, National Archives. FO 371/24251, February 27, 1940, National Archives. Historian David Irving puts the amount of U.S. gold accumulation at the time at $22 billion. Irving, *Churchill's War*, 518. Senator Elmer Thomas of Oklahoma introduced a bill in Congress to resolve this extraordinary gold problem by redistributing "among the solvent nations of the world" the $18 billion gold hoard of the United States. "Britain Protects Gold Hoard and Cuts Trade with America," *Los Angeles Times*, January 14, 1940; George T. Hughes, "Redistribution of Gold Seen as Knotty Problem," *Los Angeles Times*, March 7, 1940; "Foreign Trade: Blood over Gold," *Time*, August 5, 1940; W. R. Plewman, "The War Reviewed," *Toronto Daily Star*, August 1, 1940.

89. Irving, *Churchill's War*, 518. See also Frank R. Kent, "The Great Game of Politics," *Wall Street Journal*, October 24, 1939; and the comments by Frank D. Graham of Princeton University described in "Future of Gold Institute Topic," *Los Angeles Times*, October 19, 1940.

90. "Profits in Bonds," *Time*, January 22, 1940. By late June 1940, the U.S. Treasury possessed nearly three-fourths of the world's supply of gold, worth roughly $19.5 billion. "War Gold Gains by Reich Small," *Los Angeles Times*, June 20, 1940. See also George T. Hughes, "Nazi Rejection of Gold Seen as Questionable," *Los Angeles Times*, July 4, 1940.

91. Blum, *Years of Urgency*, 109.

92. Folder G1/20, Bank of England. See also Blum, *Years of Urgency*, 295.

93. Lash, *Roosevelt and Churchill*, 66

94. Blum, *Years of Urgency*, 295.

6. Into the Furnace of the War

1. Chamberlain Archives, Birmingham, NC 18/1/1149; Self, *Downing Street Years*, 515.

2. CAB 65/612, March 13, 1940, National Archives.

3. Cipher telegram to Lord Lothian, February 7, 1940, Folder G1/46, Bank of England.

4. Letter from Frederick Phillips to Basil Catterns, File C43/40, Bank of England; The *Times*, January 23, 1940, as found in Folder G1/46, Bank of England.

5. Campbell, *Experience of World War II*, 31; Von der Porten, *German Navy*, 63–64; Thomas, *German Navy*, 189.

6. The next day, Hitler ordered the military to prepare for the invasion of Norway and Denmark (Operation Weseruebung). Hughes and Costello, *Battle of the Atlantic*, 64.

7. Macintyre, *Naval War*, 19.

8. CAB 67/6/3, April 13, 1940, National Archives.

9. The Cabinet thought that such a gold windfall would be helpful to the Germans but would not be sufficient to resolve Germany's broader financial weaknesses.

10. CAB 67/6/3, April 13, 1940, National Archives.

11. Samuel Grafton, *An American Diary* (New York: Doubleday/Doran, 1943), 50. In the first nine months of the war, Britain realized about $152 million from the sale of U.S. securities. "British Buying Power in U.S. Kept at Maximum by Reserve," *Hamilton Spectator*, September 26, 1940.

12. Keegan, *Second World War*, 51.

13. CAB/65/6/53, April 30, 1940, National Archives.

14. Ireland, *Battle of the Atlantic*, 49; Tarrant, *U-Boat Offensive*, 87.

15. Keegan, *Second World War*, 51.

16. Ansel, *Hitler Confronts England*, 62

17. Ibid.

18. Later assessments of the battle for Norway concluded that, in all, the Kriegsmarine lost ten destroyers, one heavy cruiser, and two light cruisers. In addition, Germany lost the use of a pocket battleship for a year, and two battleships sustained heavy damage. See Macintyre, *Naval War*, 47–48; Friel, *Maritime History*, 241–42; and Thomas, *German Navy*, 191. Germany's naval support resources were also overextended. Ansel, *Hitler Confronts England*, 61–62.

19. Parrish, *To Keep the British Isles Afloat*, 84.

20. Roger Parkinson, *Blood, Toil, Tears and Sweat: The War History from Dunkirk to Alamein, Based on the War Cabinet Papers of 1940 to 1942* (London: Hart-Davis MacGibbon, 1973), 3.

21. Lukacs, *Duel*, 116.

22. In addition, as a courtesy, Churchill allowed Chamberlain to remain in the prime minister's official residence at 10 Downing Street until mid-June while the new prime minister stayed in his official apartments at the Admiralty. Regarding the incoming and outgoing prime ministers' housing arrangements, see Colville, *Fringes of Power*, 126.

23. Chamberlain Archives, Birmingham, NC 8 /34/1-109.

24. Colville, *Fringes of Power*, 84.

25. Moss, *Nineteen Weeks*, 102–3.

26. Thompson, *Assignment: Churchill*, 159.

27. Letter to Ida, May 11, 1940 in Self, *Downing Street Years*, 43.

28. Harold Ickes, *The Secret Diary of Harold L. Ickes*, vol. 3, *The Lowering Clouds, 1939–1941* (New York: Simon and Schuster, 1954), 176, as quoted in Parrish, *To Keep the British Isles Afloat*, 86.

29. Kennedy, *World War II Companion*, 77.

30. Roosevelt's letter was sent to Edward R. Stettinius at the Office of Production Management and later head of the Lend-Lease program. Ibid., 78.

31. Moss, *Nineteen Weeks*, 84.

32. Ibid., 84–85; Warren F. Kimball, *Churchill and Roosevelt: The Complete Correspondence*, vol. 1, *Alliance Emerging, October 1933–November 1942* (Princeton, NJ: Princeton University Press, 1984), 3.

33. John Lukacs, "Churchill Offers Toil and Tears to FDR," *American Heritage Magazine* 58, no. 4 (Spring/Summer 2008), accessed January 23, 2013, http://www.americanheritage.com/content/churchill-offers-toil-and-tears-fdr.

34. Draper, *Operation Fish*, 143–44.

35. Kennedy, *World War II Companion*, 441.

36. Winston Churchill, "Blood, Toil, Tears and Sweat"(speech to the House of Commons, May 13, 1940), Modern History Sourcebook, accessed September 18, 2011, http://www.fordham.edu/halsall/mod/churchill-blood.html.

37. Kennedy, *World War II Companion*, 78.

38. CAB 65/612, March 13, 1940, National Archives.

39. Parrish, *To Keep the British Isles Afloat*, 93; Moss, *Nineteen Weeks*, 317.

40. Wellington Jeffers, "Finance at Large," *Globe and Mail*, June 25 and 27, 1940.

41. Stacey, *Arms, Men and Governments*, 328–29.

42. Lash, *Roosevelt and Churchill*, 135.

43. Telegram from Lord Lothian to London, 20 May 1940, as quoted in ibid., 135.

44. Colville, *Fringes of Power*, 113.

45. Abbazia, *Mr. Roosevelt's Navy*, 92.

46. Because of the sensitivity of this suggestion, Roosevelt did not want this idea to be linked to the administration. CAB 65/7/12, National Archives; Lukacs, *Duel*, 91.

47. Kennedy, *World War II Companion*, 447, 714; Parrish, *To Keep the British Isles Afloat*, 93.

48. Colville, *Fringes of Power*, 116.

49. I. C. B. Dear and M. R. D. Foot have noted that while the estimates of those rescued from Dunkirk beach vary, the British Admiralty calculated that a total of 338,226 men were saved between May 26 and June 3, 1940, 110,000 of whom were French soldiers. Dear and Foot, *Oxford Companion*, 312; Keegan, *Second World War*, 81; Thompson, *Assignment: Churchill*, 191.

50. Martin Gilbert, *Winston Churchill's War Leadership* (New York: Vintage, 2004), 23.

51. Parrish, *To Keep the British Isles Afloat*, 93; Kennedy, *World War II Companion*, 447; Manchester and Reid, *Defender of the Realm*, 86.

52. Moss, *Nineteen Weeks*, 205.

53. Winston S. Churchill, "Be Ye Men of Valour" (first broadcast to the British people as prime minister, May 19, 1940), Churchill Centre and Museum at the Churchill War Rooms, London, accessed January 23, 2013, http://www.winstonchurchill.org/component/content/article/3-speeches/91-be-ye-men-of-valour.

54. The Martin's Bank description is drawn from "Martin's at War," *Martin's Bank Magazine* (Autumn 1946), accessed June 21, 2012, http://www.martinsbank.co.uk/Martins%20 at%20War%20-%20The%20Bullion%20boys.htm.

55. The gold value is based on the assumption that 4,719 boxes—each carrying four gold bars weighing 400 ounces each—amounted to 7,550,400 ounces. This is a rough estimate because an undisclosed number of boxes contained gold coins and others held paper securities.

56. Colville, *Fringes of Power*, 114, 117; Gilbert, *Second World War*, 82–83.

57. Fleming, *Operation Sea Lion*, 60.

58. "Invasion: Preview and Prevention," *Time*, June 3, 1940, accessed September 19, 2011, http://www.time.com/time/magazine/article/0,9171,789811,00.html.

59. Moss, *Nineteen Weeks*, 122

60. Julian Jackson, *The Fall of France: The Nazi Invasion of 1940* (Oxford: Oxford University Press, 2003), 3.

61. "Invasion: Preview and Prevention," *Time*.

7. Living from Hour to Hour

1. Draper, *Operation Fish*, 149.

2. T160/1054, May 25, 1940, National Archives.

3. R. Raban-Williams and W. S. Crawford placed the value of the cargo reached at £53 million. It is unclear if the discrepancy between the official £40 million figure is explained by £13 million worth of securities. R. Raban-Williams, "The Papers of Lieutenant R. Raban-Williams RN," PP/MCR/366, 1940, Imperial War Museum; W. S. Crawford, "Journal for the Use of Midshipmen," Crawford, WS Commander RN 92/5/1, Imperial War Museum. Draper and Pickford put the value of the consignment at £47 million. See Draper, *Operation Fish*, Appendix I, 358–59; Pickford, *Lost Treasure Ships*, 185. In the Royal Navy, a midshipman was a senior petty officer, and the rank usually applied to a young naval officer in training. "Officer Ranks in the Royal Navy," Royal Navy Museum Library, accessed June 7, 2012, http://www.royalnavalmuseum.org/info_sheets_nav_rankings.htm. Contrary to the trend in wartime censorship rules, midshipmen's journals were kept as part of the evaluation process for the young officers in training. The journal's cover states that "The Journal is to be produced at the examination in Seamanship for the rank of Lieutenant."

4. The Admiralty's figures indicate that the three ships carried £5 million. Pickford's list notes that each ship delivered £10 million. See Draper, *Operation Fish*, 360–61, and Pickford, *Lost Treasure Ships*, 184.

5. Raban-Williams, "Papers."

6. Ibid.

7. Crawford, "Journal," June 8 to June 10, 1940.

8. "$600,000,000 of Gold Received in Two Days by N.Y. Reserve Bank," *Wall Street Journal*, June 5, 1940.

9. T160/1054, June 10, 1940, National Archives.

10. Draper, *Operation Fish*, 353–54.

11. T160/1054, June 10, 1940, National Archives.

12. Lash, *Roosevelt and Churchill*, 147.

13. CHAR 20/14, June 5, 1940, Churchill Archives, Cambridge.

14. Colville, *Fringes of Power*, 126.

15. Parrish, *To Keep the British Isles Afloat*, 89.

16. T231/203, EC R 19/01, October 25, 1944, National Archives; Hennessy, *Bank of England*, 98.

17. Leutze, *Journal of General Raymond E. Lee*, 5.

18. Ansel, *Hitler Confronts England*, 96.

19. Hughes and Costello, *Battle of the Atlantic*, 92.

20. Cyrus L. Sulzberger, *World War II* (New York: American Heritage, 1985), 36.

21. The cable was sent June 26, 1940. Moss, *Nineteen Weeks*, 249.

22. For more on Roosevelt's "unneutral neutrality," see Bailey and Ryan, *Hitler vs. Roosevelt*, chap. 3 and 7.

23. Comment by Dowding to Lord Halifax. Lash, *Roosevelt and Churchill*, 135.

24. Parrish, *To Keep the British Isles Afloat*, 96. Edward R. Stettinius put the value of outstanding French commitments at $500 million. Stettinius, *Lend-Lease*, 30.

25. McDowall, "Earmarked Gold," 14.

26. Ibid., 14–15, 19.

27. Ireland, *Battle of the Atlantic*, 50.

28. Pitt, *Battle of the Atlantic*, 21.

29. Abbazia, *Mr. Roosevelt's Navy*, 108–9; Mulligan, *Neither Sharks nor Wolves*, 74. The German Naval Staff Operations Division (U-boats) in Berlin concluded that French bases doubled the available number of U-boats. Hessler, *U-Boat War in the Atlantic*, vii.

30. As it turned out, it wasn't until April to December 1941 that the Germans began extending U-boat runs in significant numbers into the central and western Atlantic. Keegan, *Second World War*, 107, 110. The collapse of France also reduced the effectiveness of Britain's blockade of Germany. According to Frederick Lindemann, an economic and technology adviser to Churchill, "It seems to me the blockade is largely ruined, in which case the sole decisive weapon in our hands would be overwhelming air attack upon Germany." Colville, *Fringes of Power*, 145.

31. Contributing to the Québecers' concerns about German spies was the arrival, on July 2, 1940, of the first German war prisoners in Québec. Jean-Marie Fallu, *Le Québec et la Guerre: 1860–1954* (Québec: Les Publications de Québec), 140. See also Jeffers, "Finance at Large," June 18, 1940.

32. "Foreign Relations: Lord Lothian's Job," *Time*, July 7, 1940; Craig Edward Saucier, "Mr. Kerr Goes to Washington: Lord Lothian and the Genesis of the Anglo-American Alliance, 1939–1940" (PhD diss., Louisiana State University, 2008), 268.

33. CAB 65/7/74, June 24, 1940, National Archives.

34. Prem 4743 B/1, June 24, 1940, National Archives. Vidkun Quisling was a Norwegian traitor, and this employment of his name was coming into general use by early June 1940. Colville, *Fringes of Power*, 123.

35. Churchill, *Their Finest Hour*, 213–15; William Fortescue, *The Third Republic in France, 1870–1940: Conflicts and Continuities* (New York: Routledge, 2000), 235.

36. Arthur Greenwood, "The British War Cabinet: Economic Aid from the New World to the Old," microfilm reel, 4567, Library and Archives Canada; CAB 66/8/39, June 16, 1940, National Archives.

8. Keeping Mum

1. Colville, *Fringes of Power*, 39–40.

2. Ibid., 163. In addition, according to one government official, "*prima facia* Germany has most of the cards; but the real test is whether the morale of our fighting personnel and civil population will counter-balance the numerical superiority and material advantage which Germany enjoys." Parkinson, *Blood, Toil, Tears and Sweat*, 3.

3. Colville, *Fringes of Power*, 151–52.

4. Amanda Smith, ed., *Hostage to Fortune: The Letters of Joseph P. Kennedy* (New York: Viking, 2001), 425, as quoted in Parrish, *To Keep the British Isles Afloat*, 93. See also Moss, *Nineteen Weeks*, 103.

5. Draper, *Operation Fish*, 160.

6. Churchill, *Their Finest Hour*, 723.

7. T160/1054, June 17, 1940, National Archives.

8. Draper, *Operation Fish*, 148.

9. T 236/721, February 12, 1940, National Archives.

10. Draper, *Operation Fish*, 160.

11. Breuer, *Top Secret Tales*, 60.

12. Letter from the Bank of England to Gordon, October 11, 1939, File A18-17-2 1936-1945, Gold Earmarked for B. of E. Arrangements Shipped from B. of C. to NY, Bank of Canada Archives.

13. Letter from Marble to S. A. Staden, October 12, 1939, File A18-17-2 1936-1945, Gold Earmarked for B. of E. Arrangements Shipped from B. of C. to NY, Bank of Canada Archives.

14. Ibid., October 16, 1939.

15. February 14, 1940, "Gold Shipments—Bank of England," dictated by Dean G. Marble, File A18-17-2 1936–1945, Gold Earmarked for B. of E. Arrangements Shipped from B. of C. to NY, Bank of Canada Archives.

16. Letter from Dean Marble of the Bank of Canada to George Bolton of the Bank of England, November 10, 1939, A18-17-2, Gold Earmarked for B of E Shipped via Vancouver, Nov. 8/40–June 28/40, Bank of Canada Archives; and "Gold Shipments—Bank of England," February 14, 1940. The Canadian government appointed H. B. (Bruce) Jefferson, a senior journalist and newspaper editor, as regional censor of publications in the fall of 1939. His duties included reviewing "all news material being prepared for publication or broadcast, decide what could or could not be said, then advise editors and producers accordingly. Sixteen daily newspapers, 68 weeklies and ten radio stations were under

Jefferson's jurisdiction, stretching across Nova Scotia, New Brunswick and Prince Edward Island." "The Censor and the City: H. B. Jefferson Captures Wartime Halifax," Nova Scotia Archives, accessed September 19, 2011, http://www.gov.ns.ca/nsarm/virtual/eastcoastport/results.asp?Search=ch3&Language=English.

17. As noted earlier, the Royal Navy did permit young officers in training to keep "Midshipman's Journals." These were kept for official, not private, purposes.

18. Colville was aware of Britain's precarious financial conditions but was apparently not informed about the shipments of gold and securities. See, for example, Colville, *Fringes of Power*, 213.

19. Stowe, "Secret Voyage," 26.

20. Ibid.

21. In Canada, the newspaper *Globe and Mail* periodically ran a column titled "Finance at Large," but the column usually contained only general references to gold. For example, in late 1939, it mentioned nothing about specific gold shipments or the quantity of gold that had arrived and was expected to arrive in Canada. It did mention, though, that the world gold market had "now become highly controlled and purely mechanistic in its functioning." Wellington Jeffers, "Finance at Large," *Globe and Mail*, December 20, 1939. See also "British Buying Power in U.S. Kept at Maximum by Reserve," *Hamilton Spectator*, September 26, 1939; and McDowall, "Earmarked Gold," 12. McDowall cites the *Toronto Star*, May 15, 1939; the *Wall Street Journal*, July 5, 1939; and the *Montréal Gazette*, August 22, 1939.

22. The *Wall Street Journal* routinely printed figures from the Federal Reserve Bank of New York of gold arriving in New York and, on occasion, San Francisco. The articles, titled "New York Gold Movement," however, rarely provided ship names or consignment values. In addition, the newspaper ceased such articles in mid-1939 as the war approached.

23. "Europe Accelerates Flow of Gold to United States," *Wall Street Journal*, April 22, 1939.

24. "Canada Latest Haven for European Capital in Search of Safety," *Wall Street Journal*, July 3, 1939.

25. "Britannic Arrives on 2D War Voyage," *New York Times*, January 11, 1940.

26. "Cameronia Delayed 2 Days by Storms," *New York Times*, February 11, 1940.

27. "$3,000,000 Gold Arrives," *New York Times*, February 12, 1940.

28. "Britannic Arrives with 375 Refugees," *New York Times*, February 20, 1940.

29. "'Hush Hush' Signs on Arriving Liners," *New York Times*, April 2, 1940.

30. Ibid.

31. "A Passenger Hears about the Sea," *New York Times*, May 12, 1940.

32. "$39,444,000 of Gold Discharged Here," *New York Times*, June 22, 1940.

33. "15 British Children Arrive Here on Vessel Recently a Freighter," *New York Times*, July 17, 1940.

34. It should be noted that the Admiralty records of Britain's gold shipments indicate that the *Eastern Prince* delivered only £6 million ($24 million), roughly half of what was reported by the *New York Times*. Draper, *Operation Fish*, 362.

35. "Business World," *New York Times*, July 30, 1940; "Two British Liners Bring 372 Children," *New York Times*, July 30, 1940.

36. Draper, *Operation Fish*, 50, 358. A different perspective of what was likely the same event may be found in Theodore W. Warden, "Follow That Train!" WW2 People's War, BBC, accessed May 16, 2013, http://www.bbc.co.uk/history/ww2peopleswar/stories/65/a3501965.shtml.

37. See the letters among Walter Winsby, Dean Marble, and F. T. Palfrey of the Bank of Canada in mid-December 1939, and the December 30, 1939, letter from the Assistant Deputy Postmaster General to Marble, in A18-17-2, Gold Earmarked for B of E Shipped via Vancouver, Nov. 8/40–June 28/40, Bank of Canada Archives.

38. In early December 1940, representatives of the Bank of England warned about the shoddy packing methods used by their representatives in the Orient: "Boxes from India are strapped with metal straps, so the boxes usually arrive intact—from the Orient, the boxes are usually sealed very poorly—result, many seals cracked or broken." This description explains the January 12, 1940, report by Dean Marble of the Bank of Canada to George Bolton of the Bank of England: "The first Indian shipment received a few days ago was in quite a mixed condition." See the December 4, 1939, interoffice correspondence from Walter Winsby to the secretary Bank of Canada, and the letter from Marble to Bolton, January 12, 1940, in A18-17-2, Gold Earmarked for B of E Shipped via Vancouver, Nov. 8/40–June 28/40, and the interoffice correspondence from Winsby to Marble, March 19 1940, "Re: Gold Shipment," A18-17-2, Gold Earmarked for B of E Shipped via Vancouver, Nov. 8/40–June 28/40, Bank of Canada Archives.

39. Interoffice correspondence from the agent in Halifax to the secretary in Ottawa, June 10, 1940, "Shipment No. 24 to Bank of Canada," File A18-17-1, Gold Earmarked for B. of E. Routine Shipments via Eastern Ports June–July 40, Bank of Canada Archives.

40. Interoffice correspondence from Bank of Canada agent Walter Winsby to the secretary in Ottawa, A18-17-2, Gold Earmarked for B of E Shipped via Vancouver, Nov. 8/40–June 28/40; Interoffice correspondence Winsby to the secretary in Ottawa, October 8, 1940, A18-17-2, Gold Earmarked for B of E Shipped via Vancouver, July 2/40–Dec. 31/40, Bank of Canada Archives.

41. Marble's story is relayed by George S. Watts in "The 'Shadow Bank' of England in Canada and Other Related Matters," File GSW-89-20, GWS—Memoranda 1976–1977, Bank of Canada Archives.

42. Agar, *Footprints in the Sea*, 245.

43. Interoffice correspondence from Walter Winsby in Vancouver to the secretary in Ottawa, October 8, 1940, Bank of Canada Archives.

44. Norman Catherall, "A Lucky Escape: Life in the Merchant Navy," WW2 People's War, BBC, accessed May 16, 2013, http://www.bbc.co.uk/history/ww2peopleswar/stories/20/a2493920.shtml. Note that this is the only known reference to this gold shipment.

45. Bolton, who provided no further details, is the only known source for these gold losses. Richard Fry, ed., *A Banker's World: The Revival of the City 1957–1970, Speakings and Writings of Sir George Bolton* (New York: Taylor & Francis, 2005), 111.

46. Letter, June 3, 1940, Chamberlain Archives, Birmingham, NC 8 /34/1-109.

47. Nasaw, *Patriarch*, 448–49.

48. "First Shipment of English Gold Due Here Today," *New York Times*, August 10, 1915.

49. William B. Breuer, *Hitler's Undercover War: The Nazi Espionage Invasion of the U.S.A.* (New York: St. Martin's Press, 1989), 284.

50. Gilbert, *Second World War*, 37; William B. Breuer, *The Air-Raid Warden Was a Spy: And Other Tales from Home-Front America in World War II* (Hoboken, NJ: Wiley, 2003), 167; Associated Press, "Woman Convicted of Espionage Plot," *Deseret News*, February 19, 1945; David Kahn, *Hitler's Spies: German Military Intelligence in World War II* (Boston: Da Capo Press, 2000), 333–35.

51. Marie Koedel was given a seven and a half year sentence; her father fifteen years. "Sentenced for Espionage," *New York Times*, March 2, 1945; Kahn, *Hitler's Spies*, 335.

52. Karl Dönitz, "F.d.U./B.d.U.'S War Log: 1–15 July 1940," War Diary and War Standing Orders of Commander in Chief, Submarines, Naval Historical Center, Washington, DC, accessed September 20, 2011, http://www.uboatarchive.net/BDUKTB30268.htm.

53. Hessler, *U-Boat War*, 12–13.

54. Hans L. Trefousse, "The Failure of German Intelligence in the United States, 1935–1945," *Mississippi Valley Historical Review* 42, no. 1 (June 1955): 84–100.

55. Lukacs, *Duel*, 188.

56. Fleming, *Operation Sea Lion*, 57–58.

57. Christopher Andrew, *Defend the Realm: The Authorized History of MI5* (New York: Knopf, 2009), 224.

58. Ibid., 223.

59. Ansel, *Hitler Confronts England*, 113.

60. Ray Bearse and Anthony Read, *Conspirator: The Untold Story of Tyler Kent* (New York: Doubleday, 1991), 135.

61. Robert T. Crowley, "Introduction," in Bearse and Read, *Conspirator*, xiv.

62. Bearse and Read, *Conspirator*, 95–96; Paul Lashmar, "The Who's Who of British Nazis," *The Independent*, January 9, 2000.

63. The title "Lord Haw Haw" originated with an earlier German propaganda broadcaster who was first heard in April 1939. Dear and Foot, *Oxford Companion to World War II*, 640. Joyce was born in the United States but moved with his English mother and Irish-American father to England in 1921. In the 1930s, he joined the Nazi movement in England and fled to Germany just before the start of World War II. He took up a prominent post as a broadcaster for Joseph Goebbel's Propaganda Ministry. British radio listeners could hear his broadcasts weekly throughout the war, which he always started by saying "Germany calling." The British hanged him for treason in 1946. James Evans, "The Capture of Lord Haw Haw," WW2 People's War, BBC, accessed September 19, 2011, http://www.bbc.co.uk/ww2peopleswar/stories/29/a2015029.shtml.

64. Andrew, *Defend the Realm*, 194.

65. Bearse and Read, *Conspirator*, 95, 169; Lashmar, "Who's Who"; Persico, *Roosevelt's Secret War*, 19–31.

66. Kennedy, *World War II Companion*, 80.

67. Louis de Jong, *The German Fifth Column in the Second World War*, trans. C. M. Geyl, (New York: Howard Fertig, 1973), 102.

68. Mack and Humphries, *London at War*, 28; Campbell, *Experience of World War II*, 157.

69. On June 14, for example, the *Daily Express* reported that the Nazis had used "every kind of trick to sap confidence and cause confusion," including poisoned chocolates and wine, and spies disguised as priests, postmen, and housemaids. De Jong, *German Fifth Column*, 95.

70. PREM 3/215, National Archives.

71. In addition, according to German intelligence records captured after the war, MI5 found that nearly 115 or so agents targeted against Britain during the war were successfully identified and caught. Others were turned into double agents working for the British. Andrew, *Defend the Realm*, 224. "History World War II," Security Service MI5, accessed June 20, 2012, https://www.mi5.gov.uk/output/world-war-2.html.

72. Membership in the pro-Nazi German-American Bund peaked at twenty thousand. "War and Peace: Attack from Within," *Time*, June 24, 1940, accessed April 28, 2009, http://www.time.com/time/magazine/article/0,9171,764056,00.html; Moss, *Nineteen Weeks*, 64; Olson, *Those Angry Days*, 124.

73. George Britt, *The Fifth Column Is Here* (New York: W. Funk, 1940); "War and Peace: Science of Treason," *Time*, August 26 1940, accessed February 2, 2010, http://www.time.com/time/magazine/article/0,9171,764451,00.html.

74. Moss, *Nineteen Weeks*, 243–44.

75. The articles, written by Edgar Ansel Mowrer and Col. William J. Donovan, dealt with the Tyler Kent spy case. Bearse and Read, *Conspirator*, 229.

76. Moss, *Nineteen Weeks*, 243.

77. Persico, *Roosevelt's Secret War*, 32; Kennedy, *World War II Companion*, 79.

78. Lash, *Roosevelt and Churchill*, 138–40.

79. De Jong, *German Fifth Column*, 106.

80. Kennedy, *World War II Companion*, 75, 79.

81. Moss, *Nineteen Weeks*, 244. Regarding sabotage specifically, the FBI concluded that, although "many allegations of sabotage were investigated by the FBI during World War II, not one instance was found of enemy-inspired sabotage. Every suspect act traced to its source was the result of vandalism, pique, resentment, a desire for relief from boredom, the curiosity of children 'to see what would happen,' or other personal motive." See the "George John Dasch and the Nazi Saboteurs (FBI Handout)," from the report "German Espionage and Sabotage against the U.S. in World War II," Naval History and Heritage Command, accessed August 2, 2012, http://www.history.navy.mil/faqs/faq114-2.htm.

82. De Jong, *German Fifth Column*, 214; Olson, *Those Angry Days*, 122 and 293.

83. Lukacs, *Duel*, 120–21.

84. The following documents are found in RG 25 G-1, Vol. 1991, Library and Archives Canada: the June 4, 1940, letter from RCMP S. T. Wood to O. D. Skelton; the July 9, 1940, letter from the Commissioner for Justice to O. D. Skelton; and the August 14, 1940, letter from Undersecretary of State for External Affairs to L. E. Emerson, Commissioner for Justice and Defense, St. John's, Newfoundland.

85. Gregory S. Kealey and Reg Whitaker, eds., *R.C.M.P. Security Bulletins: The War Series, 1939–1941* (St. John's, NL: Committee on Canadian Labour History, 1989), 259, 261, 265, 278.

86. Ibid., 260.

87. Ibid.

88. Under the Defence of Canada Regulations, committees determined which of the individuals should be released or detained. Those posing a security risk were then sent to Army authorities for internment. Later in the war, the more serious concern for Canada was the emergence of a pro-Soviet espionage network. S. W. Horrall, *The Pictorial History of the Royal Canadian Mounted Police* (Toronto: McGraw-Hill Ryerson, 1973), 226.

89. "German Espionage and Sabotage against the United States in World War II: German Intelligence Service," Naval History and Heritage Command, accessed August 2, 2012, http://www.history.navy.mil/faqs/faq114-1.htm.

9. Taking Fearful Risks

1. Winston Churchill, "Their Finest Hour" (speech to the House of Commons June 18, 1940), Churchill Museum and Centre and Museum at the Churchill War Rooms, London, accessed June 1, 2012, http://www.winstonchurchill.org/learn/speeches/speeches-of -winston-churchill/122-their-finest-hour.

2. Draper, *Operation Fish*, 17.

3. Ibid.

4. Ibid.

5. Ibid., 155–56.

6. Thompson, *Assignment: Churchill*, 157.

7. T160/1054, National Archives. May, 26, 1940.

8. Pitt, *Battle of the Atlantic*, 63, 65.

9. By the end of June 1940, the number of unpaid local defense volunteers (later named the Home Guard) reached 1.5 million. Richard Hough and Denis Richards, *The Battle of Britain: The Greatest Air Battle of World War II* (New York: Norton, 1989), 106–8.

10. Chamberlain Archives, Birmingham, NC 8 /34/1-109.

11. T160/1054, May 25, 1940, National Archives.

12. T 236/721, National Archives.

13. "Commander in Chief, Canadian Northwest Atlantic—Bullion shipments, 1940–42," RG24, Box 11098, folder 48-3-46, Library and Archives Canada.

14. Ibid.

15. Leland Stowe, "HMS *Emerald*: Cmdr. Capt. Francis Cyril Flynn (His Story)," (unpublished), July 1955, Wisconsin Historical Society; Haskins, *Irish Flagship*, 40; Draper, *Operation Fish*, 209–10. Stowe ultimately put the value of the consignment of gold and securities at nearly a half billion dollars. Stowe, "Secret Voyage," 19; Hennessy, *Bank of England*, 98.

16. Leland Stowe, "Announcement of Shipment to Canada," May 30, 1955, Leland Stowe Papers, Wisconsin Historical Society.

17. Stowe, "HMS *Emerald*," 19.

18. Stowe, "Secret Voyage," 19.

19. Written in pencil on the document is "Emerald." Letter from Nelles to Marble, June 24, 1940, "Commander in Chief, Canadian Northwest Atlantic—Bullion shipments, 1940–42," Box 11098, RG24, file 48-3-46, Library and Archives Canada.

20. In addition, Nelles wrote, a "second H.M. Ship, estimated arrival at Halifax 29th June, carries Gold valued at Five Million Pounds." The ship could have been the *Duchess of Bedford*, the *Scythia*, the *Duchess of Atholl*, or the *Samaria*, all of which delivered £5 million to North America in June 1940. Letter from Nelles to Marble, June 24, 1940, "Commander in Chief, Canadian Northwest Atlantic—Bullion shipments, 1940–42," Box 11098, RG24, File 48-3-46, Library and Archives Canada.

21. Leland Stowe note, "Alexander S. Craig," June 30, 1955, Wisconsin Historical Society. The account of the *Emerald* is drawn from Stowe, "Secret Voyage," 19–20. See also Draper, *Operation Fish*, 212, 214; and Haskins, *Irish Flagship*, 40–41. Bank of England historian Elizabeth Hennessy claims that "large numbers of U-boats" were about, but as we saw in chapter 5, the Kriegsmarine was usually capable of running at most only sixteen U-boats in the North Atlantic during this phase of the war. Hennessy, *Bank of England*, 98.

22. Haskins, *Irish Flagship*, 40, fn 4; Stowe, "HMS *Emerald*."

23. Stowe, "HMS *Emerald*."

24. Ibid.

25. Stowe, "Announcement of Shipment."

26. Sidney Perkins, "Account of Sidney John Perkins, Formerly Agent, Ottawa Branch, Bank of Canada, Pertaining to Major Transfer of British Funds July 1940 Under Operation XFF," June 15–18, 1955, 18, Leland Stowe Papers, Wisconsin Historical Society; Stowe, "Secret Voyage," 20.

27. The information here is drawn from Perkins, "Account of Sidney John Perkins." See also Draper, *Operation Fish*, 236.

28. Capt. Francis Cyril Flynn of the *Emerald* put the box count at 480. Perkins, "Account of Sidney John Perkins."

29. Stowe interview notes of David Mansur in "Emerald's Cargo: Arrival & Delivery Montreal: Notes on the 'Deposit,'" June 14, 1955, Leland Stowe Papers, Wisconsin Historical Society.

30. See Leland Stowe interview notes, May 25, 1955, Leland Stowe Papers, Wisconsin Historical Society; and Stowe, "Secret Voyage," 21.

10. Britain's Most Valuable Convoy

1. *Maclean's*, July 1, 1940, as quoted in Stacey, *Arms, Men and Governments*, 31.

2. Dilks, *Diaries of Sir Alexander Cadogan*, 308; Draper, *Operation Fish*, 187. Gen. Raymond Lee, the American military attaché in London, wrote in his diary the next day (July 2, 1940) that it was odd "to be living in a spot which at any moment may be the arena of a war such as has never been seen. The beginning of it tonight is very widely prophesied. Some people think so because the old fool Madame [Geneviève] Tambouis has foretold it." Tambouis, a French journalist, was renowned for her "uncanny" predictions about

international events. The military mind of Lee, as well as that of his good friend Lt. Gen. Sir John Dill, chief of the Imperial General Staff, preferred an explanation that focused on the new moon and a high tide. Lee's initial expectation was not met. But in his diary entry on July 15, he wrote, "I have fixed in my own mind as the edge of the blitzkrieg season. I believe Hitler will attack this island with everything he has at any moment from now on. I also believe that if he is not successful by the fifteenth of September, he will never be." Leutze, *Journal of General Raymond E. Lee*, 9, 16.

3. Colville, *Fringes of Power*, 150, 161; Best, *Churchill at War*, 289.

4. In the end, though, only five thousand children left for the Dominions. Fewer than two thousand were sent to the United States. Fleming, *Operation Sea Lion*, 93.

5. Dönitz, *War Diary*, 86.

6. Fleming, *Operation Sea Lion*, 41.

7. Dear and Foote, *Oxford Companion to World War II*, 739–40.

8. Colville, *Fringes of Power*, 151.

9. Stowe calculated that the gold was worth $773 million, the remainder being the 299 boxes of securities. Stowe, "Secret Voyage," 21.

10. Perkins, "Account of Sidney John Perkins."

11. Hughes and Costello, *Battle of the Atlantic*, 73.

12. The description is drawn from W. S. Crawford, who described the admiral a year later when he left the *Revenge*: The "[l]ower deck was cleared this forenoon for the Captain [Archer] to make his farewell speech. He has been in *Revenge* since she was commissioned in 1939 and is leaving to take up a new appointment. Extremely popular and well-liked by all with whom he came in contact, both afloat and ashore, there are none who do not view his departure with genuine regret." Archer's next posting was as captain of the *Buxton*. Crawford, "Journal for the Use of Midshipmen," Crawford, WS Commander June 10, 1941, RN 92/5/1, Imperial War Museum, London.

13. Stowe, "Secret Voyage," 22.

14. Draper, *Operation Fish*, 215.

15. Stowe, "Secret Voyage," 21.

16. Hennessy, *Bank of England*, 37.

17. Watts was the Bank of Canada's first archivist. George S. Watts, "A Note on the 'Shadow' Bank of England in Ottawa, 1940," October 9, 1940, File GSW-89-20, GWS—Memoranda 1981–1984, Bank of Canada Archives.

18. Draper, *Operation Fish*, 216–17; Leland Stowe, "Project XFF: England—Archer," July 2, 1955, Wisconsin Historical Society.

19. Crawford, "Journal."

20. Gordon Swoger, *The Strange Odyssey of Poland's National Treasures, 1939–1961: A Polish-Canadian Story* (Toronto: Dundurn Group, 2004), 21–24; "How Poland's National Treasures Ended Up in Canada," *YouNxt* (blog), May 7, 2010, accessed September 19, 2011, http://younxt.wordpress.com/2010/05/07/how-polands-national-treasures-ended-up-in-canada/.

21. Swoger, *Strange Odyssey*.

22. Map I and map VII in Swoger, *Strange Odyssey*, 11, 15.

23. Stowe, "Secret Voyage," 21.

24. Crawford, "Journal."

25. Stowe, "Secret Voyage," 22.

26. Swoger, *Strange Odyssey*, 55. One of the ships alluded to by Polkowski was probably SS *Arandora Star*, which was torpedoed and sunk off the northern coast of Ireland, on July 2, by captain Günther Prien in U-47.

27. Colville, *Fringes of Power*, 154, 158.

28. T160/1054 and T 236/721, July 11, 1940, National Archives.

29. Stowe, "Secret Voyage," 21. Swoger makes no mention of the *Batory*'s engine troubles. He based his information on the account of Polkowski, who incorrectly claimed that the damaged ship was the *Pilsudski*, which was not a part of the convoy. Swoger, *Strange Odyssey*, 56.

30. Crawford incorrectly notes the *Sobieski* as the damaged ship. Crawford, "Journal."

31. See Stowe, "Secret Voyage," 21–22, and Draper, *Operation Fish*, 221–22.

32. Draper, *Operation Fish*, 231.

33. Swoger, *Strange Odyssey*, 57; Pat MacAdam, "Evacuated Polish Royal Treasures onboard of M/S BATORY & the Amazing Story of Keeping It Safe in Canada, 1940–1961," *Ottawa Citizen*, April 10, 1999, accessed September 19, 2011, edited and supplemented at http://stefanbatoryoceanliner.weebly.com/voyage.html.

34. The newspaper also reported that the size "of the British shipments caused considerable comment in local international quarters where it was pointed out that the gold cargoes on the vessels arriving from England were apparently equal to record shipments during peacetime, although small as compared with the $241 million which recently arrived from France on the American cruiser Vincennes." "Heavy Gold Shipments Received in New York: Major Part from Britain," *Wall Street Journal*, July 9, 1940.

35. Draper, *Operation Fish*, 233.

36. Winston Churchill, "War of the Unknown Warriors" (BBC Broadcast, London, July 14, 1940), Churchill Centre and Museum at the Churchill War Rooms, London, accessed January 23, 2013, http://www.winstonchurchill.org/learn/speeches/speeches-of-winston-churchill/126-war-of-the-unknown-warriors. Emphasis in the original.

37. Keegan, *Second World War*, 91.

38. Kennedy, *World War II Companion*, 453–54.

11. Clearing the Decks in Halifax

1. "War Comes to the City," Nova Scotia Archives, accessed September 19, 2011, http://www.gov.ns.ca/nsarm/virtual/eastcoastport/results.asp?Search=ch2&Language=English. For other descriptions of Halifax that summer, see Raban-Williams, "The Papers of Lieutenant R. Raban-Williams RN"; and Anne Westcott Winter, "A Memoir: 1939–1945," 91/37/1, Imperial War Museum, chap. 2, 1. For a description of Halifax in the winter of 1940–41, see Thomas Arthur Russell, "Approach of the Storm," WW2 People's War, BBC, accessed June 18, 2012, http://www.bbc.co.uk/ww2peopleswar/stories/63/a7354163.shtml.

2. File A18-17-1, Gold Earmarked for B. of E. Routine Shipments via Eastern Ports June–July 40, July 17, 1940, Bank of Canada Archives.

3. The precise figure was $114,714.26. Letter from L. Mundy of the Bank of Canada signing for the secretary to chief cashier at the Bank of England, July 23, 1940, File A18-17-1, Gold Earmarked for B. of E. Routine Shipments via Eastern Ports June–July 40, Bank of Canada Archives.

4. Letter from Secretary Dean Marble to George Bolton, December 30, 1940, File A18-17-2, "Gold Earmarked for B of E Shipped via Vancouver, July 2/40–Dec. 31/40," Bank of Canada Archives.

5. Perkins, "Account of Sidney John Perkins."

6. Ibid., 12–13; Draper, *Operation Fish*, 222–23.

7. Stowe puts the number of boxes of securities at 299, an implausibly low number. A precise value for the securities is impossible to calculate because their value depended on market conditions that fluctuated daily. See Perkins, "Account of Sidney John Perkins," 12–13; and Stowe, "Secret Voyage," 21.

8. Perkins, "Account of Sidney John Perkins," 13–15.

9. Ibid.

10. The figure is derived from the current value of gold at $1,450 an ounce.

11. Stowe, "Secret Voyage," 22.

12. Ibid., 23; and Perkins, "Account of Sidney John Perkins," 16.

13. Stowe, "Secret Voyage," 23.

14. Swoger, *Strange Odyssey*, 55.

15. Draper, *Operation Fish*, 220.

16. Winter is likely referring to Leland Stowe's 1955 *Reader's Digest* article "The Secret Voyage of Britain's Treasure," which publicized the treasure shipments for the first time.

17. Winter, "A Memoir: 1939–1945," chap. 1, 13–14.

18. Patricia Cave, *War Guest: Recollections of Being Evacuated to Canada in 1940* (Warminster: Adept Services Publishing, 1995), 19–20.

19. John Cooke, "Safe Keeping," September 2008, accessed September 19, 2011, http://www.hidden-worlds.com/safekeeping_sample.htm.

20. Cooke, "Safe Keeping."

21. Ibid.

22. Isaiah Berlin, *Letters, 1928–1946 / Isaiah Berlin*, ed. Henry Hardy (Cambridge: Cambridge University Press, 2004).

23. Two other "problem ships" with child evacuees, the *Duchess of York* and *Samaria*, also made several gold runs in 1940. Carlton Jackson, *Who Will Take Our Children? The Story of the Evacuation in Britain, 1939–1945* (London: Methuen, 1985), 86–87.

24. Michael Ignatieff, *Isaiah Berlin: A Life* (New York: Holt, 1998), 97.

25. Frances Gray, "Evacuated from England to America," WW2 People's War, BBC, accessed May 16, 2013, http://www.bbc.co.uk/history/ww2peopleswar/stories/32/a7917032.shtml.

26. Ibid.

27. Perkins, "Account of Sidney John Perkins," 25.

28. Ibid., 19.

29. Ibid.

30. Draper, *Operation Fish*, 226.

31. William Naftel, "Letters April 2008," accessed June 20, 2010, http://historytoday
.com/MainArticle.aspx?m=32613&amid=30254376 (site discontinued).

32. Perkins, "Account of Sidney John Perkins," 18.

33. Ibid., 21.

34. Ibid., 22.

35. Ibid., 8.

36. Stowe, "Secret Voyage," 20.

37. Perkins, "Account of Sidney John Perkins," 8.

38. Leland Stowe, "Emerald's Cargo—Arrival & Delivery Montreal: Notes on the
'Deposit,'" June 14, 1955, Wisconsin Historical Society.

39. The Sun Life in-house newsletter merely reported that "little can be said about it."
Draper, *Operation Fish*, 255–56.

40. Stowe, "Announcement of Shipment."

41. Stowe, "Secret Voyage," 24.

42. Ibid., 21, 24.

43. Stowe, "Emerald's Cargo."

44. Draper, *Operation Fish*, 153, 247.

45. Perkins, "Account of Sidney John Perkins," 23–24; TheShipList, "Ship Descriptions—D," accessed September 19, 2011, http://www.theshipslist.com/ships/descriptions/
ShipsD.html. Draper makes the unsubstantiated claim that the *Duchess of Atholl* was torpedoed but survived during this July 1940 voyage. Draper, *Operation Fish*, 154.

46. Hennessy, *Bank of England*, 98–99. Hennessy quotes the Bank of England's files
M5/535, p. 604ff, E6/20; Stowe, "Emerald's Cargo."

47. Draper, *Operation Fish*, 246.

48. Stowe, "Secret Voyage," 24.

49. Stowe, "Secret Voyage," 24–25.

50. Hennessy, *Bank of England*, 91, 98.

51. Draper, *Operation Fish*, 228; Perkins, "Account of Sidney John Perkins," 18.

52. Stowe, "Secret Voyage," 23.

53. McDowall, "Earmarked Gold," 12.

54. Perkins, "Account of Sidney John Perkins," 230.

55. Stowe, "Secret Voyage," 23.

56. File 580-44-14A, Vol. 3908-4612, Gold Held in Safekeeping Bank of England, 1939–
1946, Bank of Canada Archives.

57. Ibid.

58. Letter from C. F. Cobbold to the Bank of Canada, July 17, 1940, File A18-17, Banking
Operations, Bank of Canada Archives.

59. File 580-44-14A, Vol. 3908-4612, Gold Held in Safekeeping Bank of England, 1939–
1946, Bank of Canada.

60. The Associated Press reported that shipments of gold, swelled by large British Empire transfers for purchase of war matériel, were about $1.2 billion larger in 1940 than in 1939, the previous high. The newspaper account also noted that most of the gold was sold to the U.S. Treasury and that in 1940 earmarked gold went from $1,163,004,000 to $1,807,673,000. "1940 Gold Imports up to $4,749,467,000," *New York Times*, January 14, 1941.

61. "Gold Shipped to New York for Account of Bank of England: September 1, 1939 to September 9, 1940" and File 580-42-14C, "Gold Shipments/Bank of England—Year 1940," Bank of Canada Archives.

62. In addition to the Admiralty and Pickford shipping lists (see appendix 1), see, for example, the telegram from Britain's Foreign Office to Frederick Phillips at the Treasury, January 10, 1941, Folder G1/21, Bank of England; and the "Most Secret" memo from the Admiralty, June 28, 1942, ADM 116/5485, National Archives.

63. T 236/721, November 6, 1940, National Archives.

64. CAB 65/14/23, August 22, 1940, National Archives. By then, the war was costing Britain $45 million a day. The cost of the war at the end of 1940 derives from Sir Frederick Phillips, undersecretary of the British Treasury. "Our Finances Never Better, Briton Tells U.S.," *Globe and Mail*, December 29, 1940. For statements about Britain's ongoing financial troubles, see Lash, *Roosevelt and Churchill*, 135. Bank of England documents included this December statement from Bank governor Montagu Norman: "As our ability at all times to honor our commitments in gold now seem likely to be brought into question. I rely on your full support of the Bank of England in any eventuality which may thus arise." T160/1054, December 31, 1940, National Archives. See also CAB 65/14/23, August 22, 1940, and CAB 66/11/42, September 4, 1940, National Archives.

65. CAB 65/14/23, August 22, 1940, National Archives.

66. For both the West Indies and pot scraping issues, see CAB 65/14/23, August 22, 1940, National Archives. See also Colville, *Fringes of Power*, 192. U.S. Treasury Secretary Henry Morgenthau Jr. included in the definition of "scraping the pot" works of art and South American investments in the United States (which he believed could only be sold at "rubbish" prices). Blum, *Years of Urgency*, 198–99.

67. Further evidence of Britain's financial problems may be found in the following sources: CAB 66/11/4, August 21, 1940, National Archives; T160/1089, September 23, 1940, National Archives; Folder G1/20, November 21, 1940, Bank of England.

68. "Foreign News: War of Sterling," *Time*, September 2, 1940, accessed September 19, 2011, http://www.time.com/time/printout/0,8816,764533,00.html.

69. Lee's comment was made on July 30, 1940. Leutze, *Journal of General Raymond E. Lee.*, xliv.

70. G. V. Ormsby, "British Assets," *Wall Street Journal*, July 19, 1940. See also the memo by Thelma Wells describing the public announcements regarding the securities. T231/203, EC R 19/01, October 25, 1944, National Archives.

71. According to the report, arrangements "are being completed to establish a United Kingdom security deposit in Montréal to hold in custody British-held United States and

Canadian securities sent to Canada under instructions of the British Treasury, official sources disclosed today." The report also mentioned that A. S. Craig of the Bank of England, along with five unnamed officials, would supervise the facility. T. J. Carlyle Gifford is mentioned as the special British Treasury representative in charge of liquidating all British-owned U.S. securities. "Britain Will Deposit U.S. Issues in Canada," *New York Times*, July 25, 1940. See also Thelma Wells, T231/203, EC R 19/01, October 25, 1944, National Archives.

72. "Hold Deposits for Treasury," *Globe and Mail*, July 25, 1940; "English-Owned U.S. Securities to Be Deposited in Montreal," *Wall Street Journal*, July 25, 1940; and "Britain Will Deposit," *New York Times*.

73. Blum, *Years of Urgency*, 220.

74. Stettinius, *Lend-Lease*, 4.

75. Moss, *Nineteen Weeks*, 349.

76. One possible exception is the HMAS *Sydney*, an Australian ship headed for North America in November 1941 but sunk by the German raider *Kormoran*. There is some dispute about whether the ship carried gold or not. James H. Eagles suggests that the *Sydney* was a part of Britain's treasury evacuation; the bullion came from British banks in Hong Kong and Singapore. According to Eagles, the gold may have first been stored in two Dutch submarines and then transferred to the *Sydney*. The Australian Defense Department's final report into the sinking of the *Sydney* describes Eagles's claim as a conspiracy theory. James H. Eagles, *The HMAS Sydney and Operation Fish 1941*, ed. Anne Eagles (Townsend, Australia: James and Ann Eagles, 2003), accessed July 31, 2009, http://www.defence.gov.au/sydneyii/ SUBM/SUBM.001.0212_R.pdf; James H. Eagles, "Transferring Gold at Sea, in the Instance of HMAS Sydney 17 November 1941," accessed July 31, 2009, http://www.defence.gov.au/ sydneyii/SUBM/SUBM.002.0079.pdf; Mal Booth, "HMAS *Sydney*," Australian War Memorial, March 19, 2008, accessed July 31, 2009, http://www.awm.gov.au/blog/2008/03/19/ hmas-sydney/#comment-1935; Naval History, "The Search for and Discovery of HMAS SYDNEY and German Raider KORMORAN Both Lost 19 November 1941," accessed January 26, 2013, http://www.naval-history.net/xGM-Chrono-06CL-SydneySearch.htm; HMAS Sydney II Search, "Search Diary," accessed January 26, 2013, http://presspass.findingsydney.com/ blogs/default.aspx?GroupID=6; Wesley Olson, *Bitter Victory: The Death of HMAS Sydney* (Nedlands: University of Western Australia Press, 2000); and James Eagles, "Speculation and Conspiracy: Mr James Eagles," in *The Loss of HMAS Sydney II*, vol.3, chap. 29, accessed January 26, 2013, http://www.defence.gov.au/sydneyii/finalreport/Report/Chapter%2029.pdf.

77. "War and Peace," Manchester Liners Old Shipmates Association, accessed September 19, 2011, http://www.manchesterliners.co.uk/war.htm.

78. "Aracataca (British Steam merchant)," U-boat.net, accessed September 19, 2011, http://www.uboat.net/allies/merchants/ships/682.html; "Elders & Fyffes & Geest Line," TheShipList, accessed September 19, 2011, http://www.theshipslist.com/ships/lines/elder-sfyffes.html; and "Aracataca Cargo Ship, 1924–1940," Wreck Site, accessed September 19, 2011, http://www.wrecksite.eu/wreck.aspx?134800.

79. Draper, *Operation Fish*, appendix I, 358–59; and "HMS Ramillies," Cranston Fine Arts, accessed January 19, 2013, http://www.battleships-cruisers.co.uk/ramillies.htm.

80. The exact number of children is not clear. Norman Moss puts the figure at six hundred. The *Batory* would also become known as the "Lucky Ship" for having survived its many wartime voyages. Peter Grajda, "TSS Stefan Batory—Polish Ocean Liner 1968/1988: Predecessors," accessed January 26, 2013, http://stefanbatoryoceanliner.weebly.com/predecessors.html, and "M/S Pilsudski & M/S Batory," http://www.derbysulzers.com/shipbatory.html, put the number at 480. Peter Plowman puts the figure at 477. See Moss, *Nineteen Weeks*, 189; Peter Plowman, *Across the Sea to War: Australian and New Zealand Troop Convoys from 1865 through Two World Wars to Korea and Vietnam* (Dural, Australia: Rosenberg, 2003), 161–62; Emmy E. Werner, *Through the Eyes of Innocents: Children Witness World War II* (Boulder, CO: Westview, 2000), 43–44; Meta Maclean, *The Singing Ship: An Odyssey of Evacuee Children* (Sydney: Chivers, 1975); and David Walker, "The Batory Story," WW2 People's War, BBC, accessed January 26, 2013, http://www.bbc.co.uk/print/ww2peopleswar/stories/26/a7683726.shtml.

81. "HMS Southampton (83) of the Royal Navy," Uboat.net, accessed September 19, 2011, http://www.uboat.net/allies/warships/ship/1235.html.

82. Ibid.; "HMS Bonaventure (31) of the Royal Navy," Uboat.net, accessed September 19, 2011, http://www.uboat.net/allies/warships/ship/4015.html; "Shipping Snippets April 1941," *Old Mersey Times*, accessed January 26, 2013, http://www.old-merseytimes.co.uk/shipwrecksG.html.

83. See "Parthenia: North Channel," Scotland Places, accessed September 19, 2011, http://www.scotlandsplaces.gov.uk/search_item/index.php?service=RCAHMS&id=102528; "Lloyd's Law Reports," I-law.com, accessed September 19, 2011, http://www.i-law.com/ilaw/browse_lawreports.htm?year=1942&name=lloyd's%20law%20reports; "Parthenia Cargo Ship 1917–1940," Wreck Site, accessed September 19, 2011, http://www.wrecksite.eu/wreck.aspx?31289.

84. "Bangalore Cargo Ship 1928–1941," Wreck Site, accessed September 19, 2011, http://www.wrecksite.eu/wreck.aspx?58378; "Richmond Castle (British Motor merchant)," Uboat.net, accessed September 19, 2011, http://www.uboat.net/allies/merchants/2001.html; "75282 Squadron Leader Robert Wallis Beresford," Balloon Barrage Reunion Club, accessed September 19, 2011, http://www.bbrclub.org/75282_squadron_leader_robert_wal.htm. In addition, while sailing from Liverpool to New York, the *Samaria* collided with an escorting warship on December 16, 1939. It survived the incident but was forced to return to Liverpool. "Ship Descriptions—S," TheShipList, accessed September 19, 2011, http://www.theshipslist.com/ships/descriptions/ShipsS.html.

85. "Revenge Class Battleship—HMS Revenge," Shipnostalgia.com, accessed September 19, 2011, http://www.shipsnostalgia.com/guides/Revenge_Class_Battleship_-_HMS_Revenge?cruise_forum_g__session=eae4eb8bfa9d81d6e02516318ee302b7.

12. Speculation

1. Richard Ned Lebow, *Forbidden Fruit: Counterfactuals and International Relations* (Princeton, NJ: Princeton University Press, 2010), 15.

2. Ibid., 17.

3. Noel Hendrickson, "Counterfactual Reasoning: A Basic Guide for Analysts, Strategists, and Decision Makers," *Proteus Monograph Series* 2, no.5 (October 2008), U.S. Army War College, 2.

4. Ibid., 6.

5. Richard Ned Lebow, "Counterfactual Thought Experiments: A Necessary Teaching Tool," *History Teacher* 40, no. 2 (February 2007), accessed September 19, 2011, http://www.historycooperative.org/journals/ht/40.2/lebow.html.

6. Kimball, *Alliance Forged*, 49–51; Draper, *Operation Fish*, 238.

7. Manchester and Reid, *Defender of the Realm*, 77 and 126.

8. Kimball, *Alliance Forged*, 49–51.

9. "The Battle of Britain," Imperial War Museum, accessed September 19, 2011, http://www.iwm.org.uk/upload/package/27/battleofbritain/intro.htm.

10. Lash, *Roosevelt and Churchill*, 146.

11. Ibid., 135.

12. Ansel, *Hitler Confronts England*, 320; Irving, *Churchill's War*, 379; Manchester and Reid, *Defender of the Realm*, 119.

13. Even as Hitler postponed Operation Sea Lion, he told the German naval staff that he wanted *the threat* of invasion of Britain to persist. Irving, *Churchill's War*, 379.

14. Fleming, *Operation Sea Lion*, fn 2, 91–92.

15. Ibid., 52; Kennedy, *World War II Companion*, 456. During the "Blitz," forty thousand British civilians were killed. Keegan, *Second World War*, 100.

16. T160/1089, Telegram no. 19, September 23, 1940, National Archives.

17. Martin Gilbert, *The Churchill War Papers: The Ever Widening War*, Vol. 3, *1941* (New York: W. W. Norton, 2000), xi.

18. Colville, *Fringes of Power*, 279, 284.

19. In addition, a month later, U.S. skepticism of Britain's financial problems forced Lothian to advise the Foreign Office to avoid giving any impression that Britain had any "hidden assets." Abbazia, *Mr. Roosevelt's Navy*, 93; T160/1089, September 23, 1940, National Archives.

20. Parrish, *To Keep the British Isles Afloat*, 107. For the next three days, the *Chicago Tribune*'s headlines ran "Envoy Lothian Claims Britain Is Going Broke," "British Envoy's US Talks Stirs Uproar at Home," and "Storm Brewing over US Fiscal Help to Britain." See also Saucier, "Mr. Kerr Goes to Washington," 366–67.

21. T160/1054, January 15, 1941, National Archives. In addition, as the letter from Sir Andrew Duncan to Arthur Purvis suggests, the Roosevelt administration seemed to have had an exaggerated view of how much Britain's direct investments in the United States were worth. Letter from Sir Andrew Duncan to Arthur Purvis, January 10, 1941, Folder G1/21, Bank of England.

22. "Securities: A Deal in British Stocks?" *Time*, January 20, 1941, accessed September 19, 2011, http://www.time.com/time/magazine/article/0,9171,772645,00.html. After a year of war, the British government was subsidizing foodstuffs on the order of £100 million a year, with additional government assistance for essential goods and services. Broadberry

and Howlett, "The United Kingdom: 'Victory at All Costs,'" in Harrison, *Economics of World War II*, 49.

23. Letter from Henry Morgenthau to Sol Bloom, chair of the House Committee on Foreign Relations, T160/1054, January 21, 1941, National Archives.

24. T160/1054, January 26, 1941, National Archives.

25. Churchill was often wrong about when the United States would enter the war or under what conditions the United States would enter. In mid-June 1940, as France was falling to the Germans, Churchill told those close to him that "he personally was convinced that the carnage and destruction in this country would bring the U.S. into the war." Colville, *Fringes of Power*, 128. Again, however, neither Congress nor the American public had any real interest in joining the war effort—despite how bad things looked for Britain.

26. McDowall, "Earmarked Gold."

27. CAB 66/11/4, August 21, 1940, National Archives.

28. Draper, *Operation Fish*, 202.

29. Graham Towers Memorandum, August 31 1940, File GFT75-12, Comments in Respect to Mr. Churchill's Cable of August 25, 1940: File "French Gold in Canada," Bank of Canada Archives.

30. McDowall, "Earmarked Gold," 15.

31. Ibid.

32. T160/1054, November 9, 1940, National Archives.

33. There still seemed hope for the British weeks later. On December 11, 1940, Phillips believed the U.S. secretary of the treasury, Henry Morgenthau Jr., expected Britain to take all French gold in Canada. "Morgenthau," wrote Phillips, "certainly wants to put pressure on us to secure Allied gold." Whatever pressure was ultimately brought to bear, the Canadians held firm. December 11, 1940, Folder G1/20, Bank of England; and in the same folder, correspondence from Frederick Phillips on December 10 and 12, 1940.

34. McDowall, "Earmarked Gold," 14–15, 19.

35. Ibid., 14–15. Negative attitudes toward Britain also derived from Québec's experience during World War I, when the province opposed conscription. Its views were ignored by a coalition government that had no French-speaking representation. Dear and Foot, *Oxford Companion to World War II*, 415.

36. Macintyre, *Naval War*, 562.

37. Harris, *Book of Submarines*, 285; Ireland, *Battle of the Atlantic*, 52.

38. Mine warfare, attacks by surface ships, and German planes added further to this toll. Tarrant, *U-Boat Offensive*, 93.

39. Also, between June 1940 and October 1940, U-boats plagued Allied shipping. Against ships in convoys, the Allies lost 18 percent of their ships. When Allied ships were sailing independently, the loss rate was 82 percent. Tarrant, *U-Boat Offensive*, 89, 94. Abbazia found slightly smaller numbers. According to him, from June to October 1940, U-boats sank a total of 274 merchant ships (over 1.3 million tons). Abbazia, *Mr. Roosevelt's Navy*, 109. The difference in ships sunk may be explained by alternative dating methods for the Happy Time. See also Hughes and Costello, *Battle of the Atlantic*, 63, 88, 94, 166.

40. Harris, *Book of Submarines*, 286.

41. In addition, from November 1940 through March 1941, surface ships sank 90 ships totaling 472,381 tons. Ibid., 288.

42. The Royal Navy lost two battleships, two battle cruisers, two aircraft carriers, ten cruisers, twenty-three destroyers, and twelve submarines. Merchant shipping losses were also extensive. Kennedy, *World War II Companion*, 276.

43. The rescue vessels were the *Bassethound*, *Valldemosa*, and *Olaf Fostenes*. The *Volendam* was later repaired and served as a troop ship for the remainder of the war. C.H. Hindley, Geoffrey Shakespeare, Lord Provost Dollan, "Newspaper Article about Torpedoing of SS Volendam," WW2 People's War, BBC, accessed September 19, 2011, http://www.bbc.co.uk/ww2peopleswar/stories/34/a4297034.shtml; "Volendam (Dutch Steam passenger ship)," Uboat.net, accessed September 19, 2011, http://www.uboat.net/allies/merchants/ships/505.html.

44. Information from the British Admiralty, reprinted in Draper, put the gold shipment value at £2 million, but Canadian naval records indicate "up to" £1 million. Draper, *Operation Fish*, 361; and correspondence between Percy W. Nelles, rear admiral, chief of Naval Staff, Royal Canadian Navy, and Dean Marble, secretary at the Bank of Canada, June 17, 1940, Bank of Canada Archives. See also "Sulairia Cargo Ship 1929–1940," Wreck Site, accessed September 19, 2011, http://www.wrecksite.eu/wreck.aspx?12927; "Kapitän-leutnant Manfred Buchmann: Patrol #8," 9. U-Boat Flotilla, Brest, accessed January 26, 2011, http://www.9thflottilla.de/9mbp8.htm; "Donaldson Line," TheShipList, accessed September 19, 2011, http://www.theshipslist.com/ships/lines/donaldson.html; and "Sulairia (British Steam merchant)," Uboat.net, accessed September 19, 2011, http://www.uboat.net/allies/merchants/ships/554.html.

45. "Port Gisborne (British Motor merchant)," Uboat.net, accessed September 19, 2011, http://www.uboat.net/allies/merchants/ships/585.html; "SeaWaves Today in History October 11, 2010," accessed September 19, 2011, http://www.seawaves.com/TDIH/october/11Oct.txt.

46. Correspondence from Rear Adm. Percy W. Nelles to Dean Marble of the Bank of Canada, June 4, 1940, Commander in Chief, Canadian Northwest Atlantic—Bullion shipments, 1940–42, RG24, Box 11098, File 48-3-46, Library and Archives Canada; "Manchester Brigade (British Steam merchant)," Uboat.net; Lawrence Paterson, *First U-Boat Flotilla* (Annapolis, MD: Naval Institute Press, 2002), 78; "U-110—Greenock Report—U-boat Attacks on Convoy OB 318," Uboatarchive.net, accessed September 19, 2011, http://www.uboatarchive.net/U-110GreenockReport.htm.

47. There is some controversy as to whether or not the *Empress of Britain* went down with a consignment of gold. Pickford, *Lost Treasury Ships*, 111–23; Dönitz, *Memoirs*, 109; File 580-42-14D, Bank of England 1938 1939, and File 135–6, Gold under Earmark Abroad 1938, Bank of Canada Archives; and Rohwer, *War at Sea*, 44.

48. Martienssen, *Hitler and His Admirals*, 19. See also a 1938 memo from a Naval High Command Staff officer that concurred with the Chief of the Army's general staff

generaloberst Ludwig Beck that a war Britain, France, and the Soviet Union would likely involve the United States, and, in the end, would be disastrous. Mulligan, *Neither Sharks nor Wolves*, 224.

49. Von der Porten, *German Navy*, 31. Surprisingly, according to a Kriegsmarine survey of problems at the outbreak of the war, up to the end of 1938 "neither the government nor the Navy had considered Britain as a possible enemy." Hessler, *U-Boat War*, 3.

50. Mulligan, *Neither Sharks nor Wolves*, 74.

51. Tarrant, *U-Boat Offensive*, 93, 94. Earlier in the war, the German Navy's Beobachtungs-Dienst (B Dienst Intel Service) had broken the British codes and could accurately forecast the movements of British air and sea units. During the Germans' campaign against Norway, for example, 50 percent of the British naval signal traffic had been intercepted and translated within hours of its transmission. Aware of the problem, the Admiralty attempted to stymie the Germans by printing new codebooks, but these in turn were broken in a matter of weeks. Hughes and Costello, *Battle of the Atlantic*, 51, 72.

52. Tarrant, *U-Boat Offensive*, 95.

13. Credit

1. Pickford, *Lost Treasure Ships*, 187.

2. Some of the gold sent to North America belonged to private citizens and had been requisitioned by the British government. When, on February 24, 1946, the British Parliament repealed the Emergency Powers Act, the Bank of England started releasing this gold under the Sundry Personal Accounts at the Bank of Canada in Ottawa. Over time, gold held by private citizens was then claimed. On June 7, 1955, the last of the personal deposits was claimed and settled. McDowall, "Earmarked Gold," 36–37.

3. Letter from Senior Treasury official Ernest Rowe-Dutton to his colleague Sir Wilfred Eady, T231/203, EC R 19/01, September 28, 1944, National Archives.

4. Letter from D. E. Johns to E. Rowe-Dutton, T231/203, EC R 19/01, September 27, 1944, National Archives; letter from E. Rowe-Dutton to F. W. Mattershead, T231/203, EC R 19/01, June 15, 1945, National Archives; Hennessy, *Bank of England*, 108. According to Draper, a single ship was chosen over several so as to shorten the time in which securities trading would be suspended. Draper, *Operation Fish*, 352–54. In another exchange with Rowe-Dutton, Johns made it clear that "a proper escort" would be needed to accompany the securities at all times. Johns also noted that the securities would not be insured while in transit. Letter from D. E. Johns to E. Rowe-Dutton, T231/203, EC R 19/01, December 6, 1944, National Archives.

5. Letter from D. E. Johns to E. Rowe-Dutton, T231/203, EC R 19/01, June 16, 1945, National Archives.

6. "Display Ad 71—No Title," *New York Times*, July 9, 1945.

7. Ownership of the *Leander* shifted from New Zealand to Britain in 1943. "HMS Leander (75) of the Royal Navy," Uboat.net, accessed September 20, 2011, http://www.uboat.net/allies/warships/ship/7946.html; "HMS Leander (Light Cruiser, 1933–1949)," Global Security.org, accessed September 20, 2011, http://www.globalsecurity.org/military/world/

europe/hms-leander.htm; and "HMS/MMNZS Leander," *Naval Warfare* (blog), September 18, 2007, accessed September 20, 2011, http://navalwarfare.blogspot.com/2007/09/hmshmnzs-leander.html.

8. Draper, *Operation Fish*, 354.

9. "1,000 Cases of Securities Sent from Canada to British Owners," *Globe and Mail*, September 1, 1945. One newspaper noted that the securities displaced 450 6-inch shells from the ship's ammunition lockers. Draper, *Operation Fish*, 355.

10. Draper, *Operation Fish*, 356.

11. Unaware of the story Higson had just alluded to, the interviewer then simply asked, "Do you remember where you were when the war was over?" Harry Higson, "Interview with Harry Higson, 8 June 2005," Bolton Remembers the War, accessed September 20, 2011, http://www.boltonswar.org.uk/tr-harry-higson.htm#16.

12. Leland Stowe, "Were British Crown & Crown Jewels Brought to Canada?" Leland Stowe Papers, Wisconsin Historical Society. The document is not dated but is most likely from 1955—like the other documents in the file and the year of the rest of Stowe's research. Harold Kent is referred to in several of Stowe's notes as "Z." Kent later told Stowe to remove mention of Chiselhurst and of the caves to "places not far from London, suitable places giving maximum security." John P. Melvin, the deputy chief of Currency Division at the Bank of Canada in 1940, said, "We never had any British Crown jewels in our [Bank of Canada] vault. . . . I know that. I was in charge and working there every day. . . . If the British Crown was here in Ottawa, they kept it in some other bank." Melvin did mention that the Bank of Canada held the Dutch crown jewels. David Mansur, deputy governor of the Bank of Canada, also said that he had no knowledge of the location of Britain's crown jewels during the war.

13. "The Crown Jewels in the Vaults of the Sun Life," *L'Action Catholique*, December 27, 1945; Stuart Nulman, *Beyond the Mountain: True Tales about Montreal* (Kirkland, QC: Callawind, 2002).

14. Stowe, "Crown Jewels Brought to Canada?"

15. Hennessy, *Bank of England*, 108–9.

16. In the summer of 2011, Venezuela announced its desire to repatriate the country's gold, much of it held in United States and Europe. The Venezuelan government was acting on fears that the gold might be frozen for political reasons relating President Hugo Chávez's policies. Shortly thereafter, lively press and Internet speculation ensued about how to safely transport 211 tons of gold. In contrast to Britain's situation in 1939 and 1940, Venezuela was at peace and many media organizations around the world covered the story. See, for example, Melissa Block, "All Things Considered," National Public Radio, August 22, 2011; Richard Miniter, "Why Is Hugo Chávez Moving Venezuela's Gold Holdings Home?" *Forbes*, September 18, 2011, accessed September 26, 2011, http://www.forbes.com/sites/richardminiter/2011/09/18/why-is-hugo-chavez-moving-venezuelas-gold-holdings-home/; "Chavez to Nationalize Gold Industry," *Reuters*, August 18, 2011.

17. Agar, *Footprints in the Sea*, 235. Drake's actual exhortation in 1578 was "I must have the gentleman to haul and draw with the mariner, and the mariner with the gentleman."

N. A. M. Rodger, *The Safeguard of the Sea: A Naval History of Britain, 660–1649* (New York: Norton, 1998), 302.

Appendix 1

1. Stowe, "Secret Voyage."

2. Letter from Sidney Perkins to Leland Stowe, June 18, 1955, Wisconsin Historical Society; Draper, *Operation Fish*, 217. R. Raban-Williams of the *Revenge* also referred to gold as margarine. Raban-Williams, "The Papers of Lieutenant R. Raban-Williams RN."

3. Ralph Bennett, "Geheimschreiber," in Dear and Foot, *Oxford Companion to World War II*, 432; Kennedy, *World War II Companion*, 377, 730.

4. Draper, *Operation Fish*, 246.

5. According to David Mansur of the Bank of Canada. Stowe, "Secret Voyage," 24.

6. Others have used the expression "Bundles from Britain" to refer to the children evacuated to North America. Alistair Horne, *A Bundle from Britain* (New York: St. Martin's Press, 1994). Moss, *Nineteen Weeks*, 289; "Bundles from Britain," *Time*, February 24, 1941, accessed September 20, 2011, http://www.time.com/time/magazine/article/0,9171,789990,00.html; and Draper, *Operation Fish*, 147. In 2000 Norman Shannon used the same expression in his summary of the operation. Norman Shannon, "World War II: Bundles from Britain," *Esprit de Corps*, November 1, 2000, accessed May 13, 2013, http://www.highbeam.com/doc/1G1-30124735.html.

Appendix 2

1. Stowe, "Secret Voyage," 17–26.

2. Draper, *Operation Fish*, 358–68.

3. Pickford, *Lost Treasure Ships*, 183–87.

4. See the entries from March 12, 1940 ($4,162,314) to March 14, 1950 ($3,097,822), Gold Held in Safekeeping Bank of England, 1939–1946, File 580-44-14A, Vol. 3908-4612, Bank of Canada.

5. "Crews of Warship Honored for Record Gold Transport," *Los Angeles Times*, December 24, 1939.

6. The website uses information from Arthur R. Moore, *"A Careless Word—A Needless Sinking": A History of the Staggering Losses Suffered by the U.S. Merchant Marine, Both in Ships and Personnel in World War II* (Kings Point, NY: American Merchant Marine Museum, 1983).

Bibliography

Primary documents were procured from the following archives and banks:

Bank of Canada Archives in Ottawa
Bank of England Archives in London
The Churchill Archives Centre at Churchill College in Cambridge
The Imperial War Museum in London
The Leland Stowe Papers at the Wisconsin Historical Society in Madison
Library and Archives Canada in Ottawa
The National Archives, Kew, London
The Papers of Neville Chamberlain Collection at the University of Birmingham, England

Media accounts were derived primarily from these sources:

BBC, in particular the WW2 People's War project (www.bbc.co.uk/history/ww2
    peopleswar/)
Globe and Mail
Los Angeles Times
New York Times
Time
Wall Street Journal

Books and articles

Abbazia, Patrick. *Mr. Roosevelt's Navy: The Private War of the U.S. Atlantic Fleet, 1939–1942.*
    Annapolis, MD: Naval Institute Press, 1975.
Agar, Augustus. *Footprints in the Sea.* London: Evans Bros., 1959.
Ahamed, Liaquat. "Currency Wars, Then and Now." *Foreign Affairs* 90 (March/April 2011).
Andrew, Christopher. *Defend the Realm: The Authorized History of MI5.* New York: Knopf,
    2009.
Ansel, Walter. *Hitler Confronts England.* Durham, NC: Duke University Press, 1960.
Bailey, Thomas A., and Paul B. Ryan. *Hitler vs. Roosevelt: The Undeclared Naval War.* New
    York: Free Press, 1979.

Bearse, Ray, and Anthony Read. *Conspirator: The Untold Story of Tyler Kent.* New York: Doubleday, 1991.

Beaty, David. *The Water Jump: The Story of the Transatlantic Flight.* London: Secker & Warburg, 1976.

Bekker, Cajus. *Hitler's Naval War.* Translated and edited by Frank Ziegler. Garden City, NY: Doubleday, 1974.

Bennett, Ralph. "Geheimschreiber." In Dear and Foot, *Oxford Companion to World War II,* 340.

Berlin, Isaiah. *Letters, 1928–1946 / Isaiah Berlin.* Edited by Henry Hardy. Cambridge: Cambridge University Press, 2004.

Best, Geoffrey. *Churchill and War.* London: Hambledon and Continuum, 2005.

Block, Melissa. *All Things Considered.* National Public Radio, August 22, 2011.

Blum, John Morton. *Years of Urgency: 1938–1941.* Vol. 2 of *From the Morgenthau Diaries.* Boston: Houghton Mifflin, 1965.

Brennecke, Jochen. *The Hunters and the Hunted: German U-Boats, 1939–1945.* Translated by R. H. Stevens. New York: W. W. Norton, 1958.

Breuer, William B. *The Air-Raid Warden Was a Spy: And Other Tales from Home-Front America in World War II.* Hoboken, NJ: Wiley, 2003.

———. *Hitler's Undercover War: The Nazi Espionage Invasion of the U.S.A.* New York: St. Martin's Press, 1989.

———. *Top Secret Tales of World War II.* New York: Wiley, 2000.

Britt, George. *The Fifth Column Is Here.* New York: W. Funk, 1940.

Broadberry, Stephen, and Peter Howlett. "The United Kingdom: 'Victory at All Costs.'" In *The Economics of World War II: Six Great Powers in International Comparison,* edited by Mark Harrison, 43–81. Cambridge: Cambridge University Press, 1998.

Brown, Seyom. *The Causes and Prevention of War.* 2nd ed. New York: St. Martin's Press, 1994.

Budiansky, Stephen. "The Difficult Beginnings of US-British Codebreaking Cooperation." In *American-British-Canadian Intelligence Relations, 1939–2000,* edited by David Stafford and Rhodri Jeffreys-Jones, 49–73. Portland, OR: Frank Cass, 2000.

Campbell, John, ed. *The Experience of World War II.* New York: Oxford University Press, 1989.

Caputi, Robert J. *Neville Chamberlain and Appeasement.* Cranbury, NJ: Associated University Presses, 2000.

Cave, Patricia. *War Guest: Recollections of Being Evacuated to Canada in 1940.* Warminster: Adept Services Publishing, 1995.

Churchill, Winston. *Their Finest Hour.* Vol. 2 of *The Second World War.* Boston: Houghton Mifflin, 1949.

Colville, John. *The Fringes of Power: Downing Street Diaries, 1939–1955.* London: Phoenix, 2005.

Crowley, Robert T. "Introduction." In Bearse and Read, *Conspirator,* xi–xiv.

Dear, I. C. B., and M. R. D. Foot, eds. *The Oxford Companion to World War II.* Oxford: Oxford University Press, 1995.

Dilks, David, ed. *The Diaries of Sir Alexander Cadogan, O.M.: 1938–1945*. New York: Putnam, 1972.

Dobson, Alan P. *US Wartime Aid to Britain, 1940–1946*. London: Croom Helm, 1986.

Doenecke, Justus D. *The Battle against Intervention, 1939–1941*. Malabar, FL: Krieger, 1997.

———. "Non-Interventionism of the Left: The Keep America out of the War Congress, 1938–41." *Journal of Contemporary History* 12, no. 2 (April 1977): 221–36.

Dönitz, Karl. "F.d.U./B.d.U.'S War Log: 1–15 July 1940." War Diary and War Standing Orders of Commander in Chief, Submarines. Naval Historical Center, Washington, DC. Accessed September 19, 2011. http://www.uboatarchive.net/BDUKTB30268.htm.

———. *Memoirs: Ten Years and Twenty Days*. Translated by R. H. Stevens and David Woodward. Annapolis, MD: Naval Institute Press, 1990.

Douglas, William A. B., and Brereton Greenhous. *Out of the Shadows: Canada in the Second World War*. Toronto: Oxford University Press, 1977.

Draper, Alfred. *Operation Fish: The Race to Save Europe's Wealth, 1939–1945*. Don Mills, Ontario: General Publishing Co. Limited, 1979.

Dulles, Allen W. "Cash and Carry Neutrality." *Foreign Affairs* 18, no. 2 (January 1940): 179–95.

Dutton, Raymond. *What No Isambard? (A Sort of Autobiography)*. Dutton R 85/49/1, Imperial War Museum, London.

Fallu, Jean-Marie. *Le Québec et la Guerre: 1860–1954*. Québec: Les Publications de Québec, 2003.

Feiling, Keith. *The Life of Neville Chamberlain*. London: Macmillan, 1970.

Fleming, Peter. *Operation Sea Lion: The Projected Invasion of England in 1940, an Account of the German Preparations and the British Countermeasures*. New York: Simon and Schuster, 1957.

Fortescue, William. *The Third Republic in France, 1870–1940: Conflicts and Continuities*. New York: Routledge, 2000.

Friel, Ian. *Maritime History of Britain and Ireland*. London: British Museum Press, 2003.

Fry, Richard, ed. *A Banker's World: The Revival of the City 1957–1970, Speakings and Writings of Sir George Bolton*. New York: Taylor and Francis, 2005.

Fullerton, Douglas H. *Graham Towers and His Times: A Biography*. Toronto: McClelland and Stewart, 1986.

Gilbert, Martin. *Churchill and America*. New York: Free Press, 2005.

———. *The Ever Widening War, 1941*. Vol. 3 of *The Churchill War Papers*. New York: W. W. Norton, 2000.

———. *The Second World War: A Complete History*. New York: H. Holt, 1989.

———. *Winston Churchill's War Leadership*. New York: Vintage, 2004.

Gordon, Keith. *Deep Water Gold: The Story of RMS Niagara—The Quest for New Zealand's Greatest Shipwreck Treasure*. Whangarei, New Zealand: SeaROV Technologies, 2005.

Grafton, Samuel. *An American Diary*. New York: Doubleday/Doran, 1943.

Granatstein, J. L., *Canada's War: The Politics of the Mackenzie King Government, 1939–1945*. Toronto: Oxford University Press, 1975.

Grinnell-Milne, Duncan William. *The Silent Victory, September 1940*. London: White Lion, 1976.

Hadley, Michael L. *U-Boats against Canada: German Submarines in Canadian Waters*. Kingston: McGill-Queen's University Press, 1985.

Hall, H. Duncan. *North American Supply*. London: Her Majesty's Stationery Office, 1955.

Harris, Brayton. *The Navy Times Book of Submarines: A Political, Social, and Military History*. New York: Berkley Books, 1997.

Harrison, Mark. "The Economics of World War II: An Overview." In *The Economics of World War II: Six Great Powers in International Comparison*, edited by Mark Harrison, 1–42. Cambridge: Cambridge University Press, 1998.

Haskins, Geoffrey. *The Irish Flagship: The Story of HMS* Emerald *1925–1948*. London: Arcturus, 2000.

Hawkins, Ian, ed. *Destroyer: An Anthology of First-Hand Accounts of the War at Sea, 1939–1945*. London: Conway Maritime Press, 2003.

Hendrickson, Noel. "Counterfactual Reasoning: A Basic Guide for Analysts, Strategists, and Decision Makers." *Proteus Monograph Series* 2, no. 5 (October 2008), U.S. Army War College.

Hennessy, Elizabeth. *A Domestic History of the Bank of England, 1930–1960*. Cambridge: Cambridge University Press, 1992.

Hessler, Günter. *The U-Boat War in the Atlantic, 1939–1945*. London: Her Majesty's Stationery Office, 1989.

Home, William Douglas, ed. *The Prime Ministers: Stories and Anecdotes from Number 10*. London: W. H. Allen, 1987.

Horne, Alistair. *A Bundle from Britain*. New York: St. Martin's Press, 1994.

Horrall, S. W. *The Pictorial History of the Royal Canadian Mounted Police*. Toronto: McGraw-Hill Ryerson, 1973.

Hough, Richard, and Denis Richards. *The Battle of Britain: The Greatest Air Battle of World War II*. New York: W. W. Norton, 1989.

Hughes, Terry, and John Costello. *The Battle of the Atlantic*. New York: Dial Press, 1977.

Ignatieff, Michael. *Isaiah Berlin: A Life*. New York: Holt, 1998.

Ireland, Bernard. *The Battle of the Atlantic*. Annapolis, MD: Naval Institute Press, 2003.

Irving, David. *Churchill's War: The Struggle for Power*. Maryborough, Australia: Veritas, 1987.

Jackson, Carlton. *Who Will Take Our Children? The Story of the Evacuation in Britain, 1939–1945*. London: Methuen, 1985.

Jackson, Julian. *The Fall of France: The Nazi Invasion of 1940*. Oxford: Oxford University Press, 2003.

Jong, Louis. *The German Fifth Column in the Second World War*. Translated by C. M. Geyl. New York: Howard Fertig, 1973.

Kahn, David. *Hitler's Spies: German Military Intelligence in World War II*. Boston: De Capo Press, 2000.

Kealey, Gregory S., and Reg Whitaker, eds., *R.C.M.P. Security Bulletins: The War Series, 1939–1941*. St. John's, NL: Committee on Canadian Labour History, 1989.

Kee, Robert. *Munich: The Eleventh Hour*. London: H. Hamilton, 1988.

Keegan, John. *The Second World War*. New York: Viking, 1990.

Kennedy, David M., ed. *The Library of Congress World War II Companion*. New York: Simon and Schuster, 2007.

Kennedy, John F. *Why England Slept*. New York: W. Funk, 1940.

Kimball, Warren F., ed. *Alliance Emerging, October 1933–November 1942*. Vol. 1 of *Churchill and Roosevelt: The Complete Correspondence*. Princeton, NJ: Princeton University Press, 1984.

———. *Alliance Forged, November 1942–February 1944*. Vol. 2 of *Churchill and Roosevelt: The Complete Correspondence*. Princeton, NJ: Princeton University Press, 1984.

King, William Lyon Mackenzie. *Canada and the Fight for Freedom*. Freeport, NY: Books for Libraries Press, 1944.

Lampe, David. *The Last Ditch*. New York: Putnam, 1968.

Langworth, Richard, ed. *Churchill by Himself: The Definitive Collection of Quotations*. New York: PublicAffairs, 2011.

Lash, Joseph P. *Roosevelt and Churchill, 1939–1941: The Partnership That Saved the West*. New York: W. W. Norton, 1976.

Lashmar, Paul. "The Who's Who of British Nazis." *The Independent*, January 9, 2000.

Lauderbaugh, Richard A. *American Steel Makers and the Coming of the Second World War*. Ann Arbor, MI: UMI Research Press, 1980.

Lebow, Richard Ned. "Counterfactual Thought Experiments: A Necessary Teaching Tool." *History Teacher* 40, no. 2 (February 2007). Accessed September 19, 2011. http://www .historycooperative.org/journals/ht/40.2/lebow.html.

———. *Forbidden Fruit: Counterfactuals and International Relations*. Princeton, NJ: Princeton University Press, 2010.

Leutze, James, ed. *The London Journal of General Raymond E. Lee: 1940–1941*. Boston: Little, Brown, 1971.

Lewin, Ronald. *Hitler's Mistakes*. New York: Morrow, 1984.

Lukacs, John. "Churchill Offers Toil and Tears to FDR." *American Heritage Magazine* 58, no. 4 (Spring/Summer 2008). Accessed January 23, 2013. http://www.americanheritage .com/content/churchill-offers-toil-and-tears-fdr.

———. *The Duel: The Eighty-Day Struggle between Churchill and Hitler*. New Haven, CT: Yale University Press, 2001.

Macintyre, Donald. *The Naval War against Hitler*. New York: Scribner, 1971.

Mack, Joanna, and Steve Humphries. *London at War: The Making of Modern London, 1939–1945*. London: Sidgwick & Jackson, 1985.

Macksey, Kenneth. *Invasion: The German Invasion of England, July 1940*. New York: Macmillan, 1980.

Maclean, Meta. *The Singing Ship: An Odyssey of Evacuee Children*. Sydney: Chivers, 1975.

Manchester, William, and Paul Reid. *Defender of the Realm, 1940–1965*. Vol. 3 of *The Last Lion: Winston Spencer Churchill*. Boston: Little, Brown, 2012.

Martienssen, Anthony. *Hitler and His Admirals*. New York: Dutton, 1949.

McDowall, Duncan. "Earmarked Gold in Canada 1935–56." In *Due Diligence: A Report on the Bank of Canada's Handling of Foreign Gold during World War II*. Ottawa: Bank of Canada, November 27, 1997. Accessed September 19, 2011. http://www.bankofcanada.ca/wp-content/uploads/2010/07/gold97-4.pdf.

McKercher, B. J. C. *Transition of Power: Britain's Loss of Global Pre-eminence to the United States, 1930–1945*. Cambridge: Cambridge University Press, 1999.

Milner, Marc. *Battle of the Atlantic*. St. Catherines, ON: Vanwell Pub., 2003.

Moss, Norman. *Nineteen Weeks: America, Britain, and the Fateful Summer of 1940*. Boston: Houghton Mifflin, 2003.

Mulligan, Timothy P. *Neither Sharks nor Wolves: The Men of Nazi Germany's U-boat Arm, 1939–1945*. Annapolis, MD: Naval Institute Press, 1999.

Napier, Elers. *The Life and Correspondence of Admiral Sir Charles Napier*. London: Hurst & Brackett, 1862.

Nasaw, David. *The Patriarch: The Remarkable Life and Turbulent Times of Joseph P. Kennedy*. New York: Penguin Press, 2012.

Nulman, Stuart. *Beyond the Mountain: True Tales about Montreal*. Kirkland, QC: Callawind, 2002.

Nye, Joseph S. *Understanding International Conflicts: An Introduction to Theory and History*, 5th ed. New York: Pearson/Longman, 2005.

O'Brien, Michael. *John F. Kennedy: A Biography*. New York: St. Martin's Press, 2005.

Office of the Historian. "Milestones 1921–1936: The Neutrality Acts, 1930s." U.S. Department of State. Accessed September 28, 2011. http://history.state.gov/milestones/1921-1936/Neutrality_acts.

Olson, Lynne. *Those Angry Days: Roosevelt, Lindbergh, and America's Fight over World War II, 1939–1941*. New York: Random House, 2013.

Olson, Wesley. *Bitter Victory: The Death of HMAS Sydney*. Nedlands: University of Western Australia Press, 2000.

Overy, Richard. *1939: Countdown to War*. New York: Viking, 2010.

———. *Why the Allies Won*. New York: W. W. Norton, 1995.

Parkinson, J. F., ed. *Canadian War Economics*. Toronto: University of Toronto Press, 1941.

Parkinson, Roger. *Blood, Toil, Tears and Sweat: The War History from Dunkirk to Alamein, Based on the War Cabinet Papers of 1940 to 1942*. London: Hart-Davis MacGibbon, 1973.

Parrish, Thomas, ed., *The Simon and Schuster Encyclopedia of World War II*. New York: Simon and Schuster, 1978.

———. *To Keep the British Isles Afloat: FDR's Men in Churchill's London, 1941*. New York: Smithsonian Books/HarperCollins, 2009.

Paterson, Lawrence. *First U-Boat Flotilla*. Annapolis, MD: Naval Institute Press, 2002.

Persico, Joseph E. *Roosevelt's Secret War: FDR and World War II Espionage*. New York: Random House, 2001.

Pickford, Nigel. *Lost Treasure Ships of the 20th Century*. Washington, DC: National Geographic, 1999.

Pigott, Peter. *Royal Transport: An Inside Look at the History of Royal Travel*. Toronto: Dundurn Group, 2005.

Pitt, Barrie. *The Battle of the Atlantic*. Alexandria, VA: Time-Life Books, 1977.

Plowman, Peter. *Across the Sea to War: Australian and New Zealand Troop Convoys from 1865 through Two World Wars to Korea and Vietnam*. Dural, Australia: Rosenberg, 2003.

Reynolds, David. *The Creation of the Anglo-American Alliance, 1937–41: A Study in Competitive Co-operation*. Chapel Hill: University of North Carolina Press, 1981.

———. "FDR's Foreign Policy and the British Royal Visit to the U.S.A., 1939." *The Historian* 45, no. 4 (August 23, 1983): 461–72.

Robbins, Keith. *Appeasement*. London: Basil Blackwell, 1988.

Rohwer, Jürgen. "Codes and Ciphers: Radio Communication and Intelligence." In *To Die Gallantly: The Battle of the Atlantic*, edited by Timothy J. Runyan and Jan M. Copes, 38–54. Boulder: Westview, 1994.

———. *War at Sea: 1939–1945* (Annapolis, MD: Naval Institute Press, 1996).

Roskill, Stephen Wentworth. *A Merchant Fleet in War: Alfred Holt & Co., 1939–1945*. London: Collins, 1962.

Sainsbury, Keith. *Churchill and Roosevelt at War: The War They Fought and the Peace They Hoped to Make*. New York: New York University Press, 1994.

Saucier, Craig Edward. "Mr. Kerr Goes to Washington: Lord Lothian and the Genesis of the Anglo-American Alliance, 1939–1940." PhD diss., Louisiana State University, 2008.

Self, Robert. *Neville Chamberlain: A Biography*. Aldershot, England: Ashgate, 2006.

———, ed. *The Downing Street Years, 1934–1940*. Vol. 4 of *The Neville Chamberlain Diary Letters*. Aldershot, England: Ashgate, 2005.

Smith, Kevin. *Conflict over Convoys: Anglo-American Logistics Diplomacy in the Second World War*. New York: Cambridge University Press, 1996.

Stacey, Charles P. *Arms, Men and Governments: The War Policies of Canada, 1939–1945*. Ottawa: Queen's Printer, 1970.

Stansky, Peter. *Churchill: A Profile*. New York: Hill and Wang, 1973.

Stettinius, Edward R. *Lend-Lease: Weapon for Victory*. New York: Macmillan, 1944.

Stowe, Leland. *No Other Road to Freedom*. New York: Knopf, 1941.

———. "The Secret Voyage of Britain's Treasure." *Reader's Digest* (November 1955): 17–26.

Sulzberger, Cyrus L. *World War II*. New York: American Heritage, 1985.

Swoger, Gordon. *The Strange Odyssey of Poland's National Treasures, 1939–1961: A Polish-Canadian Story*. Toronto: Dundurn Group, 2004.

Tarrant, V. E. *The U-Boat Offensive 1914–1945*. London: Arms & Armour, 1989.

Thomas, Charles S. *The German Navy in the Nazi Era*. Annapolis, MD: Naval Institute Press, 1990.

Thompson, Walter H. *Assignment: Churchill*. New York: Farrar, Straus and Young, 1955.

Trefousse, Hans L. "The Failure of German Intelligence in the United States, 1935–1945." *Mississippi Valley Historical Review* 42, no. 1 (June 1955): 84–100.

Vandenberg, A. H., Jr., and J. A. Morris, eds. *The Private Papers of Senator Vandenberg*. Boston: Houghton Mifflin, 1952.

Von der Porten, Edward P. *The German Navy in World War II*. New York: Cromwell, 1969.

Werner, Emmy E. *Through the Eyes of Innocents: Children Witness World War II*. Boulder, CO: Westview, 2000.

White, David Fairbank. *Bitter Ocean: The Battle of the Atlantic, 1939–1945*. New York: Simon and Schuster, 2006.

Williams, Andrew. *The Battle of the Atlantic: The Allies' Submarine Fight against the Hitler's Grey Wolves of the Sea*. Large print ed. London: BBC Worldwide, 2002.

Wykes, Alan. *Air Atlantic: A History of Civil and Military Transatlantic Flying*. New York: David White, 1968.

Wynn, Kenneth. *Career Histories, U1-U510*. Vol. 1 of *U-Boat Operations of the Second World War*. Annapolis, MD: Naval Institute Press, 1997.

Index

Page numbers in *italics* denote illustrations.

About the Author

Robert Switky holds a PhD in political science from the Claremont Graduate University and has written numerous articles on international affairs and European politics. He is a coauthor of *World Politics in the 21st Century* and coeditor of *The Political Consequences of Regional Trading Blocs*. His research for *Wealth of an Empire* led him to primary source documents in national archives in Ottawa and London, museums, and central banks, as well as archives in Madison, Wisconsin, and Cambridge and Birmingham, England. He teaches political science at Sonoma State University in California.